Ellipse Fitting for Computer Vision

Implementation and Applications

Synthesis Lectures on Computer Vision

Editors

Synthesis Lectures on Computer Vision is edited by Gérard Medioni of the University of Southern California and Sven Dickinson of the University of Toronto. The series publishes 50- to 150 page publications on topics pertaining to computer vision and pattern recognition. The scope will largely follow the purview of premier computer science conferences, such as ICCV, CVPR, and ECCV. Potential topics include, but not are limited to:

- Applications and Case Studies for Computer Vision
- Color, Illumination, and Texture
- Computational Photography and Video
- Early and Biologically-inspired Vision
- Face and Gesture Analysis
- Illumination and Reflectance Modeling
- Image-Based Modeling
- Image and Video Retrieval
- Medical Image Analysis
- Motion and Tracking
- Object Detection, Recognition, and Categorization
- Segmentation and Grouping
- Sensors
- Shape-from-X
- Stereo and Structure from Motion
- Shape Representation and Matching

Ellipse Fitting for Computer Vision

Implementation and Applications

Synthesis Lectures on Computer Vision

Editors
Gérard Medioni, ***University of Southern California***
Sven Dickinson, ***University of Toronto***

Synthesis Lectures on Computer Vision is edited by Gérard Medioni of the University of Southern California and Sven Dickinson of the University of Toronto. The series publishes 50- to 150 page publications on topics pertaining to computer vision and pattern recognition. The scope will largely follow the purview of premier computer science conferences, such as ICCV, CVPR, and ECCV. Potential topics include, but not are limited to:

- Applications and Case Studies for Computer Vision
- Color, Illumination, and Texture
- Computational Photography and Video
- Early and Biologically-inspired Vision
- Face and Gesture Analysis
- Illumination and Reflectance Modeling
- Image-Based Modeling
- Image and Video Retrieval
- Medical Image Analysis
- Motion and Tracking
- Object Detection, Recognition, and Categorization
- Segmentation and Grouping
- Sensors
- Shape-from-X
- Stereo and Structure from Motion
- Shape Representation and Matching

- Statistical Methods and Learning
- Performance Evaluation
- Video Analysis and Event Recognition

Ellipse Fitting for Computer Vision: Implementation and Applications
Kenichi Kanatani, Yasuyuki Sugaya, and Yasushi Kanazawa
2016

Background Subtraction: Theory and Practice
Ahmed Elgammal
2014

Vision-Based Interaction
Matthew Turk and Gang Hua
2013

Camera Networks: The Acquisition and Analysis of Videos over Wide Areas
Amit K. Roy-Chowdhury and Bi Song
2012

Deformable Surface 3D Reconstruction from Monocular Images
Mathieu Salzmann and Pascal Fua
2010

Boosting-Based Face Detection and Adaptation
Cha Zhang and Zhengyou Zhang
2010

Image-Based Modeling of Plants and Trees
Sing Bing Kang and Long Quan
2009

Ellipse Fitting for Computer Vision: Implementation and Applications
Kenichi Kanatani, Yasuyuki Sugaya, and Yasushi Kanazawa

ISBN: 978-3-031-00687-6 paperback
ISBN: 978-3-031-01815-2 ebook

DOI 10.1007/978-3-031-01815-2

A Publication in the Springer series
SYNTHESIS LECTURES ON COMPUTER VISION

Lecture #8
Series Editors: Gérard Medioni, *University of Southern California*
Sven Dickinson, *University of Toronto*
Series ISSN
Print 2153-1056 Electronic 2153-1064

Ellipse Fitting for Computer Vision

Implementation and Applications

Kenichi Kanatani
Okayama University, Okayama, Japan

Yasuyuki Sugaya
Toyohashi University of Technology, Toyohashi, Aichi, Japan

Yasushi Kanazawa
Toyohashi University of Technology, Toyohashi, Aichi, Japan

SYNTHESIS LECTURES ON COMPUTER VISION #8

ABSTRACT

Because circular objects are projected to ellipses in images, ellipse fitting is a first step for 3-D analysis of circular objects in computer vision applications. For this reason, the study of ellipse fitting began as soon as computers came into use for image analysis in the 1970s, but it is only recently that optimal computation techniques based on the statistical properties of noise were established. These include *renormalization* (1993), which was then improved as *FNS* (2000) and *HEIV* (2000). Later, further improvements, called *hyperaccurate correction* (2006), *HyperLS* (2009), and *hyper-renormalization* (2012), were presented. Today, these are regarded as the most accurate fitting methods among all known techniques. This book describes these algorithms as well implementation details and applications to 3-D scene analysis.

We also present general mathematical theories of statistical optimization underlying all ellipse fitting algorithms, including rigorous covariance and bias analyses and the theoretical accuracy limit. The results can be directly applied to other computer vision tasks including computing fundamental matrices and homographies between images.

This book can serve not simply as a reference of ellipse fitting algorithms for researchers, but also as learning material for beginners who want to start computer vision research. The sample program codes are downloadable from the website: `https://sites.google.com/a/morganclaypool.com/ellipse-fitting-for-computer-vision-implementation-and-applications/`.

KEYWORDS

geometric distance minimization, hyperaccurate correction, HyperLS, hyper-renormalization, iterative reweight, KCR lower bound, maximum likelihood, renormalization, robust fitting, Sampson error, statistical error analysis, Taubin method

Contents

Preface

Because circular objects are projected to ellipses in images, ellipse fitting is a first step for 3-D analysis of circular objects in computer vision applications. For this reason, the study of ellipse fitting began as soon as computers came into use for image analysis in the 1970s. The basic principle was to compute the parameters so that the sum of squares of expressions that should ideally be zero is minimized, which is today called *least squares* or *algebraic distance minimization*. In the 1990s, the notion of optimal computation based on the statistical properties of noise was introduced by researchers including the authors. The first notable example was the authors' *renormalization* (1993), which was then improved as *FNS* (2000) and *HEIV* (2000) by researchers in Australia and the U.S. Later, further improvements, called *hyperaccurate correction* (2006), *HyperLS* (2009), and *hyper-renormalization* (2012), were presented by the authors. Today, these are regarded as the most accurate fitting methods among all known techniques. This book describes these algorithms as well as underlying theories, implementation details, and applications to 3-D scene analysis.

Most textbooks on computer vision begin with mathematical fundamentals followed by the resulting computational procedures. This book, in contrast, *immediately* describes computational procedures after a short statement of the purpose and the principle. The theoretical background is briefly explained as *Comments*. Thus, readers need not worry about mathematical details, which often annoy those who only want to build their vision systems. Rigorous derivations and detailed justifications are given later in separate sections, but they can be skipped if the interest is not in theories. Sample program codes of the authors are provided via the website[1] of the publisher. At the end of each chapter is given a section called *Supplemental Note*, describing historical backgrounds, related issues, and reference literature.

Chapters 1–4 specifically describe ellipse fitting algorithms. Chapter 5 discusses 3-D analysis of circular objects in the scene extracted by ellipse fitting. In Chapter 6, performance comparison experiments are conducted among the methods described in Chapters 1–4. Also, some real image applications of the 3-D analysis of Chapter 5 are shown. In Chapter 7, we point out how procedures of ellipse fitting can straightforwardly be extended to fundamental matrix and homography computation, which play a central role in 3-D analysis by computer vision. Chapters 8 and 9 give general mathematical theories of statistical optimization underlying all ellipse fitting algorithms. Finally, Chapter 10 gives a rigorous analysis of the theoretical accuracy limit. However, beginners and practice-oriented readers can skip these last three chapters.

The authors used the materials in this book as student projects for introductory computer vision research at Okayama University, Japan, and Toyohashi University of Technology, Japan. By implementing the algorithms themselves, students can learn basic programming know-hows

[1]https://sites.google.com/a/morganclaypool.com/ellipse-fitting-for-computer-vision-implementation-and-applications/

and also understand the theoretical background of vision computation as their interest deepens. We are hoping that this book can serve not simply as a reference of ellipse fitting algorithms for researchers, but also as learning material for beginners who want to start computer vision research.

The theories in this book are the fruit of the authors' collaborations and interactions with their colleagues and friends for many years. The authors thank Takayuki Okatani of Tohoku University, Japan, Mike Brooks and Wojciech Chojnacki of the University of Adelaide, Australia, Peter Meer of Rutgers University, U.S., Wolfgang Förstner, of the University of Bonn, Germany, Michael Felsberg of Linköping University, Sweden, Rudolf Mester of the University of Frankfurt, Germany, Prasanna Rangarajan of Southern Methodist University, U.S., Ali Al-Sharadqah of University of East Carolina, U.S., and Alexander Kukush of the University of Kiev, Ukraine. Special thanks are to (late) Professor Nikolai Chernov of the University of Alabama at Birmingham, U.S., without whose inspiration and assistance this work would not have been possible.

Kenichi Kanatani, Yasuyuki Sugaya, and Yasushi Kanazawa
March 2016

CHAPTER 1
Introduction

This chapter describes the basic mathematical formulation to be used in subsequent chapters for fitting an ellipse to observed points. The main focus is on the description of statistical properties of noise in the data in terms of covariance matrices. We point out that two approaches exist for ellipse fitting: "algebraic" and "geometric." Also, some historical background is mentioned, and related mathematical topics are discussed.

1.1 ELLIPSE FITTING

Ellipse fitting means fitting an ellipse equation to points extracted from an image. This is one of the fundamental tasks of computer vision for various reasons. First, we observe many circular objects in man-made scenes indoors and outdoors, and a circle is projected as an ellipse in camera images. If we extract elliptic segments, say, by an edge detection filter, and fit an ellipse equation to them, we can compute the 3-D position of the circular object in the scene (we will discuss such applications in Chapter 5). Figure 1.1a shows edges extracted from an indoor scene, using an edge detection filter. This scene contains many elliptic arcs, as indicated there. Figure 1.1b shows ellipses fitted to them superimposed on the original image. We observe that fitted ellipses are not necessarily exact object shapes, in particular when the observed arc is only a small part of the circumference or when it is continuously connected to a non-elliptic segment (we will discuss this issue in Chapter 4).

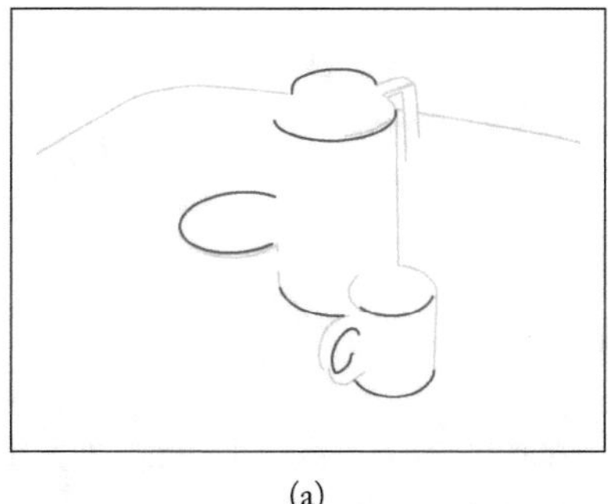

(a)

(b)

Figure 1.1: (a) An edge image and selected elliptic arcs. (b) Ellipses are fitted to the arcs in (a) and superimposed on the original image.

Ellipse fitting is also used for detecting not only circular objects in the image but also objects of approximately elliptic shape, e.g., human faces. An important application of ellipse fitting is *camera calibration* for determining the position and internal parameters of a camera by taking images of a reference pattern, for which circles are often used for the ease of image processing. Ellipse fitting is also important as a mathematical prototype of various geometric estimation problems for computer vision. Typical problems include the computation of fundamental matrices and homographies (we will briefly describe these in Chapter 7).

1.2 REPRESENTATION OF ELLIPSES

The equation of an ellipse has the form

$$Ax^2 + 2Bxy + Cy^2 + 2f_0(Dx + Ey) + f_0^2 F = 0, \tag{1.1}$$

where f_0 is a constant for adjusting the scale. Theoretically, it can be 1, but for finite-length numerical computation it should be chosen so that x/f_0 and y/f_0 have approximately the order of 1; this increases the numerical accuracy, avoiding the loss of significant digits. In view of this, we take the origin of the image xy coordinate system at the center of the image, rather than the upper-left corner as is customarily done, and take f_0 to be the length of the side of a square which we assume to contain the ellipse to be extracted. For example, if we know that an ellipse exists in a 600×600 pixel region, we let $f_0 = 600$. Since Eq. (1.1) has scale indeterminacy, i.e., the same ellipse is represented if A, B, C, D, E, and F are simultaneously multiplied by a nonzero constant, we need some kind of normalization. Various types of normalizations have been considered in the past, including

$$F = 1, \tag{1.2}$$

$$A + C = 1, \tag{1.3}$$

$$A^2 + B^2 + C^2 + D^2 + E^2 + F^2 = 1, \tag{1.4}$$

$$A^2 + B^2 + C^2 + D^2 + E^2 = 1, \tag{1.5}$$

$$A^2 + 2B^2 + C^2 = 1, \tag{1.6}$$

$$AC - B^2 = 1. \tag{1.7}$$

Among these, Eq. (1.2) is the simplest and most familiar one, but Eq. (1.1) with $F = 1$ cannot express an ellipse that passes through the origin $(0, 0)$. Equation (1.3) remedies this. Each of the above normalization equations has its own reasoning, but in this book we adopt Eq. (1.4) (see Supplemental Note (page 6) below for the background).

If we define the 6-D vectors

$$\boldsymbol{\xi} = \begin{pmatrix} x^2 \\ 2xy \\ y^2 \\ 2f_0x \\ 2f_0y \\ f_0^2 \end{pmatrix}, \qquad \boldsymbol{\theta} = \begin{pmatrix} A \\ B \\ C \\ D \\ E \\ F \end{pmatrix}, \tag{1.8}$$

Eq. (1.4) can be written as

$$(\boldsymbol{\xi}, \boldsymbol{\theta}) = 0, \tag{1.9}$$

where and hereafter we denote the inner product of vectors $\boldsymbol{a}$ and $\boldsymbol{b}$ by $(\boldsymbol{a}, \boldsymbol{b})$. Since the vector $\boldsymbol{\theta}$ in Eq. (1.9) has scale indeterminacy, it must be normalized in correspondence with Eqs. (1.2)–(1.7). Note that the left sides of Eqs. (1.2)–(1.7) can be seen as quadratic forms in A, ..., F; Eqs. (1.2) and (1.3) are linear equations, but we may regard them as $F^2 = 1$ and $(A + C)^2 = 1$, respectively. Hence, Eqs. (1.2)–(1.7) are all written in the form

$$(\boldsymbol{\theta}, \boldsymbol{N}\boldsymbol{\theta}) = 1, \tag{1.10}$$

for some normalization matrix $\boldsymbol{N}$. The use of Eq. (1.4) corresponds to $\boldsymbol{N} = \boldsymbol{I}$ (the identity), in which case Eq. (1.10) is simply $\|\boldsymbol{\theta}\| = 1$, i.e., normalization to unit norm.

1.3 LEAST SQUARES APPROACH

Fitting an ellipse in the form of Eq. (1.1) to a sequence of points (x_1, y_1), ..., (x_N, y_N) in the presence of noise (Fig. 1.2) is to find A, B, C, D, E, and F such that

$$Ax_\alpha^2 + 2Bx_\alpha y_\alpha + Cy_\alpha^2 + 2f_0(Dx_\alpha + Ey_\alpha) + f_0^2F \approx 0, \qquad \alpha = 1, ..., N. \tag{1.11}$$

If we write $\boldsymbol{\xi}_\alpha$ for the value obtained by replacing x and y in the 6-D vector $\boldsymbol{\xi}$ of Eq. (1.8) by x_α and y_α, respectively, Eq. (1.11) can be equivalently written as

$$(\boldsymbol{\xi}_\alpha, \boldsymbol{\theta}) \approx 0, \qquad \alpha = 1, ..., N. \tag{1.12}$$

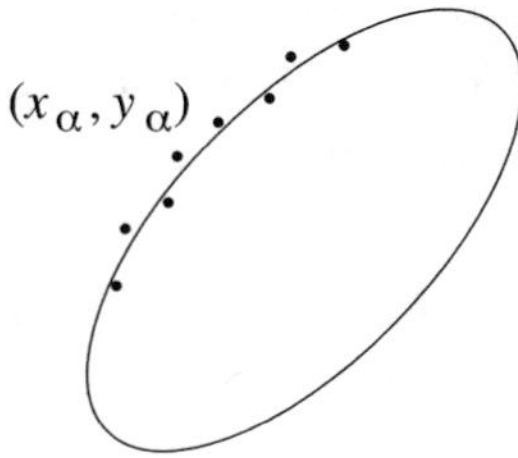

Figure 1.2: Fitting an ellipse to a noisy point sequence.

Our task is to compute such a unit vector $\boldsymbol{\theta}$. The simplest and the most naive method is the following *least squares*.

Procedure 1.1 (Least squares)

1. Compute the 6×6 matrix

$$\boldsymbol{M} = \frac{1}{N}\sum_{\alpha=1}^{N} \boldsymbol{\xi}_\alpha \boldsymbol{\xi}_\alpha^\top. \tag{1.13}$$

2. Solve the eigenvalue problem

$$\boldsymbol{M}\boldsymbol{\theta} = \lambda\boldsymbol{\theta}, \tag{1.14}$$

and return the unit eigenvector $\boldsymbol{\theta}$ for the smallest eigenvalue λ.

Comments. This is a straightforward generalization of line fitting to a point sequence ($\hookrightarrow$ Problem 1.1); we minimize the sum of the squares

$$J = \frac{1}{N}\sum_{\alpha=1}^{N}(\boldsymbol{\xi}_\alpha, \boldsymbol{\theta})^2 = \frac{1}{N}\sum_{\alpha=1}^{N}\boldsymbol{\theta}^\top \boldsymbol{\xi}_\alpha \boldsymbol{\xi}_\alpha^\top \boldsymbol{\theta} = (\boldsymbol{\theta}, \Big(\frac{1}{N}\sum_{\alpha=1}^{N}\boldsymbol{\xi}_\alpha \boldsymbol{\xi}_\alpha^\top\Big)\boldsymbol{\theta}) = (\boldsymbol{\theta}, \boldsymbol{M}\boldsymbol{\theta}), \tag{1.15}$$

subject to $\|\boldsymbol{\theta}\| = 1$. As is well known in linear algebra, the minimum of this quadratic form in $\boldsymbol{\theta}$ is given by the unit eigenvector $\boldsymbol{\theta}$ of $\boldsymbol{M}$ for the smallest eigenvalue. Equation (1.15) is often called the *algebraic distance*, and Procedure 1.1 is also known as *algebraic distance minimization*. It is sometimes called *DLT* (*direct linear transformation*). Since the computation is very easy and the solution is immediately obtained, this method has been widely used. However, when the input point sequence covers only a small part of the ellipse circumference, it often produces a small and flat ellipse very different from the true shape (we will see such examples in Chapter 6). Still, this is a prototype of all existing ellipse fitting algorithms. How we can improve this method is the main theme of this book.

1.4 NOISE AND COVARIANCE MATRICES

The reason for the poor accuracy of Procedure 1.1 is that the properties of image noise are not considered; for accurate fitting, we need to take the statistical properties of noise into consideration. Suppose the data x_α and y_α are disturbed from their true values $\bar{x}_\alpha$ and $\bar{y}_\alpha$ by Δx_α and Δy_α:

$$x_\alpha = \bar{x}_\alpha + \Delta x_\alpha, \qquad y_\alpha = \bar{y}_\alpha + \Delta y_\alpha. \tag{1.16}$$

Substituting this into $\boldsymbol{\xi}_\alpha$, we can write

$$\boldsymbol{\xi}_\alpha = \bar{\boldsymbol{\xi}}_\alpha + \Delta_1\boldsymbol{\xi}_\alpha + \Delta_2\boldsymbol{\xi}_\alpha, \tag{1.17}$$

where $\bar{\xi}_\alpha$ is the value of ξ_α obtained by replacing x_α and y_α by their true values $\bar{x}_\alpha$ and $\bar{y}_\alpha$, respectively, while $\Delta_1\xi_\alpha$ and $\Delta_2\xi_\alpha$ are, respectively, the first-order noise term (the linear expression in Δx_α and Δy_α) and the second-order noise term (the quadratic expression in Δx_α and Δy_α). From Eq. (1.8), we obtain the following expressions:

$$\Delta_1\xi_\alpha = \begin{pmatrix} 2\bar{x}_\alpha \Delta x_\alpha \\ 2\Delta x_\alpha \bar{y}_\alpha + 2\bar{x}_\alpha \Delta y_\alpha \\ 2\bar{y}_\alpha \Delta y_\alpha \\ 2f_0\Delta x_\alpha \\ 2f_0\Delta y_\alpha \\ 0 \end{pmatrix}, \qquad \Delta_2\xi_\alpha = \begin{pmatrix} \Delta x_\alpha^2 \\ 2\Delta x_\alpha \Delta y_\alpha \\ \Delta y_\alpha^2 \\ 0 \\ 0 \\ 0 \end{pmatrix}. \tag{1.18}$$

We regard the noise terms Δx_α and Δy_α as random variables and define the covariance matrix of ξ_α by

$$V[\xi_\alpha] = E[\Delta_1\xi_\alpha \Delta_1\xi_\alpha^\top], \tag{1.19}$$

where $E[\cdot]$ denotes expectation over the noise distribution. If we assume that Δx_α and Δy_α are sampled from independent Gaussian distributions of mean 0 and standard deviation σ, we obtain

$$E[\Delta x_\alpha] = E[\Delta y_\alpha] = 0, \qquad E[\Delta x_\alpha^2] = E[\Delta y_\alpha^2] = \sigma^2, \qquad E[\Delta x_\alpha \Delta y_\alpha] = 0. \tag{1.20}$$

Substituting Eq. (1.18) and using this relationship, we obtain the covariance matrix in Eq. (1.19) in the following form:

$$V[\xi_\alpha] = \sigma^2 V_0[\xi_\alpha], \qquad V_0[\xi_\alpha] = 4\begin{pmatrix} \bar{x}_\alpha^2 & \bar{x}_\alpha\bar{y}_\alpha & 0 & f_0\bar{x}_\alpha & 0 & 0 \\ \bar{x}_\alpha\bar{y}_\alpha & \bar{x}_\alpha^2 + \bar{y}_\alpha^2 & \bar{x}_\alpha\bar{y}_\alpha & f_0\bar{y}_\alpha & f_0\bar{x}_\alpha & 0 \\ 0 & \bar{x}_\alpha\bar{y}_\alpha & \bar{y}_\alpha^2 & 0 & f_0\bar{y}_\alpha & 0 \\ f_0\bar{x}_\alpha & f_0\bar{y}_\alpha & 0 & f_0^2 & 0 & 0 \\ 0 & f_0\bar{x}_\alpha & f_0\bar{y}_\alpha & 0 & f_0^2 & 0 \\ 0 & 0 & 0 & 0 & 0 & 0 \end{pmatrix}. \tag{1.21}$$

Since all the elements of $V[\xi_\alpha]$ have the multiple σ^2, we factor it out and call $V_0[\xi_\alpha]$ the *normalized covariance matrix*. We also call the standard deviation σ the *noise level*. The diagonal elements of the covariance matrix $V[\xi_\alpha]$ indicate the noise susceptibility of each component of ξ_α, and the off-diagonal elements measure their pair-wise correlation.

The covariance matrix of Eq. (1.19) is defined in terms of the first-order noise term $\Delta_1\xi_\alpha$ alone. It is known that incorporation of the second-order term $\Delta_2\xi_\alpha$ has little influence over final results. This is because $\Delta_2\xi_\alpha$ is very small as compared with $\Delta_1\xi_\alpha$. Note that the elements of $V_0[\xi_\alpha]$ in Eq. (1.21) contain true values $\bar{x}_\alpha$ and $\bar{y}_\alpha$. They are replaced by observed values x_α and y_α in actual computation. It is known that this replacement has practically no effect in the final results.

1.5 ELLIPSE FITTING APPROACHES

In the following chapters, we describe typical ellipse fitting methods that incorporate the above noise properties. We will see that all the methods we consider *do not require knowledge of the noise level* σ, which is very difficult to estimate in real problems. The qualitative properties of noise are all encoded in the normalized covariance matrix $V_0[\boldsymbol{\xi}_\alpha]$, which gives sufficient information for designing high accuracy fitting schemes. In general terms, there exist two approaches for ellipse fittings: algebraic and geometric.

Algebraic methods: We solves some algebraic equation for computing $\boldsymbol{\theta}$. The resulting solution may or may not minimize some cost function. In other words, the equation need not have the form of $\nabla_{\boldsymbol{\theta}} J = 0$ for some cost function J. Rather, we can modify the equation in any way so that the resulting solution $\boldsymbol{\theta}$ is as close to its true value $\bar{\boldsymbol{\theta}}$ as possible. Thus, our task is to find *a good equation to solve*. To this end, we need detailed statistical error analysis.

Geometric methods: We minimize some cost function J. Hence, the solution is uniquely determined once the cost J is defined. Thus, our task is to find *a good cost to minimize*. For this, we need to consider the geometry of the ellipse and the data points. We also need to devise a convenient minimization algorithm, since minimization of a given cost is not always easy.

The meaning of these two approaches will be better understood by seeing the actual procedures described in the subsequent chapters. There are, however, a lot of overlaps between the two approaches.

1.6 SUPPLEMENTAL NOTE

The study of ellipse fitting began as soon as computers came into use for image analysis in the 1970s. Since then, numerous fitting techniques have been proposed, and even today new methods appear one after another. Since we are unable cite all the literature, we mention only some of the earliest work: Albano [1974], Bookstein [1979], Cooper and Yalabik [1979], Gnanadesikan [1977], Nakagawa and Rosenfeld [1979], Paton [1970]. Beside fitting an ellipse to data points, a voting scheme called *Hough transform* for accumulating evidences in the parameter space was also studied as a means of ellipse fitting [Davis, 1989].

In the 1990s, a paradigm shift occurred. It was first thought that the purpose of ellipse fitting was to find an ellipse that *approximately* passes *near observed points*. However, some researchers, including the authors, turned their attention to finding an ellipse that *exactly* passes *through the true points* that would be observed in the absence of noise. Thus, the problem turned to a *statistical* problem for *estimating* the true points *subject to the constraint that they are on some ellipse*. It follows that the goodness of the fitted ellipse is measured not by how close it is to the observed points but by how close it is to the *true* shape. This type of paradigm shift has also occurred in other problems including fundamental matrix and homography computation for 3-D analysis. Today, statistical analysis is one of the main tools for accurate geometric computation for computer vision.

The ellipse fitting techniques discussed in this book are naturally extended to general curves and surfaces in a general space in the form

$$\theta_1\xi_1 + \theta_2\xi_2 + \cdots + \theta_n\xi_n = 0, \tag{1.22}$$

where ξ_1, ..., ξ_n are functions of coordinates x_1, x_2, ..., and θ_1, ..., θ_n are unknowns to be determined. This equation is written in the form of $(\boldsymbol{\xi}, \boldsymbol{\theta}) = 0$ in terms of the vector $\boldsymbol{\xi} = (\xi_i)$ of observations and the vector $\boldsymbol{\theta} = (\theta_i)$ of unknowns. Then, all techniques and analysis for ellipse fitting can apply. Evidently, Eq. (1.22) includes all polynomial curves in 2-D and all polynomial surfaces in 3-D, but all algebraic functions also can be expressed in the form of Eq. (1.22) after canceling denominators. For general nonlinear surfaces, too, we can usually write the equation in the form of Eq. (1.22) after an appropriate reparameterization, as long as the problem is to estimate the "coefficients" of linear/nonlinear terms. Terms that are not multiplied by unknown coefficients are regarded as being multiplied by 1, which is also regarded as an unknown. The resulting set of coefficients can be viewed as a vector of unknown magnitude, or a "homogeneous vector," and we can write the equation in the form $(\boldsymbol{\xi}, \boldsymbol{\theta}) = 0$. Thus, the theory in this book has wide applicability beyond ellipse fitting.

In Eq. (1.1), we introduce the scaling constant f_0 to make x/f_0 and y/f_0 have the order of 1, and this also make the vector $\boldsymbol{\xi}$ in Eq. (1.8) have magnitude $O(f_0^2)$ so that $\boldsymbol{\xi}/f_0^2$ is approximately a unit vector. The necessities and effects of such scaling for numerical computation is discussed by Hartley [1997] in relation to fundamental matrix computation (we will discuss this in Chapter 7), which is also a fundamental problem of computer vision and has the same mathematical structure as ellipse fitting. In this book, we introduce the scaling constant f_0 and take the coordinate origin at the center of the image based on the same reasoning.

The normalization using Eq. (1.2) was adopted by Albano [1974], Cooper and Yalabik [1979], and Rosin [1993]. Many authors used Eq. (1.4), but some authors preferred Eq. (1.5) [Gnanadesikan, 1977]. The use of Eq. (1.6) was proposed by Bookstein [1979], who argued that it leads to "coordinate invariance" in the sense that the ellipse fitted by least squares after the coordinate system is translated and rotated is the same as the originally fitted ellipse translated and rotated accordingly. In this respect, Eqs. (1.3) and (1.7) also have that invariance. The normalization using Eq. (1.7) was proposed by Fitzgibbon et al. [1999] so that the resulting least-squares fit is guaranteed to be an ellipse, while other equations can theoretically produce a parabola or a hyperbola (we will discuss this in Chapter 4).

Today, we need not worry about the coordinate invariance, which is a concern of the past. As long as we regard ellipse fitting as statistical estimation and use Eq. (1.10) for normalization, all statistically meaningful methods are automatically invariant to the choice of the coordinate system. This is because the normalization matrix $\boldsymbol{N}$ in Eq. (1.10) is defined as a function of the covariance matrix $V[\boldsymbol{\xi}_\alpha]$ of Eq. (1.19). If we change the coordinate system, e.g., adding translation, rotation, and other arbitrary mapping, the covariance matrix $V[\boldsymbol{\xi}_\alpha]$ defined by Eq. (1.19) also changes, and the fitted ellipse after the coordinate change using the transformed covariance matrix is the same as the ellipse fitted in the original coordinate system using the original covariance matrix and transformed afterwards.

The fact that the all the normalization equations of Eqs. (1.2)–(1.7) are written in the form of Eq. (1.10) poses an interesting question: What $\boldsymbol{N}$ is the "best," if we are to minimize the algebraic distance of Eq. (1.15) subject to $(\boldsymbol{\theta}, \boldsymbol{N}\boldsymbol{\theta}) = 1$? This problem was studied by the authors' group [Kanatani and Rangarajan, 2011, Kanatani et al., 2011, Rangarajan and Kanatani, 2009], and the matrix $\boldsymbol{N}$ that gives rise to the highest accuracy was found after a detailed error analysis. The method was named *HyperLS* (this will be described in the next chapter).

Minimizing the sum of squares in the form of Eq. (1.15) is a natural idea, but readers may wonder why we minimize $\sum_{\alpha=1}^{N}(\boldsymbol{\xi}_\alpha, \boldsymbol{\theta})^2$. Why not minimize, say, the absolute sum $\sum_{\alpha=1}^{N}|(\boldsymbol{\xi}_\alpha, \boldsymbol{\theta})|$ or the maximum $\max_{\alpha=1}^{N}|(\boldsymbol{\xi}_\alpha, \boldsymbol{\theta})|$? This is the issue of the choice of the *norm*. A class of criteria, called L_p*-norms*, exist for measuring the magnitude of an n-D vector $\boldsymbol{x} = (x_i)$:

$$\|\boldsymbol{x}\|_p \equiv \left(\sum_{i=1}^{n}|x_i|^p\right)^{1/p}. \tag{1.23}$$

The L_2-norm, or the *square norm*,

$$\|\boldsymbol{x}\|_2 \equiv \sqrt{\sum_{i=1}^{n}|x_i|^2}, \tag{1.24}$$

is widely used for linear algebra. If we let $p \to \infty$ in Eq. (1.23), it approaches

$$\|\boldsymbol{x}\|_\infty \equiv \max_{i=1}^{n}|x_i|, \tag{1.25}$$

called the L_∞*-norm*, or the *maximum norm*, where components with large $|x_i|$ have a dominant effect and those with small $|x_i|$ are ignored. Conversely, if let $p \to 0$ in Eq. (1.23), those components with large $|x_i|$ are ignored. The L_1*-norm*

$$\|\boldsymbol{x}\|_1 \equiv \sum_{i=1}^{n}|x_i| \tag{1.26}$$

is often called the *average norm*, because it effectively measures the average $(1/N)\sum_{i=1}^{n}|x_i|$. In the limit of $p \to 0$, we obtain

$$\|\boldsymbol{x}\|_0 \equiv |\{i \mid |x_i| \neq 0\}|, \tag{1.27}$$

where the right side means the number of nonzero components. This is called the L_0*-norm*, or the *Hamming distance*.

Least squares for minimizing the L_2-norm is the most widely used approach for statistical optimization for two reasons. One is the computational simplicity: differentiation of a sum of squares leads to linear expressions, so the solution is immediately obtained by solving linear equations or an eigenvalue problem. The other reason is that it corresponds to *maximum likelihood* estimation (we will discuss this in Chapter 9), provided the discrepancies to be minimized arise from independent and identical Gaussian noise. Indeed, the scheme of least squares was invented by Gauss, who introduced the "Gaussian distribution," which he himself called the "normal distribution," as the standard noise model (physicists usually use the former term, while statisticians prefer the latter). In spite of added computational complexity, however, minimization of the L_p-norm for $p < 2$, typically $p = 1$, has its merit, because the effect of those terms with large absolute values are suppressed. This suggests that terms irrelevant for estimation, called *outliers*, are automatically ignored. Estimation methods that are not very susceptible to outliers are said to be *robust* (we will discuss robust ellipse fitting in Chapter 4). For this reason, L_1-minimization is frequently used in some computer vision applications.

PROBLEMS

1.1. Fitting a line in the form $n_1 x + n_2 y + n_3 f_0 = 0$ to points (x_α, y_α), $\alpha = 1, ..., N$, can be viewed as the problem for computing $\boldsymbol{n} = (n_i)$, which can be normalized to a unit vector, such that $(\boldsymbol{\xi}_\alpha, \boldsymbol{n}) \approx 0$, $\alpha = 1, .., N$, with

$$\boldsymbol{\xi}_\alpha = \begin{pmatrix} x_\alpha \\ y_\alpha \\ f_0 \end{pmatrix}, \qquad \boldsymbol{n} = \begin{pmatrix} n_1 \\ n_2 \\ n_3 \end{pmatrix}. \tag{1.28}$$

(1) Write down the least-squares procedure for this computation.

(2) If the noise terms Δx_α and Δy_α are sampled from independent Gaussian distributions of mean 0 and variance σ^2, how is their covariance matrix $V[\boldsymbol{\xi}_\alpha]$ defined?

CHAPTER 2

Algebraic Fitting

We now describe computational procedures for typical algebraic fitting methods: "iterative reweight," the "Taubin method," "renormalization," "HyperLS," and "hyper-renormalization." We point out that all these methods reduce to solving a generalized eigenvalue problem of the same form; different choices of the matrices involved result in different methods.

2.1 ITERATIVE REWEIGHT AND LEAST SQUARES

The following *iterative reweight* is an old and well-known method:

Procedure 2.1 (Iterative reweight)

1. Let $\boldsymbol{\theta}_0 = \mathbf{0}$ and $W_\alpha = 1$, $\alpha = 1, \ldots, N$.
2. Compute the 6×6 matrix
$$\boldsymbol{M} = \frac{1}{N}\sum_{\alpha=1}^{N} W_\alpha \boldsymbol{\xi}_\alpha \boldsymbol{\xi}_\alpha^\top, \tag{2.1}$$
where $\boldsymbol{\xi}_\alpha$ is the vector defined in Eq. (1.8) for the αth point.
3. Solve the eigenvalue problem
$$\boldsymbol{M}\boldsymbol{\theta} = \lambda\boldsymbol{\theta}, \tag{2.2}$$
and compute the unit eigenvector $\boldsymbol{\theta}$ for the smallest eigenvalue λ.
4. If $\boldsymbol{\theta} \approx \boldsymbol{\theta}_0$ up to sign, return $\boldsymbol{\theta}$ and stop. Else, update
$$W_\alpha \leftarrow \frac{1}{(\boldsymbol{\theta}, V_0[\boldsymbol{\xi}_\alpha]\boldsymbol{\theta})}, \qquad \boldsymbol{\theta}_0 \leftarrow \boldsymbol{\theta}, \tag{2.3}$$
and go back to Step 2.

Comments. This method is motivated to minimize the weighted sum of squares $\sum_{\alpha=1}^{N} W_\alpha (\boldsymbol{\xi}_\alpha, \boldsymbol{\theta})^2$; the approach known as *weighted least squares*. In fact, we see that

$$\frac{1}{N}\sum_{\alpha=1}^{N} W_\alpha(\boldsymbol{\xi}_\alpha, \boldsymbol{\theta})^2 = \frac{1}{N}\sum_{\alpha=1}^{N} W_\alpha(\boldsymbol{\theta}, \boldsymbol{\xi}_\alpha\boldsymbol{\xi}_\alpha^\top\boldsymbol{\theta}) = (\boldsymbol{\theta}, \Big(\frac{1}{N}\sum_{\alpha=1}^{N} W_\alpha\boldsymbol{\xi}_\alpha\boldsymbol{\xi}_\alpha^\top\Big)\boldsymbol{\theta}) = (\boldsymbol{\theta}, \boldsymbol{M}\boldsymbol{\theta}), \tag{2.4}$$

and this quadratic form is minimized by the unit eigenvector of $\boldsymbol{M}$ for the smallest eigenvalue. According to the theory of statistics, the weights W_α are optimal if they are inversely proportional to the variance of each term, being small for uncertain terms and large for certain terms. Since $(\boldsymbol{\xi}_\alpha, \boldsymbol{\theta}) = (\bar{\boldsymbol{\xi}}_\alpha, \boldsymbol{\theta}) + (\Delta_1\boldsymbol{\xi}_\alpha, \boldsymbol{\theta}) + (\Delta_2\boldsymbol{\xi}_\alpha, \boldsymbol{\theta})$ and $(\bar{\boldsymbol{\xi}}_\alpha, \boldsymbol{\theta}) = 0$, the variance is

$$E[(\boldsymbol{\xi}_\alpha, \boldsymbol{\theta})^2] = E[(\boldsymbol{\theta}, \Delta_1\boldsymbol{\xi}_\alpha \Delta_1\boldsymbol{\xi}_\alpha^\top \boldsymbol{\theta})] = (\boldsymbol{\theta}, E[\Delta_1\boldsymbol{\xi}_\alpha \Delta_1\boldsymbol{\xi}_\alpha^\top]\boldsymbol{\theta}) = \sigma^2(\boldsymbol{\theta}, V_0[\boldsymbol{\xi}_\alpha]\boldsymbol{\theta}), \tag{2.5}$$

omitting higher-order noise terms. Thus, we should let $W_\alpha = 1/(\boldsymbol{\theta}, V_0[\boldsymbol{\xi}_\alpha]\boldsymbol{\theta})$, but $\boldsymbol{\theta}$ is not known yet. So, we instead use the weights W_α determined in the preceding iteration to compute $\boldsymbol{\theta}$ and update the weights as in Eq. (2.3). Let us call the solution $\boldsymbol{\theta}$ computed in the initial iteration the *initial solution*. Initially, we let $W_\alpha = 1$, so Eq. (2.4) implies that we are minimizing $\sum_{\alpha=1}^{N}(\boldsymbol{\xi}_\alpha, \boldsymbol{\theta})^2$. In other words, the initial solution is the least-squares solution, from which the iterations start. The phrase "up to sign" in Step 4 reflects the fact that eigenvectors have sign indeterminacy. So, we align $\boldsymbol{\theta}$ and $\boldsymbol{\theta}_0$ by reversing the sign $\boldsymbol{\theta} \leftarrow -\boldsymbol{\theta}$ whenever $(\boldsymbol{\theta}, \boldsymbol{\theta}_0) < 0$.

2.2 RENORMALIZATION AND THE TAUBIN METHOD

It is well known that the iterative reweight method has a large bias, in particular when the input elliptic arc is short. As a result, we often obtain a smaller ellipse than expected. The following *renormalization* was introduced to remedy this.

Procedure 2.2 (Renormalization)

1. Let $\boldsymbol{\theta}_0 = \boldsymbol{0}$ and $W_\alpha = 1$, $\alpha = 1, ..., N$.

2. Compute the 6×6 matrices

$$\boldsymbol{M} = \frac{1}{N}\sum_{\alpha=1}^{N} W_\alpha \boldsymbol{\xi}_\alpha \boldsymbol{\xi}_\alpha^\top, \qquad \boldsymbol{N} = \frac{1}{N}\sum_{\alpha=1}^{N} W_\alpha V_0[\boldsymbol{\xi}_\alpha]. \tag{2.6}$$

3. Solve the generalized eigenvalue problem

$$\boldsymbol{M}\boldsymbol{\theta} = \lambda \boldsymbol{N}\boldsymbol{\theta}, \tag{2.7}$$

   and compute the unit generalized eigenvector $\boldsymbol{\theta}$ for the generalized eigenvalue λ of the smallest absolute value.

4. If $\boldsymbol{\theta} \approx \boldsymbol{\theta}_0$ up to sign, return $\boldsymbol{\theta}$ and stop. Else, update

$$W_\alpha \leftarrow \frac{1}{(\boldsymbol{\theta}, V_0[\boldsymbol{\xi}_\alpha]\boldsymbol{\theta})}, \qquad \boldsymbol{\theta}_0 \leftarrow \boldsymbol{\theta}, \tag{2.8}$$

   and go back to Step 2.

Comments. This method was motivated as follows. Since the true values $\bar{\xi}_\alpha$ satisfy $(\bar{\xi}_\alpha, \theta) = 0$, we can immediately see that $\bar{M}\theta = \mathbf{0}$, where $\bar{M}$ is the true value of the matrix M in Eq. (2.6) defined by the true values $\bar{\xi}_\alpha$. Thus, if we know $\bar{M}$, the solution θ is obtained as its unit eigenvector for eigenvalue 0. However, $\bar{M}$ is unknown, so we estimate it. The expectation of M is

$$\begin{aligned} E[M] &= E[\frac{1}{N}\sum_{\alpha=1}^{N} W_\alpha(\bar{\xi}_\alpha + \Delta\xi_\alpha)(\bar{\xi}_\alpha + \Delta\xi_\alpha)^\top] = \bar{M} + E[\frac{1}{N}\sum_{\alpha=1}^{N} W_\alpha \Delta\xi_\alpha \Delta\xi_\alpha^\top] \\ &= \bar{M} + \frac{1}{N}\sum_{\alpha=1}^{N} W_\alpha E[\Delta\xi_\alpha \Delta\xi_\alpha^\top] = \bar{M} + \frac{1}{N}\sum_{\alpha=1}^{N} W_\alpha \sigma^2 V_0[\xi_\alpha] \\ &= \bar{M} + \sigma^2 N. \end{aligned} \tag{2.9}$$

Since $\bar{M} = E[M] - \sigma^2 N \approx M - \sigma^2 N$, we solve $(M - \sigma^2 N)\theta = \mathbf{0}$, or $M\theta = \sigma^2 N\theta$, for some unknown σ^2, which is supposed to be very small. Thus, we solve Eq. (2.7) for the smallest absolute value λ. As is well known in linear algebra, solving Eq. (2.7) is equivalent to minimizing the quadratic form $(\theta, M\theta)$ subject to the constraint $(\theta, N\theta)$ = constant. Since we start from $W_\alpha = 1$, the initial solution minimizes $\sum_{\alpha=1}^{N}(\xi_\alpha, \theta)^2$ subject to $(\theta, \left(\sum_{\alpha=1}^{N} V_0[\xi_\alpha]\right)\theta)$ = constant. This is known as the *Taubin method* (↪ Problem 2.1).

Standard numerical tools for solving the generalized eigenvalue problem in the form of Eq. (2.7) assume that N is positive definite (some eigenvalues are negative). However, Eq. (1.21) implies that the sixth column and the sixth row of the matrix $V_0[\xi_\alpha]$ all consist of zero, so N is not positive definite. On the other hand, Eq. (2.7) is equivalently written as

$$N\theta = \frac{1}{\lambda}M\theta. \tag{2.10}$$

If the data contain noise, the matrix M is positive definite, so we can apply a standard numerical tool to compute the unit generalized eigenvector θ for the generalized eigenvalue $1/\lambda$ of the *largest* absolute value. The matrix M is not positive definite only when there is no noise. We need not consider that case in practice, but if M happens to have eigenvalue 0, which implies that the data are all exact, the corresponding unit eigenvector θ is exactly the true solution.

2.3 HYPER-RENORMALIZATION AND HYPERLS

According to experiments, the accuracy of the Taubin method is higher than iterative reweight, and renormalization has even higher accuracy. The accuracy can be further improved by the following *hyper-renormalization*.

Procedure 2.3 (Hyper-renormalization)

1. Let $\theta_0 = \mathbf{0}$ and $W_\alpha = 1$, $\alpha = 1, \ldots, N$.

2. Compute the 6×6 matrices

$$
\begin{aligned}
M &= \frac{1}{N}\sum_{\alpha=1}^{N} W_\alpha \xi_\alpha \xi_\alpha^\top, \\
N &= \frac{1}{N}\sum_{\alpha=1}^{N} W_\alpha \Big(V_0[\xi_\alpha] + 2\mathcal{S}[\xi_\alpha e^\top] \Big) \\
&\quad - \frac{1}{N^2}\sum_{\alpha=1}^{N} W_\alpha^2 \Big((\xi_\alpha, M_5^- \xi_\alpha) V_0[\xi_\alpha] + 2\mathcal{S}[V_0[\xi_\alpha] M_5^- \xi_\alpha \xi_\alpha^\top] \Big),
\end{aligned}
\tag{2.11}
$$

where $\mathcal{S}[\,\cdot\,]$ is the symmetrization operator ($\mathcal{S}[A] = (A + A^\top)/2$), and e is the vector

$$
e = (1, 0, 1, 0, 0, 0)^\top. \tag{2.12}
$$

The matrix M_5^- is the pseudoinverse of M of truncated rank 5.

3. Solve the generalized eigenvalue problem

$$
M\theta = \lambda N \theta, \tag{2.13}
$$

and compute the unit generalized eigenvector θ for the generalized eigenvalue λ of the smallest absolute value.

4. If $\theta \approx \theta_0$ up to sign, return θ and stop. Else, update

$$
W_\alpha \leftarrow \frac{1}{(\theta, V_0[\xi_\alpha]\theta)}, \qquad \theta_0 \leftarrow \theta, \tag{2.14}
$$

and go back to Step 2.

Comments. This method was obtained in an effort to improve renormalization by modifying the matrix N in Eq. (2.7) so that the resulting solution θ has the highest accuracy. It has been found by rigorous error analysis that the choice of N in Eq. (2.11) attains the highest accuracy (the derivation of Eq. (2.11) will be given in Chapter 8). The vector e in Eq. (2.12) is defined in such a way that

$$
E[\Delta_2 \xi_\alpha] = \sigma^2 e \tag{2.15}
$$

holds for the second-order noise term $\Delta_2 \xi_\alpha$. From Eqs. (1.18) and (1.20), we obtain Eq. (2.12). The pseudoinverse M_5^- of truncated rank 5 is computed from the eigenvalues $\mu_1 \geq \cdots \geq \mu_6$ of M and the corresponding unit eigenvectors θ_1, ..., θ_6 of M in the form

$$
M_5^- = \frac{1}{\mu_1}\theta_1\theta_1^\top + \cdots + \frac{1}{\mu_5}\theta_5\theta_5^\top, \tag{2.16}
$$

where the term for μ_6 and θ_6 is removed. The matrix $\boldsymbol{N}$ in Eq. (2.11) is not positive definite, but we can use a standard numerical tool by rewriting Eq. (2.13) in the form of Eq. (2.10) and computing the unit generalized eigenvector for the generalized eigenvalue $1/\lambda$ of the largest absolute value. The initial solution minimizes $\sum_{\alpha=1}^{N}(\boldsymbol{\xi}_\alpha, \boldsymbol{\theta})^2$ subject to $(\boldsymbol{\theta}, \boldsymbol{N}\boldsymbol{\theta})$ = constant for the matrix $\boldsymbol{N}$ obtained by letting $W_\alpha = 1$ in Eq. (2.11). This corresponds to the method called *HyperLS* ($\hookrightarrow$ Problem 2.2).

2.4 SUMMARY

We have seen that all the above methods compute the $\boldsymbol{\theta}$ that satisfies

$$\boldsymbol{M}\boldsymbol{\theta} = \lambda \boldsymbol{N}\boldsymbol{\theta}, \tag{2.17}$$

where the matrices $\boldsymbol{M}$ and $\boldsymbol{N}$ are defined in terms of the observations $\boldsymbol{\xi}_\alpha$ and the unknown $\boldsymbol{\theta}$. Different choices of them lead to different methods:

$$\boldsymbol{M} = \begin{cases} \dfrac{1}{N}\displaystyle\sum_{\alpha=1}^{N} \boldsymbol{\xi}_\alpha \boldsymbol{\xi}_\alpha^\top, & \text{(least squares, Taubin, HyperLS)} \\ \dfrac{1}{N}\displaystyle\sum_{\alpha=1}^{N} \dfrac{\boldsymbol{\xi}_\alpha \boldsymbol{\xi}_\alpha^\top}{(\boldsymbol{\theta}, V_0[\boldsymbol{\xi}_\alpha]\boldsymbol{\theta})}, & \text{(iterative reweight, renormalization, hyper-renormalization)} \end{cases} \tag{2.18}$$

$$\boldsymbol{N} = \begin{cases} \boldsymbol{I} \ \text{(identity)}, & \text{(least squares, iterative reweight)} \\ \dfrac{1}{N}\displaystyle\sum_{\alpha=1}^{N} V_0[\boldsymbol{\xi}_\alpha], & \text{(Taubin)} \\ \dfrac{1}{N}\displaystyle\sum_{\alpha=1}^{N} \dfrac{V_0[\boldsymbol{\xi}_\alpha]}{(\boldsymbol{\theta}, V_0[\boldsymbol{\xi}_\alpha]\boldsymbol{\theta})}, & \text{(renormalization)} \\ \dfrac{1}{N}\displaystyle\sum_{\alpha=1}^{N} \Big(V_0[\boldsymbol{\xi}_\alpha] + 2\mathcal{S}[\boldsymbol{\xi}_\alpha \boldsymbol{e}^\top]\Big) & \\ \quad - \dfrac{1}{N^2}\displaystyle\sum_{\alpha=1}^{N} \Big((\boldsymbol{\xi}_\alpha, \boldsymbol{M}_5^- \boldsymbol{\xi}_\alpha) V_0[\boldsymbol{\xi}_\alpha] + 2\mathcal{S}[V_0[\boldsymbol{\xi}_\alpha]\boldsymbol{M}_5^- \boldsymbol{\xi}_\alpha \boldsymbol{\xi}_\alpha^\top]\Big), & \\ & \text{(HyperLS)} \\ \dfrac{1}{N}\displaystyle\sum_{\alpha=1}^{N} \dfrac{1}{(\boldsymbol{\theta}, V_0[\boldsymbol{\xi}_\alpha]\boldsymbol{\theta})} \Big(V_0[\boldsymbol{\xi}_\alpha] + 2\mathcal{S}[\boldsymbol{\xi}_\alpha \boldsymbol{e}^\top]\Big) & \\ \quad - \dfrac{1}{N^2}\displaystyle\sum_{\alpha=1}^{N} \dfrac{1}{(\boldsymbol{\theta}, V_0[\boldsymbol{\xi}_\alpha]\boldsymbol{\theta})^2} \Big((\boldsymbol{\xi}_\alpha, \boldsymbol{M}_5^- \boldsymbol{\xi}_\alpha) V_0[\boldsymbol{\xi}_\alpha] + 2\mathcal{S}[V_0[\boldsymbol{\xi}_\alpha]\boldsymbol{M}_5^- \boldsymbol{\xi}_\alpha \boldsymbol{\xi}_\alpha^\top]\Big). & \\ & \text{(hyper-renormalization)} \end{cases} \tag{2.19}$$

For least squares, Taubin, and HyperLS, the matrices $\boldsymbol{M}$ and $\boldsymbol{N}$ do not contain the unknown $\boldsymbol{\theta}$, so Eq. (2.17) is a generalized eigenvalue problem, which can be directly solved without iterations. For other methods (iterative reweight, renormalization, and hyper-renormalization), the unknown $\boldsymbol{\theta}$ is contained in the denominators in the expressions of $\boldsymbol{M}$ and $\boldsymbol{N}$. Letting the part that contains $\boldsymbol{\theta}$ be $1/W_\alpha$, we compute W_α using the value of $\boldsymbol{\theta}$ obtained in the preceding iteration and solve the generalized eigenvalue problem in the form of Eq. (2.17). We then use the resulting $\boldsymbol{\theta}$ to update W_α and repeat this process.

According to experiments, HyperLS has comparable accuracy to renormalization, and hyper-renormalization has even higher accuracy. Since the hyper-renormalization iteration starts from the HyperLS solution, the convergence is very fast; usually, three to four iterations are sufficient. Numerical comparison of the accuracy and efficiency of these methods is shown in Chapter 6.

2.5 SUPPLEMENTAL NOTE

The iterative reweight was first presented by Sampson [1982]. The renormalization scheme was proposed by Kanatani [1993b]; the details are discussed in Kanatani [1996]. The method of Taubin was proposed by Taubin [1991], but his derivation was rather heuristic without considering the statistical properties of image noise. As mentioned in the Supplemental Note of Chapter 1 (page 6), the HyperLS was obtained in an effort to improve the algebraic distance minimization of $\sum_{\alpha=1}^{N}(\boldsymbol{\xi}_\alpha, \boldsymbol{\theta})^2$ subject to the normalization $(\boldsymbol{\theta}, \boldsymbol{N}\boldsymbol{\theta}) = 1$. The least squares is for $\boldsymbol{N} = \boldsymbol{I}$, while the Taubin method is for $\boldsymbol{N} = (1/N)\sum_{\alpha=1}^{N} V_0[\boldsymbol{\xi}_\alpha]$. Then, what $\boldsymbol{N}$ is the best? After detailed error analysis, the optimal $\boldsymbol{N}$ found by the authors' group [Kanatani and Rangarajan, 2011, Kanatani et al., 2011, Rangarajan and Kanatani, 2009] turned out to be the value of $\boldsymbol{N}$ in Eq. (2.11) with $W_\alpha = 1$. This HyperLS method was then generalized to the iterative hyper-renormalization scheme also by the authors' group [Kanatani et al., 2012, 2014].

The fact that all known algebraic methods can be written in the form of Eq. (2.17) was pointed out in Kanatani et al. [2014]. Since noise is regarded as random, the observed data are random variables having probability distributions. Hence, the computed value $\boldsymbol{\theta}$ is also a random variable having its probability distribution. The choice of the matrices $\boldsymbol{M}$ and $\boldsymbol{N}$ affects the probability distribution of the computed $\boldsymbol{\theta}$. According to the detailed error analysis of Kanatani et al. [2014] (which we will discuss in Chapter 8), the choice of $\boldsymbol{M}$ controls the covariance of $\boldsymbol{\theta}$ (Fig. 2.1a), while the choice of $\boldsymbol{N}$ controls its bias (Fig. 2.1b). If we choose $\boldsymbol{M}$ to be the second row of Eq. (2.18), the covariance matrix of $\boldsymbol{\theta}$ attains the theoretical accuracy limit called the *KCR lower bound* (this will be discussed in Chapter 10) except for $O(\sigma^4)$ terms. If we choose $\boldsymbol{N}$ to be the fifth row of Eq. (2.19), the bias of $\boldsymbol{\theta}$ is 0 except for $O(\sigma^4)$ terms (this will be shown in Chapter 8). Hence, the accuracy of hyper-renormalization cannot be improved any further except for higher order terms in σ. It indeed fits a very accurate ellipse, as will be demonstrated in the experiments in Chapter 6.

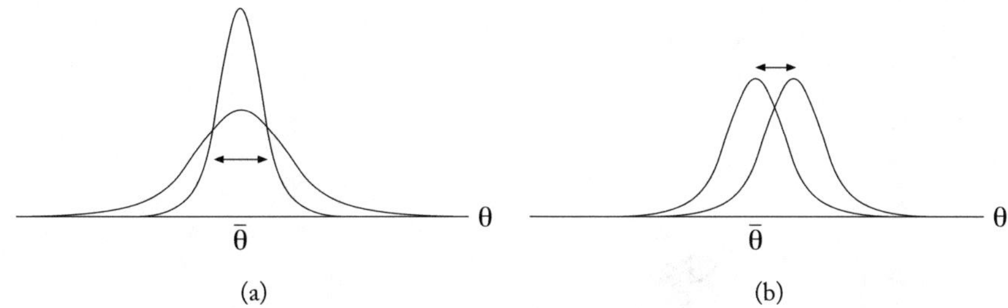

Figure 2.1: (a) The matrix $\boldsymbol{M}$ controls the covariance of $\boldsymbol{\theta}$. (b) The matrix $\boldsymbol{N}$ controls the bias of $\boldsymbol{\theta}$.

PROBLEMS

2.1. Write down the procedure of the Taubin method.

2.2. Write down the HyperLS procedure.

CHAPTER 3

Geometric Fitting

We consider geometric fitting, i.e., computing an ellipse that passes near data points as closely as possible. We first show that the closeness to the data points is measured by a function called the "Sampson error." Then, we give a computational procedure, called "FNS," that minimizes it. Next, we describe a procedure for exactly minimizing the sum of squares from the data points, called the "geometric distance," iteratively using the FNS procedure. Finally, we show how the accuracy can be further improved by a scheme called "hyperaccurate correction."

3.1 GEOMETRIC DISTANCE AND SAMPSON ERROR

Geometric fitting refers to computing the ellipse that minimizes the sum of squares of the distance d_α from observed points (x_α, y_α) to the ellipse (Fig. 3.1). Let $(\bar{x}_\alpha, \bar{y}_\alpha)$ be the point on the ellipse closest to (x_α, y_α). We compute the ellipse that minimizes

$$S = \frac{1}{N}\sum_{\alpha=1}^{N}\Big((x_\alpha - \bar{x}_\alpha)^2 + (y_\alpha - \bar{y}_\alpha)^2\Big) = \frac{1}{N}\sum_{\alpha=1}^{N} d_\alpha^2, \tag{3.1}$$

which is known as the *geometric distance*. Strictly speaking, it should be called the "square geometric distance," because it has the dimension of square length. However, the term "geometric distance" is commonly used for simplicity.

Here, the notations $\bar{x}_\alpha$ and $\bar{y}_\alpha$ are used in a slightly different sense from the previous chapters. In the geometric fitting context, they are the *variables* for *estimating* the true values of x_α

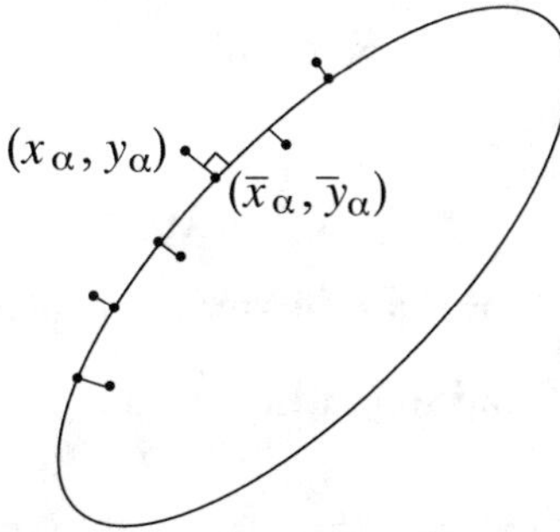

Figure 3.1: We fit an ellipse such that the geometric distance, i.e., the sum of the square distances of the data points to the ellipse, is minimized.

and y_α, rather than their true values themselves. We use this convention for avoiding overly introducing new symbols This also applies to Eq. (1.16), i.e., we now regard Δx_α and Δy_α as the *variables* for *estimating* the discrepancy between observed and estimated positions, rather than stochastic quantities. Hence, Eq. (3.1) is also written as $S = (1/N)\sum_{\alpha=1}^{N}(\Delta x_\alpha^2 + \Delta y_\alpha^2)$.

If the point (x_α, y_α) is close to the ellipse, the square distance d_α^2 is written except for high order terms in Δx_α and Δy_α as follows (see Section 3.5 below):

$$d_\alpha^2 = (x_\alpha - \bar{x}_\alpha)^2 + (y_\alpha - \bar{y}_\alpha)^2 \approx \frac{(\boldsymbol{\xi}_\alpha, \boldsymbol{\theta})^2}{(\boldsymbol{\theta}, V_0[\boldsymbol{\xi}_\alpha]\boldsymbol{\theta})}. \tag{3.2}$$

Hence, the geometric distance in Eq. (3.1) can be approximated by

$$J = \frac{1}{N}\sum_{\alpha=1}^{N} \frac{(\boldsymbol{\xi}_\alpha, \boldsymbol{\theta})^2}{(\boldsymbol{\theta}, V_0[\boldsymbol{\xi}_\alpha]\boldsymbol{\theta})}, \tag{3.3}$$

which is known as the *Sampson error*.

3.2 FNS

A well-known method for minimizing the Sampson error of Eq. (3.3) is the *FNS* (*Fundamental Numerical Scheme*). It goes as follows.

Procedure 3.1 (FNS)

1. Let $\boldsymbol{\theta} = \boldsymbol{\theta}_0 = \mathbf{0}$ and $W_\alpha = 1$, $\alpha = 1, \ldots, N$.
2. Compute the 6×6 matrices

$$\boldsymbol{M} = \frac{1}{N}\sum_{\alpha=1}^{N} W_\alpha \boldsymbol{\xi}_\alpha \boldsymbol{\xi}_\alpha^\top, \qquad \boldsymbol{L} = \frac{1}{N}\sum_{\alpha=1}^{N} W_\alpha^2 (\boldsymbol{\xi}_\alpha, \boldsymbol{\theta})^2 V_0[\boldsymbol{\xi}_\alpha]. \tag{3.4}$$

3. Compute the 6×6 matrix

$$\boldsymbol{X} = \boldsymbol{M} - \boldsymbol{L}. \tag{3.5}$$

4. Solve the eigenvalue problem

$$\boldsymbol{X}\boldsymbol{\theta} = \lambda\boldsymbol{\theta}, \tag{3.6}$$

   and compute the unit eigenvector $\boldsymbol{\theta}$ for the smallest eigenvalue λ.

5. If $\boldsymbol{\theta} \approx \boldsymbol{\theta}_0$ up to sign, return $\boldsymbol{\theta}$ and stop. Else , update

$$W_\alpha \leftarrow \frac{1}{(\boldsymbol{\theta}, V_0[\boldsymbol{\xi}_\alpha]\boldsymbol{\theta})}, \qquad \boldsymbol{\theta}_0 \leftarrow \boldsymbol{\theta}, \tag{3.7}$$

   and go back to Step 2.

Comments. This scheme solves $\nabla_{\theta} J = \mathbf{0}$ for the Sampson error J, where $\nabla_{\theta} J$ is the gradient of J, i.e., the vector whose ith component is $\partial J/\partial \theta_i$. Differentiating Eq. (3.3), we obtain the following expression (↪ Problem 3.1):

$$\nabla_{\theta} J = 2(\boldsymbol{M} - \boldsymbol{L})\boldsymbol{\theta} = 2\boldsymbol{X}\boldsymbol{\theta}. \tag{3.8}$$

Here, $\boldsymbol{M}$, $\boldsymbol{L}$, and $\boldsymbol{X}$ are the matrices given by Eqs. (3.4) and (3.5). After the iterations have converged, $\lambda = 0$ holds (see Proposition 3.5 below). Hence, Eq. (3.8) implies that we obtain the value $\boldsymbol{\theta}$ that satisfies $\nabla_{\theta} J = \mathbf{0}$. Since we start with $\boldsymbol{\theta} = \mathbf{0}$, the matrix $\boldsymbol{L}$ in Eq. (3.4) is initially the zero matrix $\boldsymbol{O}$ (all elements are 0), so Eq. (3.6) reduces to $\boldsymbol{M}\boldsymbol{\theta} = \lambda\boldsymbol{\theta}$. Thus, the FNS iterations start from the least-squares solution.

3.3 GEOMETRIC DISTANCE MINIMIZATION

Once we have computed $\boldsymbol{\theta}$ by the above FNS, we can iteratively modify it so that it strictly minimizes the geometric distance of Eq. (3.1). To be specific, we modify the data $\boldsymbol{\xi}_{\alpha}$, using the current solution $\boldsymbol{\theta}$, and minimize the resulting Sampson error to obtain the new solution $\boldsymbol{\theta}$. After a few iterations, the Sampson error coincides with the geometric distance. The procedure goes as follows.

Procedure 3.2 (Geometric distance minimization)

1. Let $J_0 = \infty$ (a sufficiently large number), $\hat{x}_{\alpha} = x_{\alpha}$, $\hat{y}_{\alpha} = y_{\alpha}$, and $\tilde{x}_{\alpha} = \tilde{y}_{\alpha} = 0$, $\alpha = 1, ..., N$.

2. Compute the normalized covariance matrix $V_0[\hat{\boldsymbol{\xi}}_{\alpha}]$ obtained by replacing $\bar{x}_{\alpha}$ and $\bar{y}_{\alpha}$ in the definition of $V_0[\boldsymbol{\xi}_{\alpha}]$ in Eq. (1.21) by $\hat{x}_{\alpha}$ and $\hat{y}_{\alpha}$, respectively.

3. Computing the following modified data $\boldsymbol{\xi}_{\alpha}^{*}$:

$$\boldsymbol{\xi}_{\alpha}^{*} = \begin{pmatrix} \hat{x}_{\alpha}^2 + 2\hat{x}_{\alpha}\tilde{x}_{\alpha} \\ 2(\hat{x}_{\alpha}\hat{y}_{\alpha} + \hat{y}_{\alpha}\tilde{x}_{\alpha} + \hat{x}_{\alpha}\tilde{y}_{\alpha}) \\ \hat{y}_{\alpha}^2 + 2\hat{y}_{\alpha}\tilde{y}_{\alpha} \\ 2f_0(\hat{x}_{\alpha} + \tilde{x}_{\alpha}) \\ 2f_0(\hat{y}_{\alpha} + \tilde{y}_{\alpha}) \\ f_0^2 \end{pmatrix}. \tag{3.9}$$

4. Compute the value $\boldsymbol{\theta}$ that minimizes the following *modified Sampson error*:

$$J^{*} = \frac{1}{N}\sum_{\alpha=1}^{N} \frac{(\boldsymbol{\xi}_{\alpha}^{*}, \boldsymbol{\theta})^2}{(\boldsymbol{\theta}, V_0[\hat{\boldsymbol{\xi}}_{\alpha}]\boldsymbol{\theta})}. \tag{3.10}$$

5. Update $\tilde{x}_\alpha$ and $\tilde{y}_\alpha$ as follows:

$$\begin{pmatrix} \tilde{x}_\alpha \\ \tilde{y}_\alpha \end{pmatrix} \leftarrow \frac{2(\boldsymbol{\xi}^*_\alpha, \boldsymbol{\theta})}{(\boldsymbol{\theta}, V_0[\hat{\boldsymbol{\xi}}_\alpha]\boldsymbol{\theta})} \begin{pmatrix} \theta_1 & \theta_2 & \theta_4 \\ \theta_2 & \theta_3 & \theta_5 \end{pmatrix} \begin{pmatrix} \hat{x}_\alpha \\ \hat{y}_\alpha \\ f_0 \end{pmatrix}. \tag{3.11}$$

6. Update $\hat{x}_\alpha$ and $\hat{y}_\alpha$ as follows:

$$\hat{x}_\alpha \leftarrow x_\alpha - \tilde{x}_\alpha, \qquad \hat{y}_\alpha \leftarrow y_\alpha - \tilde{y}_\alpha. \tag{3.12}$$

7. Compute

$$J^* = \frac{1}{N}\sum_{\alpha=1}^{N}(\tilde{x}_\alpha^2 + \tilde{y}_\alpha^2). \tag{3.13}$$

If $J^* \approx J_0$, return $\boldsymbol{\theta}$ and stop. Else, let $J_0 \leftarrow J^*$, and go back to Step 2.

Comments. Since $\hat{x}_\alpha = x_\alpha$, $\hat{y}_\alpha = y_\alpha$, and $\tilde{x}_\alpha = \tilde{y}_\alpha = 0$ in the initial iteration, the value $\boldsymbol{\xi}^*_\alpha$ of Eq. (3.9) is the same as $\boldsymbol{\xi}_\alpha$. Hence, the modified Sampson error J^* in Eq. (3.10) is the same as the Sampson error J in Eq. (3.3). Now, we rewrite Eq. (3.1) in the form

$$\begin{aligned} S &= \frac{1}{N}\sum_{\alpha=1}^{N}\Big((\hat{x}_\alpha + (x_\alpha - \hat{x}_\alpha) - \bar{x}_\alpha)^2 + (\hat{y}_\alpha + (y_\alpha - \hat{y}_\alpha) - \bar{y}_\alpha)^2\Big) \\ &= \frac{1}{N}\sum_{\alpha=1}^{N}\Big((\hat{x}_\alpha + \tilde{x}_\alpha - \bar{x}_\alpha)^2 + (\hat{y}_\alpha + \tilde{y}_\alpha - \bar{y}_\alpha)^2\Big), \end{aligned} \tag{3.14}$$

where

$$\tilde{x}_\alpha = x_\alpha - \hat{x}_\alpha, \qquad \tilde{y}_\alpha = y_\alpha - \hat{y}_\alpha. \tag{3.15}$$

In the next iteration, we regard the corrected values $(\hat{x}_\alpha, \hat{y}_\alpha)$ as the input data and minimize Eq. (3.14). Let $(\hat{\hat{x}}_\alpha, \hat{\hat{y}}_\alpha)$ be the resulting solution. Ignoring high-order small terms in $\hat{x}_\alpha - \bar{x}_\alpha$ and $\hat{y}_\alpha - \bar{y}_\alpha$ and rewriting Eq. (3.14), we obtain the modified Sampson error J^* in Eq. (3.10) (see Proposition 3.7 below). We minimize this, regarding $(\hat{\hat{x}}_\alpha, \hat{\hat{y}}_\alpha)$ as $(\hat{x}_\alpha, \hat{y}_\alpha)$, and repeat the same process. Since the current $(\hat{x}_\alpha, \hat{y}_\alpha)$ are the best approximation of $(\bar{x}_\alpha, \bar{y}_\alpha)$, Eq. (3.15) implies that $\tilde{x}_\alpha^2 + \tilde{y}_\alpha^2$ is the corresponding approximation of $(\bar{x}_\alpha - x_\alpha)^2 + (\bar{y}_\alpha - y_\alpha)^2$. So, we use (3.13) to evaluate the geometric distance S. Since the ignored high order terms decrease after each iteration, we obtain in the end the value $\boldsymbol{\theta}$ that minimizes the geometric distance S, and Eq. (3.13) coincides with S. According to experiments, however, the correction of $\boldsymbol{\theta}$ by this procedure is very small: the three or four significant digits are unchanged in typical problems; the corrected ellipse is indistinguishable from the original one when displayed or plotted. Thus, we can practically identify FNS with a method to minimize the geometric distance.

3.4 HYPERACCURATE CORRECTION

The geometric method, whether it is geometric distance minimization or Sampson error minimization, is known to have small statistical bias, meaning that the expectation $E[\boldsymbol{\theta}]$ does not completely agree with the true value $\bar{\boldsymbol{\theta}}$. We express the computed solution $\hat{\boldsymbol{\theta}}$ in the form

$$\hat{\boldsymbol{\theta}} = \bar{\boldsymbol{\theta}} + \Delta_1\boldsymbol{\theta} + \Delta_2\boldsymbol{\theta} + \cdots, \tag{3.16}$$

where $\Delta_k\boldsymbol{\theta}$ is a kth order expression in Δx_α and Δy_α. Since $\Delta_1\boldsymbol{\theta}$ is linear in Δx_α and Δy_α, we have $E[\Delta_1\boldsymbol{\theta}] = \mathbf{0}$. However, we have $E[\Delta_2\boldsymbol{\theta}] \neq \mathbf{0}$ in general. If we are able to evaluate $E[\Delta_2\boldsymbol{\theta}]$ in an analytic form by doing error analysis, it is expected that the subtraction

$$\tilde{\boldsymbol{\theta}} = \hat{\boldsymbol{\theta}} - E[\Delta_2\boldsymbol{\theta}] \tag{3.17}$$

will result in a higher accuracy than $\hat{\boldsymbol{\theta}}$; its expectation is $E[\tilde{\boldsymbol{\theta}}] = \bar{\boldsymbol{\theta}} + O(\sigma^4)$, where σ is the noise level. Note that $\Delta_3\boldsymbol{\theta}$ is a third-order expression in Δx_α and Δy_α, so $E[\Delta_3\boldsymbol{\theta}] = \mathbf{0}$. This operation for increasing accuracy by subtracting $E[\Delta_2\boldsymbol{\theta}]$ is called *hyperaccurate correction*. The procedure goes as follows.

Procedure 3.3 (Hyperaccurate correction)

1. Compute $\boldsymbol{\theta}$ by FNS (Procedure 3.1).
2. Estimate σ^2 in the form
$$\hat{\sigma}^2 = \frac{(\boldsymbol{\theta}, \boldsymbol{M}\boldsymbol{\theta})}{1 - 5/N}, \tag{3.18}$$
where $\boldsymbol{M}$ is the value of the matrix $\boldsymbol{M}$ in Eq. (3.4) after the FNS iterations have converged.
3. Compute the correction term
$$\Delta_c\boldsymbol{\theta} = -\frac{\hat{\sigma}^2}{N}\boldsymbol{M}_5^- \sum_{\alpha=1}^{N} W_\alpha(\boldsymbol{e}, \boldsymbol{\theta})\boldsymbol{\xi}_\alpha + \frac{\hat{\sigma}^2}{N^2}\boldsymbol{M}_5^- \sum_{\alpha=1}^{N} W_\alpha^2(\boldsymbol{\xi}_\alpha, \boldsymbol{M}_5^- V_0[\boldsymbol{\xi}_\alpha]\boldsymbol{\theta})\boldsymbol{\xi}_\alpha, \tag{3.19}$$
where W_α is the value of W_α in Eq. (3.7) after the FNS iterations have converged, and $\boldsymbol{e}$ is the vector in Eq. (2.12). The matrix $\boldsymbol{M}_5^-$ is the pseudoinverse of $\boldsymbol{M}$ of truncated rank 5 given by Eq. (2.16).
4. Correct $\boldsymbol{\theta}$ into
$$\boldsymbol{\theta} \leftarrow \mathcal{N}[\boldsymbol{\theta} - \Delta_c\boldsymbol{\theta}], \tag{3.20}$$
where $\mathcal{N}[\,\cdot\,]$ denotes normalization to unit norm ($\mathcal{N}[\boldsymbol{a}] = \boldsymbol{a}/\|\boldsymbol{a}\|$).

Comments. The derivation of Eq. (3.19) is given in Chapter 9. According to experiments, the accuracy of geometric distance minimization is higher than renormalization but lower than hyper-renormalization. It is known, however, that after the above hyperaccurate correction the accuracy improves and is comparable to hyper-renormalization, as will be demonstrated in Chapter 6.

3.5 DERIVATIONS

If we define the vector $\boldsymbol{x}$ and the symmetric matrix $\boldsymbol{Q}$ by

$$\boldsymbol{x} = \begin{pmatrix} x/f_0 \\ y/f_0 \\ 1 \end{pmatrix}, \qquad \boldsymbol{Q} = \begin{pmatrix} A & B & D \\ B & C & E \\ D & E & F \end{pmatrix}, \tag{3.21}$$

the ellipse equation of Eq. (1.1) is written in the form

$$(\boldsymbol{x}, \boldsymbol{Q}\boldsymbol{x}) = 0. \tag{3.22}$$

Note that the scaling factor f_0 in Eq. (3.21) makes the three component have the order $O(1)$, stabilizing finite-length numerical computation. In the following, we define

$$\boldsymbol{k} \equiv \begin{pmatrix} 0 \\ 0 \\ 1 \end{pmatrix}, \qquad \boldsymbol{P_k} \equiv \begin{pmatrix} 1 & 0 & 0 \\ 0 & 1 & 0 \\ 0 & 0 & 0 \end{pmatrix}. \tag{3.23}$$

Thus, $\boldsymbol{k}$ is the unit vector orthogonal to the xy plane, and $\boldsymbol{P_k}\boldsymbol{v}$ for any vector $\boldsymbol{v}$ is the projection of $\boldsymbol{v}$ onto the xy plane, replacing the third component of $\boldsymbol{v}$ by 0. Evidently, $\boldsymbol{P_k}\boldsymbol{k} = \boldsymbol{0}$.

Proposition 3.4 (Distance to ellipse) *The square distance d_α^2 of point (x_α, y_α) from the ellipse of Eq. (3.22) is written, up to high-order small noise terms, in the form*

$$d_\alpha^2 \approx \frac{f_0^2}{4} \frac{(\boldsymbol{x}_\alpha, \boldsymbol{Q}\boldsymbol{x}_\alpha)}{(\boldsymbol{Q}\boldsymbol{x}_\alpha, \boldsymbol{P_k}\boldsymbol{Q}\boldsymbol{x}_\alpha)}. \tag{3.24}$$

Proof. Let $(\bar{x}_\alpha, \bar{y}_\alpha)$ be the closest point on the ellipse from (x_α, y_α). Let $\bar{\boldsymbol{x}}_\alpha$ and $\boldsymbol{x}_\alpha$ be their vector representations as in Eq. (3.21). If we write

$$\Delta\boldsymbol{x}_\alpha = \boldsymbol{x}_\alpha - \bar{\boldsymbol{x}}_\alpha, \tag{3.25}$$

the distance d_α between the two points is $f_0\|\Delta\boldsymbol{x}_\alpha\|$. We compute the value $\Delta\boldsymbol{x}_\alpha$ that minimizes $\|\Delta\boldsymbol{x}_\alpha\|^2$. Since the point $\bar{\boldsymbol{x}}_\alpha$ is on the ellipse,

$$(\boldsymbol{x}_\alpha - \Delta\boldsymbol{x}_\alpha, \boldsymbol{Q}(\boldsymbol{x}_\alpha - \Delta\boldsymbol{x}_\alpha)) = 0 \tag{3.26}$$

holds. Expanding the left side and ignoring second-order terms in $\Delta\boldsymbol{x}_\alpha$, we obtain

$$(\boldsymbol{Q}\boldsymbol{x}_\alpha, \Delta\boldsymbol{x}_\alpha) = \frac{1}{2}(\boldsymbol{x}_\alpha, \boldsymbol{Q}\boldsymbol{x}_\alpha). \tag{3.27}$$

Since the third components of $\boldsymbol{x}_\alpha$ and $\bar{\boldsymbol{x}}_\alpha$ are both 1, the third component of $\Delta\boldsymbol{x}_\alpha$ is 0. This constraint is written as $(\boldsymbol{k}, \Delta\boldsymbol{x}_\alpha) = 0$, using the vector $\boldsymbol{k}$ in Eq. (3.23). Introducing Lagrange multipliers, we differentiate

$$\|\Delta\boldsymbol{x}_\alpha\|^2 - \lambda_\alpha\Big((\boldsymbol{Q}\boldsymbol{x}_\alpha, \Delta\boldsymbol{x}_\alpha) - \frac{1}{2}(\boldsymbol{x}_\alpha, \boldsymbol{Q}\boldsymbol{x}_\alpha)\Big) - \mu(\boldsymbol{k}, \Delta\boldsymbol{x}_\alpha), \tag{3.28}$$

with respect to $\Delta\boldsymbol{x}_\alpha$. Letting the result be $\boldsymbol{0}$, we obtain

$$2\Delta\boldsymbol{x}_\alpha - \lambda_\alpha\boldsymbol{Q}\boldsymbol{x}_\alpha - \mu\boldsymbol{k} = \boldsymbol{0}. \tag{3.29}$$

Multiplying $\boldsymbol{P}_{\boldsymbol{k}}$ on both sides and noting that $\boldsymbol{P}_{\boldsymbol{k}}\Delta\boldsymbol{x}_\alpha = \Delta\boldsymbol{x}_\alpha$ and $\boldsymbol{P}_{\boldsymbol{k}}\boldsymbol{k} = \boldsymbol{0}$, we obtain

$$\Delta\boldsymbol{x}_\alpha = \frac{\lambda_\alpha}{2}\boldsymbol{P}_{\boldsymbol{k}}\boldsymbol{Q}\boldsymbol{x}_\alpha. \tag{3.30}$$

Substituting this into Eq. (3.27), we have

$$(\boldsymbol{Q}\boldsymbol{x}_\alpha, \frac{\lambda_\alpha}{2}\boldsymbol{P}_{\boldsymbol{k}}\boldsymbol{Q}\boldsymbol{x}_\alpha) = \frac{1}{2}(\boldsymbol{x}_\alpha, \boldsymbol{Q}\boldsymbol{x}_\alpha), \tag{3.31}$$

from which λ_α is given in the form

$$\lambda_\alpha = \frac{(\boldsymbol{x}_\alpha, \boldsymbol{Q}\boldsymbol{x}_\alpha)}{(\boldsymbol{Q}\boldsymbol{x}_\alpha, \boldsymbol{P}_{\boldsymbol{k}}\boldsymbol{Q}\boldsymbol{x}_\alpha)}. \tag{3.32}$$

Hence, $\Delta\boldsymbol{x}_\alpha$ is given by

$$\Delta\boldsymbol{x}_\alpha = \frac{(\boldsymbol{x}_\alpha, \boldsymbol{Q}\boldsymbol{x}_\alpha)\boldsymbol{P}_{\boldsymbol{k}}\boldsymbol{Q}\boldsymbol{x}_\alpha}{2(\boldsymbol{Q}\boldsymbol{x}_\alpha, \boldsymbol{P}_{\boldsymbol{k}}\boldsymbol{Q}\boldsymbol{x}_\alpha)}. \tag{3.33}$$

Thus, we obtain

$$\|\Delta\boldsymbol{x}_\alpha\|^2 = \frac{(\boldsymbol{x}_\alpha, \boldsymbol{Q}\boldsymbol{x}_\alpha)^2\|\boldsymbol{P}_{\boldsymbol{k}}\boldsymbol{Q}\boldsymbol{x}_\alpha\|^2}{4(\boldsymbol{Q}\boldsymbol{x}_\alpha, \boldsymbol{P}_{\boldsymbol{k}}\boldsymbol{Q}\boldsymbol{x}_\alpha)^2} = \frac{(\boldsymbol{x}_\alpha, \boldsymbol{Q}\boldsymbol{x}_\alpha)^2}{4(\boldsymbol{Q}\boldsymbol{x}_\alpha, \boldsymbol{P}_{\boldsymbol{k}}\boldsymbol{Q}\boldsymbol{x}_\alpha)}, \tag{3.34}$$

where we have noted that $\boldsymbol{P}_{\boldsymbol{k}}^2 = \boldsymbol{P}_{\boldsymbol{k}}$ from the definition of $\boldsymbol{P}_{\boldsymbol{k}}$. We have also used the identity

$$\|\boldsymbol{P}_{\boldsymbol{k}}\boldsymbol{Q}\boldsymbol{x}_\alpha\|^2 = (\boldsymbol{P}_{\boldsymbol{k}}\boldsymbol{Q}\boldsymbol{x}_\alpha, \boldsymbol{P}_{\boldsymbol{k}}\boldsymbol{Q}\boldsymbol{x}_\alpha) = (\boldsymbol{Q}\boldsymbol{x}_\alpha, \boldsymbol{P}_{\boldsymbol{k}}^2\boldsymbol{Q}\boldsymbol{x}_\alpha) = (\boldsymbol{Q}\boldsymbol{x}_\alpha, \boldsymbol{P}_{\boldsymbol{k}}\boldsymbol{Q}\boldsymbol{x}_\alpha). \tag{3.35}$$

Hence, $d_\alpha^2 = f_0^2\|\Delta\boldsymbol{x}_\alpha\|^2$ is expressed in the form of Eq. (3.24). □

From the definition of the vectors $\boldsymbol{\xi}$ and $\boldsymbol{\theta}$ and the matrices $\boldsymbol{Q}$ and $V_0[\boldsymbol{\xi}_\alpha]$ ($(\bar{x}_\alpha, \bar{y}_\alpha)$ in Eq. (1.21) are replaced by (x_α, y_α)), we can confirm after substitution and expansion that the following identities hold:

$$(\boldsymbol{x}_\alpha, \boldsymbol{Q}\boldsymbol{x}_\alpha) = \frac{1}{f_0^2}(\boldsymbol{\xi}_\alpha, \boldsymbol{\theta}), \qquad (\boldsymbol{Q}\boldsymbol{x}_\alpha, \boldsymbol{P}_{\boldsymbol{k}}\boldsymbol{Q}\boldsymbol{x}_\alpha) = \frac{1}{4f_0^2}(\boldsymbol{\theta}, V_0[\boldsymbol{\xi}_\alpha]\boldsymbol{\theta}). \tag{3.36}$$

This means that Eq. (3.24) is equivalently written as Eq. (3.2).

Proposition 3.5 (Eigenvalue of FNS) *The eigenvalue λ in Eq. (3.6) is 0 after the FNS iterations have converged.*

Proof. Computing the inner product of Eq. (3.6) and $\boldsymbol{\theta}$ on both sides, we see that $(\boldsymbol{\theta}, \boldsymbol{X}\boldsymbol{\theta}) = \lambda\|\boldsymbol{\theta}\|^2 = \lambda$. If the iterations have converged, Eq. (3.7) means that $W_\alpha = 1/(\boldsymbol{\theta}, V_0[\boldsymbol{\xi}_\alpha]\boldsymbol{\theta})$ holds. Hence,

$$
\begin{aligned}
(\boldsymbol{\theta}, \boldsymbol{X}\boldsymbol{\theta}) = (\boldsymbol{\theta}, \boldsymbol{M}\boldsymbol{\theta}) - (\boldsymbol{\theta}, \boldsymbol{L}\boldsymbol{\theta}) &= \frac{1}{N}\sum_{\alpha=1}^{N} \frac{(\boldsymbol{\theta}, \boldsymbol{\xi}_\alpha \boldsymbol{\xi}_\alpha^\top \boldsymbol{\theta})}{(\boldsymbol{\theta}, V_0[\boldsymbol{\xi}_\alpha]\boldsymbol{\theta})} - \frac{1}{N}\sum_{\alpha=1}^{N} \frac{(\boldsymbol{\xi}_\alpha, \boldsymbol{\theta})^2 (\boldsymbol{\theta}, V_0[\boldsymbol{\xi}_\alpha]\boldsymbol{\theta})}{(\boldsymbol{\theta}, V_0[\boldsymbol{\xi}_\alpha]\boldsymbol{\theta})^2} \\
&= \frac{1}{N}\sum_{\alpha=1}^{N} \frac{(\boldsymbol{\xi}_\alpha, \boldsymbol{\theta})^2}{(\boldsymbol{\theta}, V_0[\boldsymbol{\xi}_\alpha]\boldsymbol{\theta})} - \frac{1}{N}\sum_{\alpha=1}^{N} \frac{(\boldsymbol{\xi}_\alpha, \boldsymbol{\theta})^2}{(\boldsymbol{\theta}, V_0[\boldsymbol{\xi}_\alpha]\boldsymbol{\theta})} = 0,
\end{aligned}
$$

which means $\lambda = 0$. □

Lemma 3.6 (Geometric distance minimization) *For the ellipse given by Eq. (3.22), the position of the point $(\bar{x}_\alpha, \bar{y}_\alpha)$ that minimizes Eq. (3.14), which we write $(\hat{\hat{x}}_\alpha, \hat{\hat{y}}_\alpha)$, is written as*

$$
\begin{pmatrix} \hat{\hat{x}}_\alpha \\ \hat{\hat{y}}_\alpha \end{pmatrix} = \begin{pmatrix} x_\alpha \\ y_\alpha \end{pmatrix} - \frac{(\hat{\boldsymbol{x}}_\alpha, \boldsymbol{Q}\hat{\boldsymbol{x}}'_\alpha) + 2(\boldsymbol{Q}\hat{\boldsymbol{x}}'_\alpha, \tilde{\boldsymbol{x}}_\alpha)}{2(\boldsymbol{Q}\hat{\boldsymbol{x}}_\alpha, \boldsymbol{P}_{\mathbf{k}}\boldsymbol{Q}\hat{\boldsymbol{x}}_\alpha)} \begin{pmatrix} A & B & D \\ B & C & E \end{pmatrix} \begin{pmatrix} \hat{x}_\alpha \\ \hat{y}_\alpha \\ f_0 \end{pmatrix}, \tag{3.37}
$$

if high-order terms in $\hat{x}_\alpha - \bar{x}_\alpha$ and $\hat{y}_\alpha - \bar{y}_\alpha$ are ignored, where A, B, C, D, and E are the elements of the matrix $\boldsymbol{Q}$ in Eq. (3.21). The vectors $\hat{\boldsymbol{x}}_\alpha$ and $\tilde{\boldsymbol{x}}_\alpha$ are defined by

$$
\hat{\boldsymbol{x}}_\alpha = \begin{pmatrix} \hat{x}_\alpha / f_0 \\ \hat{y}_\alpha / f_0 \\ 1 \end{pmatrix}, \qquad \tilde{\boldsymbol{x}}_\alpha = \begin{pmatrix} \tilde{x}_\alpha / f_0 \\ \tilde{y}_\alpha / f_0 \\ 0 \end{pmatrix}, \tag{3.38}
$$

where $(\tilde{x}_\alpha, \tilde{y}_\alpha)$ are defined by Eq. (3.15).

Proof. If we let

$$
\Delta\hat{\boldsymbol{x}}_\alpha = \hat{\boldsymbol{x}}_\alpha - \bar{\boldsymbol{x}}_\alpha, \tag{3.39}
$$

the sum of squares $\sum_{\alpha=1}^{N} \|\tilde{\boldsymbol{x}}_\alpha + \Delta\hat{\boldsymbol{x}}_\alpha\|^2$ equals the geometric distance S of Eq. (3.14) divided by f_0^2. Since $\bar{\boldsymbol{x}}_\alpha$ satisfies the ellipse equation, we have

$$
(\hat{\boldsymbol{x}}_\alpha - \Delta\hat{\boldsymbol{x}}_\alpha, \boldsymbol{Q}(\hat{\boldsymbol{x}}_\alpha - \Delta\hat{\boldsymbol{x}}_\alpha)) = 0. \tag{3.40}
$$

Expanding this and ignoring quadratic terms in $\Delta\hat{\boldsymbol{x}}_\alpha$, we obtain

$$
(\boldsymbol{Q}\hat{\boldsymbol{x}}_\alpha, \Delta\hat{\boldsymbol{x}}_\alpha) = \frac{1}{2}(\hat{\boldsymbol{x}}_\alpha, \boldsymbol{Q}\hat{\boldsymbol{x}}'_\alpha). \tag{3.41}
$$

Since the third components of $\hat{\boldsymbol{x}}_\alpha$ and $\bar{\boldsymbol{x}}_\alpha$ are both 1, the third component of $\Delta\hat{\boldsymbol{x}}_\alpha$ is 0, i.e., $(\boldsymbol{k}, \Delta\hat{\boldsymbol{x}}_\alpha) = 0$. Introducing Lagrange multipliers, we differentiate

$$\sum_{\alpha=1}^{N} \|\tilde{\boldsymbol{x}}_\alpha + \Delta\hat{\boldsymbol{x}}_\alpha\|^2 - \sum_{\alpha=1}^{N} \lambda_\alpha \Big((\boldsymbol{Q}\hat{\boldsymbol{x}}_\alpha, \Delta\hat{\boldsymbol{x}}_\alpha) - \frac{1}{2}(\hat{\boldsymbol{x}}_\alpha, \boldsymbol{Q}\hat{\boldsymbol{x}}_\alpha)\Big) - \sum_{\alpha=1}^{N} \mu_\alpha(\boldsymbol{k}, \Delta\hat{\boldsymbol{x}}_\alpha). \tag{3.42}$$

with respect to $\Delta\hat{\boldsymbol{x}}_\alpha$. Letting the result be $\boldsymbol{0}$, we obtain

$$2(\tilde{\boldsymbol{x}}_\alpha + \Delta\hat{\boldsymbol{x}}_\alpha) - \lambda_\alpha \boldsymbol{Q}\hat{\boldsymbol{x}}_\alpha - \mu_\alpha \boldsymbol{k} = \boldsymbol{0}. \tag{3.43}$$

Multiplying both sides by the matrix $\boldsymbol{P}_{\boldsymbol{k}}$ of Eq. (3.23) and noting that $\boldsymbol{P}_{\boldsymbol{k}}\tilde{\boldsymbol{x}}_\alpha = \tilde{\boldsymbol{x}}_\alpha$ from the definition of $\tilde{\boldsymbol{x}}_\alpha$, we obtain

$$2\tilde{\boldsymbol{x}}_\alpha + 2\Delta\hat{\boldsymbol{x}}_\alpha - \lambda_\alpha \boldsymbol{P}_{\boldsymbol{k}}\boldsymbol{Q}\hat{\boldsymbol{x}}_\alpha = \boldsymbol{0}, \tag{3.44}$$

from which we obtain

$$\Delta\hat{\boldsymbol{x}}_\alpha = \frac{\lambda_\alpha}{2}\boldsymbol{P}_{\boldsymbol{k}}\boldsymbol{Q}\hat{\boldsymbol{x}}_\alpha - \tilde{\boldsymbol{x}}_\alpha. \tag{3.45}$$

Substituting this into Eq. (3.41), we obtain

$$(\boldsymbol{Q}\hat{\boldsymbol{x}}_\alpha, \frac{\lambda_\alpha}{2}\boldsymbol{P}_{\boldsymbol{k}}\boldsymbol{Q}\hat{\boldsymbol{x}}_\alpha - \tilde{\boldsymbol{x}}_\alpha) = \frac{1}{2}(\hat{\boldsymbol{x}}_\alpha, \boldsymbol{Q}\hat{\boldsymbol{x}}_\alpha), \tag{3.46}$$

from which λ_α is given in the form

$$\lambda_\alpha = \frac{(\hat{\boldsymbol{x}}_\alpha, \boldsymbol{Q}\hat{\boldsymbol{x}}_\alpha) + 2(\boldsymbol{Q}\hat{\boldsymbol{x}}_\alpha, \tilde{\boldsymbol{x}}_\alpha)}{(\boldsymbol{Q}\hat{\boldsymbol{x}}_\alpha, \boldsymbol{P}_{\boldsymbol{k}}\boldsymbol{Q}\hat{\boldsymbol{x}}_\alpha)}. \tag{3.47}$$

Hence,

$$\Delta\hat{\boldsymbol{x}}_\alpha = \frac{\Big((\hat{\boldsymbol{x}}_\alpha, \boldsymbol{Q}\hat{\boldsymbol{x}}_\alpha) + 2(\boldsymbol{Q}\hat{\boldsymbol{x}}_\alpha, \tilde{\boldsymbol{x}}_\alpha)\Big)\boldsymbol{P}_{\boldsymbol{k}}\boldsymbol{Q}\hat{\boldsymbol{x}}_\alpha}{2(\boldsymbol{Q}\hat{\boldsymbol{x}}_\alpha, \boldsymbol{P}_{\boldsymbol{k}}\boldsymbol{Q}\hat{\boldsymbol{x}}_\alpha)} - \tilde{\boldsymbol{x}}_\alpha. \tag{3.48}$$

It follows that $\bar{\boldsymbol{x}}_\alpha$ is estimated to be

$$\hat{\hat{\boldsymbol{x}}}_\alpha = \boldsymbol{x}_\alpha - \frac{\Big((\hat{\boldsymbol{x}}_\alpha, \boldsymbol{Q}\hat{\boldsymbol{x}}_\alpha) + 2(\boldsymbol{Q}\hat{\boldsymbol{x}}_\alpha, \tilde{\boldsymbol{x}}_\alpha)\Big)\boldsymbol{P}_{\boldsymbol{k}}\boldsymbol{Q}\hat{\boldsymbol{x}}_\alpha}{2(\boldsymbol{Q}\hat{\boldsymbol{x}}_\alpha, \boldsymbol{P}_{\boldsymbol{k}}\boldsymbol{Q}\hat{\boldsymbol{x}}_\alpha)}. \tag{3.49}$$

Rewriting this, we obtain Eq. (3.37). □

Proposition 3.7 (Modified Sampson error) *If we replace $(\bar{x}_\alpha, \bar{y}_\alpha)$ in Eq. (3.1) by $(\hat{\hat{x}}_\alpha, \hat{\hat{y}}_\alpha)$ and use the 9-D vector $\boldsymbol{\xi}^*_\alpha$ in Eq. (3.9), the geometric distance S is written in the form of Eq. (3.10).*

Proof. In correspondence with Eq. (3.36), we can confirm, by substitution and expansion, the identities

$$(\hat{\boldsymbol{x}}_\alpha, \boldsymbol{Q}\hat{\boldsymbol{x}}_\alpha) + 2(\boldsymbol{Q}\hat{\boldsymbol{x}}_\alpha, \tilde{\boldsymbol{x}}_\alpha) = \frac{1}{f_0^2}(\boldsymbol{\xi}^*_\alpha, \boldsymbol{\theta}) \tag{3.50}$$

$$(\boldsymbol{Q}\hat{\boldsymbol{x}}_\alpha, \boldsymbol{P}_k \boldsymbol{Q}\hat{\boldsymbol{x}}_\alpha) = \frac{1}{4f_0^2}(\boldsymbol{\theta}, V_0[\hat{\boldsymbol{\xi}}_\alpha]\boldsymbol{\theta}) \tag{3.51}$$

hold, where $V_0[\hat{\boldsymbol{\xi}}_\alpha]$ is the normalized covariance matrix obtained by replacing $(\bar{x}, \bar{y})$ in Eq. (1.21) by $(\hat{x}_\alpha, \hat{y}_\alpha)$. Hence, Eq. (3.37) can be written in the form

$$\begin{pmatrix} \hat{\hat{x}}_\alpha \\ \hat{\hat{y}}_\alpha \end{pmatrix} = \begin{pmatrix} x_\alpha \\ y_\alpha \end{pmatrix} - \frac{2(\boldsymbol{\xi}_\alpha^*, \boldsymbol{\theta})}{(\boldsymbol{\theta}, V_0[\hat{\boldsymbol{\xi}}_\alpha]\boldsymbol{\theta})} \begin{pmatrix} \theta_1 & \theta_2 & \theta_4 \\ \theta_2 & \theta_3 & \theta_5 \end{pmatrix} \begin{pmatrix} \hat{x}_\alpha \\ \hat{y}_\alpha \\ f_0 \end{pmatrix}. \tag{3.52}$$

Note that

$$\begin{pmatrix} \theta_1 & \theta_2 & \theta_4 \\ \theta_2 & \theta_3 & \theta_5 \end{pmatrix} \begin{pmatrix} \hat{x}_\alpha \\ \hat{y}_\alpha \\ f_0 \end{pmatrix} = f_0 \begin{pmatrix} \theta_1 & \theta_2 & \theta_4 \\ \theta_2 & \theta_3 & \theta_5 \\ 0 & 0 & 0 \end{pmatrix} \begin{pmatrix} \hat{x}_\alpha/f_0 \\ \hat{y}_\alpha/f_0 \\ 1 \end{pmatrix} = f_0 \boldsymbol{P}_k \boldsymbol{Q}\hat{\boldsymbol{x}}_\alpha. \tag{3.53}$$

From Eq. (3.51), the square norm of this is

$$\begin{aligned} f_0^2 \|\boldsymbol{P}_k \boldsymbol{Q}\hat{\boldsymbol{x}}_\alpha\|^2 &= f_0^2 (\boldsymbol{P}_k \boldsymbol{Q}\hat{\boldsymbol{x}}_\alpha, \boldsymbol{P}_k \boldsymbol{Q}\hat{\boldsymbol{x}}_\alpha) = f_0^2 (\boldsymbol{Q}\hat{\boldsymbol{x}}_\alpha, \boldsymbol{P}_k^2 \boldsymbol{Q}\hat{\boldsymbol{x}}_\alpha) \\ &= f_0^2 (\boldsymbol{Q}\hat{\boldsymbol{x}}_\alpha, \boldsymbol{P}_k \boldsymbol{Q}\hat{\boldsymbol{x}}_\alpha) = \frac{1}{4}(\boldsymbol{\theta}, V_0[\hat{\boldsymbol{\xi}}_\alpha]\boldsymbol{\theta}). \end{aligned} \tag{3.54}$$

Hence, if we replace $(\bar{x}_\alpha, \bar{y}_\alpha)$ in Eq. (3.1) by $(\hat{\hat{x}}_\alpha, \hat{\hat{y}}_\alpha)$ and substitute Eq. (3.37), we can approximate the geometric distance S in the form

$$\begin{aligned} S &\approx \frac{1}{N}\sum_{\alpha=1}^{N}\left((x_\alpha - \hat{\hat{x}}_\alpha)^2 + (y_\alpha - \hat{\hat{y}}_\alpha)^2\right) = \frac{1}{N}\sum_{\alpha=1}^{N}\left\| \begin{pmatrix} \hat{\hat{x}}_\alpha \\ \hat{\hat{y}}_\alpha \end{pmatrix} - \begin{pmatrix} x_\alpha \\ y_\alpha \end{pmatrix} \right\|^2 \\ &= \frac{1}{N}\sum_{\alpha=1}^{N} \frac{4(\boldsymbol{\xi}_\alpha^*, \boldsymbol{\theta})^2}{(\boldsymbol{\theta}, V_0[\hat{\boldsymbol{\xi}}_\alpha]\boldsymbol{\theta})^2} \frac{(\boldsymbol{\theta}, V_0[\hat{\boldsymbol{\xi}}_\alpha]\boldsymbol{\theta})}{4} = \frac{1}{N}\sum_{\alpha=1}^{N} \frac{(\boldsymbol{\xi}_\alpha^*, \boldsymbol{\theta})^2}{(\boldsymbol{\theta}, V_0[\hat{\boldsymbol{\xi}}_\alpha]\boldsymbol{\theta})}. \end{aligned} \tag{3.55}$$

Thus, we obtain Eq. (3.35). □

3.6 SUPPLEMENTAL NOTE

The FNS scheme for minimizing the Sampson error was introduced by Chojnacki et al. [2000]. They called Eq. (3.3) the *AML* (*approximated maximum likelihood*), but later the term "Sampson error" came to be used widely. This name originates from Sampson [1982], who proposed the iterative reweight scheme (Procedure 2.1 in Chapter 2) for minimizing it. It was later pointed out, however, that iterative reweight does not minimize Eq. (3.3), because it uses the value of W_α computed in the preceding step of the iteration, which means that we are minimizing the numerator part with the denominators fixed. Hence, after the convergence of iterative reweight, we obtain a solution $\boldsymbol{\theta}$ such that for any $\boldsymbol{\theta}' \neq \boldsymbol{\theta}$

$$\frac{1}{N}\sum_{\alpha=1}^{N} \frac{(\boldsymbol{\xi}_\alpha, \boldsymbol{\theta})^2}{(\boldsymbol{\theta}, V_0[\boldsymbol{\xi}_\alpha]\boldsymbol{\theta})} \leq \frac{1}{N}\sum_{\alpha=1}^{N} \frac{(\boldsymbol{\xi}_\alpha, \boldsymbol{\theta}')^2}{(\boldsymbol{\theta}, V_0[\boldsymbol{\xi}_\alpha]\boldsymbol{\theta})}. \tag{3.56}$$

However, this does not mean that

$$\frac{1}{N}\sum_{\alpha=1}^{N}\frac{(\boldsymbol{\xi}_\alpha,\boldsymbol{\theta})^2}{(\boldsymbol{\theta},V_0[\boldsymbol{\xi}_\alpha]\boldsymbol{\theta})}\leq\frac{1}{N}\sum_{\alpha=1}^{N}\frac{(\boldsymbol{\xi}_\alpha,\boldsymbol{\theta}')^2}{(\boldsymbol{\theta}',V_0[\boldsymbol{\xi}_\alpha]\boldsymbol{\theta}')}. \tag{3.57}$$

The FNS solution $\boldsymbol{\theta}$ is guaranteed to satisfy this inequality.

In the Step 4 of Procedure 3.1, we can compute the unit eigenvector for the eigenvalue of the *smallest absolute value*, but it was experimentally found by Chojnacki et al. [2000] and Kanatani and Sugaya [2007b] that the iterations converge faster using the (possibly negative) *smallest* eigenvalue. This is explained as follows. Equation (3.6) is written as

$$(\boldsymbol{M}-\boldsymbol{L}-\lambda\boldsymbol{I})\boldsymbol{\theta}=\boldsymbol{0}. \tag{3.58}$$

The matrix $\boldsymbol{L}$ in Eq. (3.4) is generally positive semidefinite and approaches the zero matrix $\boldsymbol{O}$ in the course of the iterations; $\boldsymbol{L}$ is equal to $\boldsymbol{O}$ if the constraint $(\boldsymbol{\xi}_\alpha,\boldsymbol{\theta})=0$ exactly holds. Initially, however, $\boldsymbol{L}$ can be very different from $\boldsymbol{O}$. This effect is better canceled if we choose a *negative* λ.

There exists an alternative iterative scheme closely resembling FNS called *HEIV* (*heteroscedastic errors-in-variables method*) [Leedan and Meer, 2000, Matei and Meer, 2006] for minimizing the Sampson error of Eq. (3.3); the computed solution is the same as FNS. The general strategy of minimizing the geometric distance by repeating Sampson error minimization was presented by Kanatani and Sugaya [2010a], and its use for ellipse fitting was presented in Kanatani and Sugaya [2008].

When the noise distribution is Gaussian, the geometric distance minimization is equivalent to what is called in statistics *maximum likelihood estimation* (*ML*) (we discuss this in detail in Chapter 9). The fact that the maximum likelihood solution has statistical bias has been pointed out by many people. The cause of the bias is the fact that an ellipse is a convex curve: if a point on the curve is randomly displaced, the probability of falling outside is larger than the probability of falling inside. Given a data point, its closest point on the ellipse is the foot of the perpendicular line from it to the ellipse, and the probability as to on which side on the curve its true position is more likely to be depends on the shape and the curvature of the ellipse in the neighborhood. Okatani and Deguchi [2009a] analyzed this for removing the bias. They also used a technique called *projected score* to remove bias [Okatani and Deguchi, 2009b]. The hyperaccurate correction described in this chapter was introduced by Kanatani [2006, 2008], and Kanatani and Sugaya [2013].

PROBLEMS

3.1. Show that the derivative of Eq. (3.3) is given by Eq. (3.8).

CHAPTER 4

Robust Fitting

We consider two typical cases where standard ellipse fitting techniques fail: existence of superfluous data and scarcity of information. In the former case, we discuss how to remove unwanted segments, or "outliners," that do not belong to the ellipse under consideration. In the latter case, which occurs when the segment is too short or too noisy, a hyperbola can be fit. We describe methods that force the fit to be an ellipse, although accuracy is compromised.

4.1 OUTLIER REMOVAL

For fitting an ellipse to real image data, we must first extract a sequence of edge points from an elliptic arc. However, edge segments obtained by an edge detection filter may not belong to the same ellipse; some may be parts of other object boundaries. We call points of such segments *outliers*; those coming from the ellipse under consideration are called *inliers*. Note that we are not talking abou random dispersions of edge pixels due to image processing inaccuracy, although such pixels, if they exist, are also-called outliers. Our main concern is the parts of the extracted edge sequence that do not belong to the ellipse we are interested in (see Fig. 1.1).

Methods that are not sensitive to the existence of outliers are said to be *robust*. The general idea of robust fitting is to find an ellipse such that *the number of points close to it is as large as possible*. Then, those points that are not close to it are removed as outliers. A typical such method is *RANSAC* (*Random Sample Consensus*). The procedure goes as follows.

Procedure 4.1 (RANSAC)

1. Randomly select five points from the input sequence, and let $\boldsymbol{\xi}_1, \boldsymbol{\xi}_2, ..., \boldsymbol{\xi}_5$ be their vector representations in the form of Eq. (1.8).

2. Compute the unit eigenvector $\boldsymbol{\theta}$ of the matrix

$$M_5 = \sum_{\alpha=1}^{5} \boldsymbol{\xi}_\alpha \boldsymbol{\xi}_\alpha^\top, \tag{4.1}$$

for the smallest eigenvalue, and store it as a candidate.

3. Let n be the number of points in the input sequence that satisfy

$$\frac{(\boldsymbol{\xi}, \boldsymbol{\theta})^2}{(\boldsymbol{\theta}, V_0[\boldsymbol{\xi}]\boldsymbol{\theta})} < d^2, \tag{4.2}$$

where $\boldsymbol{\xi}$ is the vector representation of the point in the sequence in the form of Eq. (1.8), $V_0[\boldsymbol{\xi}]$ is the normalized covariance matrix defined by Eq. (1.21), and d is a threshold for admissible deviation from the fitted ellipse, e.g., $d = 2$ (pixels). Store that n.

4. Select a new set of five points from the input sequence, and do the same. Repeat this many times, and return from among the stored candidate ellipses the one for which n is the largest.

Comments. In Step 1, we select five integers over $[1, N]$, using uniform random sampling; overlapped values are discarded. Step 2 computes the ellipse that passes through the five point. We may solve the simultaneous linear equations obtained by substituting the point coordinates to Eq. (1.1) for A, B, ..., F; they are determined up to scale (and normalized afterward). However, using least squares as shown above is easier to program: we compute the unit eigenvector of the matrix $\boldsymbol{M}$ in the first row of Eq. (2.18); the coefficient $1/N$ is omitted, but the computed eigenvectors are the same. In Step 3, we measure the distance of the points from the ellipse by Eq. (3.2); by definition, both $\boldsymbol{\xi}$ and $V_0[\boldsymbol{\xi}]$ have the dimension of square length, so the left side of Eq. (4.2) also has the dimension of square length. We can directly go on to the next sampling if the count n is smaller than the stored count, and we can stop if the current value of n is not updated over a fixed number of sampling. In the end, those pixels that do not satisfy Eq. (4.2) for the chosen ellipse are removed as outliers.

In Chapter 6, some image examples are shown to demonstrate how the RANSAC procedure fits a correct ellipse to partly elliptic (i.e., inlying) and partly non-elliptic (i.e., outlying) edge segments.

4.2 ELLIPSE-SPECIFIC FITTING

Equation (1.1) does not necessarily represent an ellipse; depending on the coefficients, it can represent an hyperbola or a parabola. In special cases, it may degenerate into two lines, or no real point (x, y) may satisfy Eq. (1.1). It can be shown that Eq. (1.1) represents an ellipse if and only if

$$AC - B^2 > 0. \tag{4.3}$$

We will discuss this further in Chapter 5. Usually, an ellipse is obtained when Eq. (1.1) is fitted to an edge point sequence obtained from an ellipse, but if the sequence does not have sufficient information, typically if it is too short or too noisy, a hyperbola may result; a parabola results only when the solution exactly satisfies $AC - B^2 = 0$, but this possibility can be excluded in real situations. If a hyperbola results, we can ignore it, because it indicates data insufficiency. From a theoretical interest, however, schemes to force the fit to be an ellipse have been studied in the past. The best known is the following method of Fitzgibbon et al. [1999].

Procedure 4.2 (Method of Fitzgibbon et al.)

1. Compute the 6×6 matrices

$$M = \frac{1}{N}\sum_{\alpha=1}^{N} \xi_\alpha \xi_\alpha^\top, \qquad N = \begin{pmatrix} 0 & 0 & 1 & 0 & 0 & 0 \\ 0 & -2 & 0 & 0 & 0 & 0 \\ 1 & 0 & 0 & 0 & 0 & 0 \\ 0 & 0 & 0 & 0 & 0 & 0 \\ 0 & 0 & 0 & 0 & 0 & 0 \\ 0 & 0 & 0 & 0 & 0 & 0 \end{pmatrix}. \tag{4.4}$$

2. Solve the generalized eigenvalue problem

$$M\theta = \lambda N\theta, \tag{4.5}$$

and return the unit generalized eigenvector θ for the generalized eigenvalue λ of the smallest absolute value.

Comments. This is an algebraic method, minimizing the algebraic distance $\sum_{\alpha=1}^{N}(\xi_\alpha, \theta)^2$ subject to the normalization $AC - B^2 = 1$ so that Eq. (4.3) is always satisfied. This normalization is written as $(\theta, N\theta) = 1$ using the matrix N in Eq. (4.4). Hence, the solution is obtained by solving Eq. (4.5), as pointed out in Chapter 2. However, the normalization matrix N is not positive definite. So, as in the case of renormalization and hyper-renormalization, we rewrite Eq. (4.5) in the form of Eq. (2.10) and use a standard numerical tool to compute the unit eigenvector θ for the generalized eigenvalue $1/\lambda$ of the largest absolute value. It is known that the accuracy of this method is rather low; often a small and flat ellipse is returned, as demonstrated in the experiments in Chapter 6.

Another way to always obtain an ellipse is first to apply a standard method, e.g., by hyper-renormalization, and modify the result to an ellipse if it is not an ellipse. A simple and effective method is the use of random sampling in the same way as RANSAC: we randomly sample five points from the input sequence, fit an ellipse to them, and repeat this many times to find the best ellipse. The actual procedure goes as follows.

Procedure 4.3 (Random sampling)

1. Fit an ellipse without considering the ellipse condition. If the solution θ satisfies

$$\theta_1\theta_3 - \theta_2^2 > 0, \tag{4.6}$$

return it as the final result.

2. Else, randomly select five points from the input sequence, and let ξ_1, ξ_2, ..., ξ_5 be the corresponding vectors of the form of Eq. (1.8).

3. Compute the unit eigenvector $\boldsymbol{\theta}$ of the following matrix for the smallest eigenvalue:

$$M_5 = \sum_{\alpha=1}^{5} \xi_\alpha \xi_\alpha^\top. \tag{4.7}$$

4. If that $\boldsymbol{\theta}$ does not satisfy Eq. (4.6), discard it and select a new set of five points randomly for fitting an ellipse.

5. If $\boldsymbol{\theta}$ satisfies Eq. (4.6), store it as a candidate. Also, evaluate the corresponding Sampson error J of Eq. (3.3), and store its value.

6. Repeat this process many times, and return the value $\boldsymbol{\theta}$ whose Sampson error J is the smallest.

Comments. The random sampling in Step 2 is done in the same way as RANSAC. Step 2 computes the ellipse that passes through the five point as in RANSAC. In theory, this could fail in a pathological case, e.g., all the points are on a hyperbola so that any five points define a hyperbola. We ignore such an extreme case. In Step 5, if the evaluated J is larger than the stored J, we can directly go on to the next sampling without storing $\boldsymbol{\theta}$ and J. We can stop the sampling if the current value of J is not updated consecutively after a fixed number of iterations. This method fits a better ellipse than the method of Fitzgibbon, et al., as shown in the experiment in Chapter 6, but still the resulting fit is not very close to the true shape when a standard method, such as hyper-renormalization, returns a hyperbola.

4.3 SUPPLEMENTAL NOTE

The RANSAC technique for outlier removal was proposed by Fischler and Bolles [1981]. Its principle is to randomly select a minimum set of data points to fit a curve (or any shape) many times, each time counting the number of the data points nearby, and to output the curve to which the largest number of data points are close. In other words, a small number of data points are allowed to be far from the curve; they are regarded as outliers. Alternatively, instead of counting the number of points nearby, we may sort the square distances of all the data points from the curve, evaluate the median, and output the curve for which the median is the smallest. This is called *LMedS* (*least median of squares*) [Rousseeuw and Leroy, 1987]. This also ignores those data points that are far from the curve. Instead of ignoring far apart points, we may use a distance function that does not penalize far apart points very much. Such a method is generally called *M-estimation*, for which various types of distance function have been studied [Huber, 2009]. An alternative approach for the same purpose is the use of the L_p-norm for $p < 2$, typically $p = 1$, as mentioned in the Supplemental Note of Chapter 1 (page 6).

The ellipse-specific method of Fitzgibbon et al. was proposed by Fitzgibbon et al. [1999], and the method of random sampling was proposed by Masuzaki et al. [2013]. As an alternative ellipse-specific method, Szpak et al. [2015] minimized the Sampson error of (3.3) with a penalty term such that it diverges to infinity if the solution approaches a hyperbola. As the experiment examples in Chapter 6 show, however, all these methods do not produce a satisfactory fit when standard methods return a hyperbola. If a hyperbola is obtained by, say, hyper-renormalization, it indicates the lack of information so that it does not make sense to fit an ellipse in the first place.

CHAPTER 5

Ellipse-based 3-D Computation

Circular objects in the scene are projected as ellipses in the image. We show here how we can compute the 3-D properties of the circular objects from their images. We start with techniques for computing attributes of ellipses such as intersections, centers, tangents, and perpendiculars. Then, we describe how to compute the position and orientation of a circle and its center in the scene from its image. This allows us to generate an image of the circle seen from the front. The underlying principle is the analysis of image transformations induced by hypothetical camera rotations around its viewpoint.

5.1 INTERSECTIONS OF ELLIPSES

The ellipse equation

$$Ax^2 + 2Bxy + Cy^2 + 2f_0(Dx + Ey) + f_0^2 F = 0 \tag{5.1}$$

can be written in the following vector form:

$$(\boldsymbol{x}, \boldsymbol{Q}\boldsymbol{x}) = 0, \qquad \boldsymbol{x} = \begin{pmatrix} x/f_0 \\ y/f_0 \\ 1 \end{pmatrix}, \qquad \boldsymbol{Q} = \begin{pmatrix} A & B & D \\ B & C & E \\ D & E & F \end{pmatrix}. \tag{5.2}$$

However, Eq. (5.1) may not always represent an ellipse. It defines a smooth curve only when the matrix $\boldsymbol{Q}$ is nonsingular, i.e., $|\boldsymbol{Q}| \neq 0$, where $|\boldsymbol{Q}|$ denotes the determinant of $\boldsymbol{Q}$; if $|\boldsymbol{Q}| = 0$, two real or imaginary lines result. If $|\boldsymbol{Q}| \neq 0$, Eq. (5.1) describes an ellipse (possibly an imaginary ellipse such as $x^2 + y^2 = -1$), a parabola, or a hyperbola (↪ Problem 5.1). In a general term, these curves are called *conics*.

Suppose two ellipses $(\boldsymbol{x}, \boldsymbol{Q}_1\boldsymbol{x}) = 0$ and $(\boldsymbol{x}, \boldsymbol{Q}_2\boldsymbol{x}) = 0$ intersect. Here, we consider only real intersections; in the following, we do not consider imaginary points or imaginary curves/lines. The intersections of two ellipses are computed as follows.

Procedure 5.1 (Ellipse intersections)

1. Compute one solution of the following cubic equation in λ:

$$|\lambda \boldsymbol{Q}_1 + \boldsymbol{Q}_2| = 0. \tag{5.3}$$

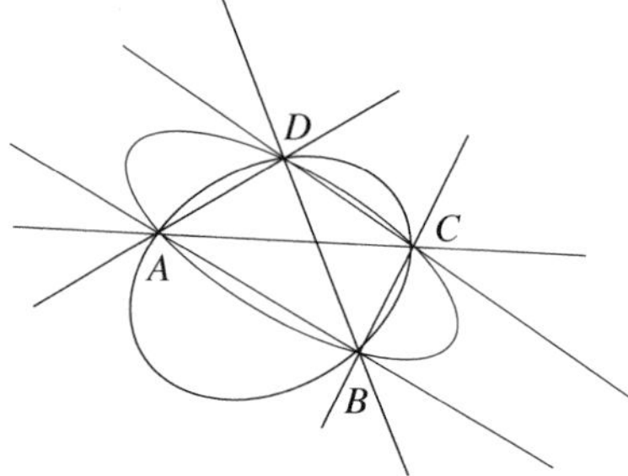

Figure 5.1: The three pairs of lines $\{AC, BD\}$, $\{AB, CD\}$, and $\{AD, BC\}$ passing through the four intersections A, B, C, and D of two ellipses.

2. Compute the two lines represented by the following quadratic equation in x and y for that λ:

$$(\boldsymbol{x}, (\lambda \boldsymbol{Q}_1 + \boldsymbol{Q}_2)\boldsymbol{x}) = 0. \tag{5.4}$$

3. Return the intersection of each of the lines with the ellipse $(\boldsymbol{x}, \boldsymbol{Q}_1\boldsymbol{x}) = 0$ (or $(\boldsymbol{x}, \boldsymbol{Q}_2\boldsymbol{x}) = 0$).

Comments. If two ellipses $(\boldsymbol{x}, \boldsymbol{Q}_1\boldsymbol{x}) = 0$ and $(\boldsymbol{x}, \boldsymbol{Q}_2\boldsymbol{x}) = 0$ intersect at $\boldsymbol{x}$, it satisfies $\lambda(\boldsymbol{x}, \boldsymbol{Q}_1\boldsymbol{x}) + (\boldsymbol{x}, \boldsymbol{Q}_2\boldsymbol{x}) = 0$ for an arbitrary λ. This is a quadratic equation in $\boldsymbol{x}$ in the form of Eq. (5.4), which describes a curve or a line pair (possibly imaginary) that passes through all the intersections of the two ellipses. If we choose the λ so that Eq. (5.3) is satisfied, Eq. (5.4) represents two real or imaginary lines ($\hookrightarrow$ Problem 5.2). Since we are assuming that real intersections exist, we obtain two real lines by factorizing Eq. (5.4) ($\hookrightarrow$ Problem 5.3). Hence, we can locate the intersections by computing the intersections of each line with either of the ellipses ($\hookrightarrow$ Problem 5.4).

If the two ellipses intersect at four points (Fig. 5.1), the cubic equation of Eq. (5.3) has three real roots, each of which defines a pair of lines; a pair of lines intersecting inside the ellipses and two pairs of lines intersecting outside the ellipses (or being parallel to each other). If the two ellipses intersect at two points, at least one real line among the six computed lines pass through them. Evidently, the above procedure can be applied if one (or both) of $(\boldsymbol{x}, \boldsymbol{Q}_1\boldsymbol{x}) = 0$ and $(\boldsymbol{x}, \boldsymbol{Q}_2\boldsymbol{x}) = 0$ is a hyperbola or a parabola, returning their intersections if they exist.

5.2 ELLIPSE CENTERS, TANGENTS, AND PERPENDICULARS

The center (x_c, y_c) of the ellipse of Eq. (5.1) has the following coordinates:

$$x_c = f_0 \frac{-CD + BE}{AC - B^2}, \qquad y_c = f_0 \frac{BD - AE}{AC - B^2}. \tag{5.5}$$

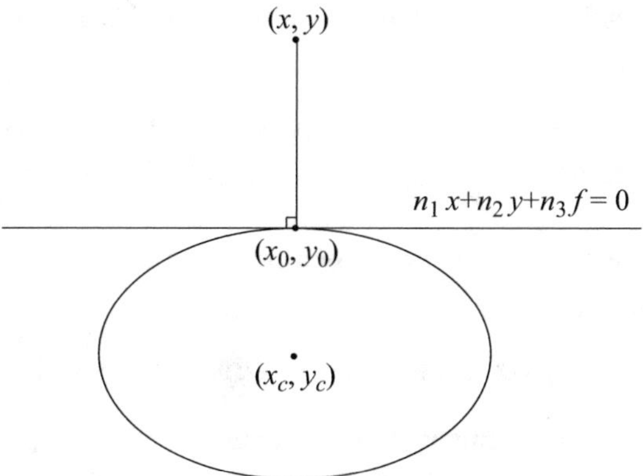

Figure 5.2: The center (x_c, y_c) of the ellipse, the tangent line $n_1x + n_2y + n_3f = 0$ at point (x_0, y_0) on the ellipse, and the perpendicular line from point (a, b) to point (x_0, y_0).

These are obtained by differentiating the ellipse equation $F(x, y) = 0$ of Eq. (5.1) and solving $\partial F/\partial x = 0$ and $\partial F/\partial y = 0$:

$$Ax + By + f_0D = 0, \qquad Bx + Cy + f_0E = 0. \tag{5.6}$$

Using Eq. (5.5), we can write Eq. (5.1) in the form

$$A(x - x_c)^2 + 2B(x - x_c)(y - y_c) + C(y - y_c)^2 = Ax_c^2 + 2Bx_cy_c + Cy_c^2 - f_0F. \tag{5.7}$$

The tangent line $n_1x + n_2y + n_3f_0 = 0$ to the ellipse of Eq. (5.1) at point (x_0, y_0) on it is given as follows (Fig. 5.2):

$$n_1 = Ax_0 + By_0 + Df_0, \quad n_2 = Bx_0 + Cy_0 + Ef_0, \quad n_3 = Dx_0 + Ey_0 + Ff_0. \tag{5.8}$$

Let $\boldsymbol{x}_0$ be the vector obtained from the vector $\boldsymbol{x}$ of Eq. (5.2) by replacing x and y by x_0 and y_0, respectively, and let $\boldsymbol{n}$ be the vector with components n_1, n_2, and n_3. We can see that Eq. (5.8) implies $\boldsymbol{n} \simeq \boldsymbol{Q}\boldsymbol{x}_0$, where $\simeq$ denotes equality up to a nonzero constant; note that the same line is represented if multiplied by arbitrary nonzero constant. The expressions in Eq. (5.8) are easily obtained by differentiating Eq. (5.1) ($\hookrightarrow$ Problem 5.5).

The foot of the perpendicular line from point (a, b) to the ellipse of Eq. (5.1), i.e., the closest point on it, is computed as follows (Fig. 5.2).

Procedure 5.2 (Perpendicular to Ellipse)

1. Define the matrix

$$\boldsymbol{D} = \begin{pmatrix} B & (C-A)/2 & (Ab - Ba + Ef_0)/2f_0 \\ (C-A)/2 & -B & (Bb - Ca - Df_0)/2f_0 \\ (Ab - Ba + Ef_0)/2f_0 & (Bb - Ca - Df_0)/2f_0 & (Db - Ea)/f_0 \end{pmatrix}. \tag{5.9}$$

2. Compute the intersections (x_0, y_0) of the ellipse $(\boldsymbol{x}, \boldsymbol{Q}\boldsymbol{x}) = 0$ and the quadratic curve $(\boldsymbol{x}, \boldsymbol{D}\boldsymbol{x}) = 0$ by Procedure 5.1.

3. From among the computed intersections, return the point (x_0, y_0) for which $(a - x_0)^2 + (b - y_0)^2$ is the smallest.

Comments. Let (x_0, y_0) be the foot of the perpendicular line from (a, b) to the ellipse. The line passing through (a, b) and (x_0, y_0) is

$$(b - y_0)x + (x_0 - a)y + (ay_0 - bx_0) = 0. \tag{5.10}$$

Let $n_1 x + n_2 y + n_3 f_0 = 0$ be the tangent line to the ellipse at (x_0, y_0) on it. The condition that this tangent line is orthogonal to the above line is

$$(b - y_0)n_1 + (x_0 - a)n_2 = 0. \tag{5.11}$$

Substituting Eq. (5.8), this condition is rearranged in the form

$$Bx_0^2 + (C - A)x_0 y_0 - By_0^2 + (Ab - Ba + Ef_0)x_0 + (Bb - Ca - Df_0)y_0 + (Db - Ea)f_0 = 0. \tag{5.12}$$

This means that if we define the matrix $\boldsymbol{D}$ of Eq. (5.9), Eq. (5.12) states that the point (x_0, y_0) is on the quadratic curve $(\boldsymbol{x}, \boldsymbol{D}\boldsymbol{x}) = 0$. Since (x_0, y_0) is a point on the ellipse $(\boldsymbol{x}, \boldsymbol{Q}\boldsymbol{x}) = 0$, we can compute it as the intersection of the two quadratic curves by Procedure 5.1, which applies even if $(\boldsymbol{x}, \boldsymbol{D}\boldsymbol{x}) = 0$ does not represent an ellipse. The above procedure is an analytical computation, but we can also compute the same result iteratively by modifying the geometric distance minimization procedure for ellipse fitting described in Chapter 3 ($\hookrightarrow$ Problem 5.6).

5.3 PERSPECTIVE PROJECTION AND CAMERA ROTATION

For analyzing the relationship between a circle in the scene and its image, we need to consider the camera imaging geometry. It is modeled by perspective projection as idealized in Fig. 5.3.

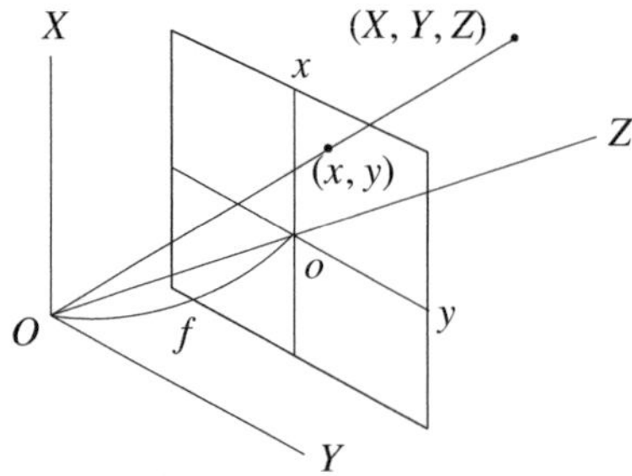

Figure 5.3: Idealized perspective projection.

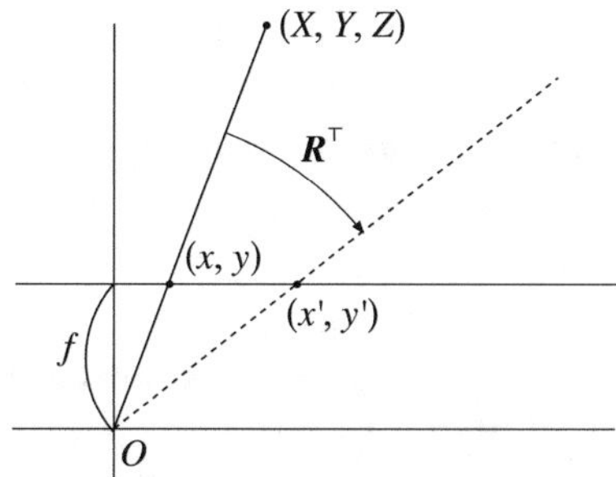

Figure 5.4: If the camera is rotated by $\boldsymbol{R}$ around its viewpoint O, the scene appears to rotate relative to the camera by $\boldsymbol{R}^{-1}$ (= $\boldsymbol{R}^\top$). As a result, the ray direction of (x, y) is rotated to the ray direction of (x', y').

We regard the origin O of the XYZ coordinate system as the center of lens, which we call the *viewpoint*, and the Z-axis as the *optical axis*, i.e., the axis of symmetry through the lens. We identify the image plane as $Z = f$, i.e., the plane orthogonal to the optical axis apart from the view point by distance f, which is commonly called the *focal length*. The intersection of the image plane with the optical axis is called the *principal point*. We define an xy image coordinate system such that its origin o is at the principal point and the x- and the y-axes are parallel to the X- and Y-axes, respectively. Thus, a point (X, Y, Z) in the scene is projected to a position (x, y) in the image given by

$$x = f\frac{X}{Z}, \qquad y = f\frac{Y}{Z}. \tag{5.13}$$

Suppose the camera is rotated around the viewpoint O. As shown in Fig. 5.3, the vector $(x, y, f)^\top$ points to the point (X, Y, Z) in the scene that we are viewing. If the camera is rotated by $\boldsymbol{R}$, the scene appears to rotate relative to the camera in the opposite sense by $\boldsymbol{R}^{-1}$ (= $\boldsymbol{R}^\top$). It follows that the direction of the vector $(x, y, f)^\top$ rotates to the direction of $\boldsymbol{R}^\top(x, y, f)^\top$ (Fig. 5.4), which is the ray direction $(x', y', f)^\top$ of the point (x', y') we observe after the rotation. Hence, we obtain

$$\begin{aligned}\begin{pmatrix} x'/f_0 \\ y'/f_0 \\ 1 \end{pmatrix} &= \begin{pmatrix} 1/f_0 & 0 & 0 \\ 0 & 1/f_0 & 0 \\ 0 & 0 & 1/f \end{pmatrix}\begin{pmatrix} x' \\ y' \\ f \end{pmatrix} \simeq \begin{pmatrix} 1/f_0 & 0 & 0 \\ 0 & 1/f_0 & 0 \\ 0 & 0 & 1/f \end{pmatrix}\boldsymbol{R}^\top\begin{pmatrix} x \\ y \\ f \end{pmatrix} \\ &= \begin{pmatrix} 1/f_0 & 0 & 0 \\ 0 & 1/f_0 & 0 \\ 0 & 0 & 1/f \end{pmatrix}\boldsymbol{R}^\top\begin{pmatrix} f_0 & 0 & 0 \\ 0 & f_0 & 0 \\ 0 & 0 & f \end{pmatrix}\begin{pmatrix} x/f_0 \\ y/f_0 \\ 1 \end{pmatrix} = \boldsymbol{H}\begin{pmatrix} x/f_0 \\ y/f_0 \\ 1 \end{pmatrix},\end{aligned} \tag{5.14}$$

where

$$\boldsymbol{H} = \begin{pmatrix} 1/f_0 & 0 & 0 \\ 0 & 1/f_0 & 0 \\ 0 & 0 & 1/f \end{pmatrix}\boldsymbol{R}^\top\begin{pmatrix} f_0 & 0 & 0 \\ 0 & f_0 & 0 \\ 0 & 0 & f \end{pmatrix}. \tag{5.15}$$

Throughout this book, we follow our convention that image coordinates are always normalized by the scaling factor f_0. In general, an image transformation that maps a point (x, y) to a point (x', y') is called a *homography* (or *projective transformation*) if

$$\boldsymbol{x}' \simeq \boldsymbol{H}\boldsymbol{x}, \tag{5.16}$$

for some nonsingular matrix $\boldsymbol{H}$, where $\boldsymbol{x}$ and $\boldsymbol{x}'$ are the vector representations of points (x, y) and (x', y') as defined in Eq. (5.2). Evidently, compositions and inverses of homographies are also homographies, and the set of all homographies constitue a group of transformations. From Eq. (5.14), we see that rotation of the camera induces a homography in the image if the image plane is sufficiently large.

Lemma 5.3 (Conic mapping by homography) *A conic is mapped to a conic by a homography.*
Proof. Consider a conic $(\boldsymbol{x}, \boldsymbol{Q}\boldsymbol{x}) = 0$, which may be an ellipse, a parabola, or a hyperbola. We map it by a homography $\boldsymbol{x}' \simeq \boldsymbol{H}\boldsymbol{x}$. Since $\boldsymbol{x} \simeq \boldsymbol{H}^{-1}\boldsymbol{x}'$, we have $(\boldsymbol{H}^{-1}\boldsymbol{x}', \boldsymbol{Q}\boldsymbol{H}^{-1}\boldsymbol{x}) = (\boldsymbol{x}', \boldsymbol{H}^{-\top}\boldsymbol{Q}\boldsymbol{H}^{-1}\boldsymbol{x}) = 0$, where $\boldsymbol{H}^{-\top}$ denotes $(\boldsymbol{H}^{-1})^{\top}$ $(= (\boldsymbol{H}^{\top})^{-1})$ ($\hookrightarrow$ Problem 5.7). This means the point $\boldsymbol{x}'$ is on the conic $(\boldsymbol{x}', \boldsymbol{Q}'\boldsymbol{x}') = 0$ with

$$\boldsymbol{Q}' \simeq \boldsymbol{H}^{-\top}\boldsymbol{Q}\boldsymbol{H}^{-1}. \tag{5.17}$$

Since $\boldsymbol{H}$ is nonsingular, we see that $|\boldsymbol{Q}'| \neq 0$ if $|\boldsymbol{Q}| \neq 0$. □

Consider a circle in the scene. We call the plane on which it lies the *supporting plane* of the circle.

Proposition 5.4 (Projection of a circle) *A circle in the scene is projected to a conic in the image.*
Proof. Let $\boldsymbol{n}$ be the unit surface normal to the supporting plane of the circle. Suppose we rotate the camera so that its optical axis becomes parallel to $\boldsymbol{n}$ (Fig. 5.5). Now that the supporting plane is front parallel to the image plane, we should observe the circle as a circle in the image if the image plane is sufficiently large. This camera rotation induces a homography, which maps a circle to a general conic. Hence, a circle is generally imaged as a conic by a camera in general position.□

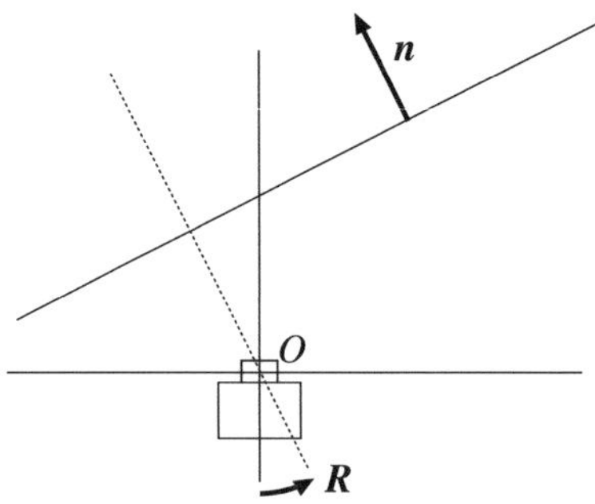

Figure 5.5: If we rotate the camera so that the optical axis is perpendicular to the supporting plane, the image of the circle becomes a circle.

5.4 3-D RECONSTRUCTION OF THE SUPPORTING PLANE

Using the camera imaging geometry described above, we can compute from an ellipse image the 3-D position of the supporting plane of the circle. Let $\boldsymbol{n}$ be its unit surface normal, and h its distance from the origin O (= the viewpoint). If we know the radius r of the circle, we can compute $\boldsymbol{n}$ and h as follows.

Procedure 5.5 (Supporting plane reconstruction)

1. Transform the coefficient matrix $\boldsymbol{Q}$ of the observed ellipse $(\boldsymbol{x}, \boldsymbol{Q}\boldsymbol{x}) = 0$ as follows:

$$\bar{\boldsymbol{Q}} = \begin{pmatrix} 1/f_0 & 0 & 0 \\ 0 & 1/f_0 & 0 \\ 0 & 0 & 1/f \end{pmatrix} \boldsymbol{Q} \begin{pmatrix} 1/f_0 & 0 & 0 \\ 0 & 1/f_0 & 0 \\ 0 & 0 & 1/f \end{pmatrix}. \tag{5.18}$$

   Then, normalize it to determinant -1:

$$\bar{\boldsymbol{Q}} \leftarrow \frac{\bar{\boldsymbol{Q}}}{\sqrt[3]{-|\bar{\boldsymbol{Q}}|}}. \tag{5.19}$$

2. Compute the eigenvalues λ_1, λ_2, and λ_3 of $\bar{\boldsymbol{Q}}$ and arrange them in the order $\lambda_2 \geq \lambda_1 > 0 > \lambda_3$. Let $\boldsymbol{u}_1$, $\boldsymbol{u}_2$, and $\boldsymbol{u}_3$ be the corresponding unit eigenvectors.

3. Compute the unit surface normal $\boldsymbol{n}$ to the supporting plane in the form

$$\boldsymbol{n} = \mathcal{N}[\sqrt{\lambda_2 - \lambda_1}\boldsymbol{u}_2 + \sqrt{\lambda_1 - \lambda_3}\boldsymbol{u}_3], \tag{5.20}$$

   where $\mathcal{N}[\,\cdot\,]$ is normalization to unit norm.

4. Compute the distance h to the supporting plane in the form

$$h = \lambda_1^{3/2} r. \tag{5.21}$$

Comments. If the matrix $\bar{\boldsymbol{Q}}$ is defined by Eq. (5.18), we see from Eq. (5.2) that

$$\bar{\boldsymbol{Q}} = \begin{pmatrix} A/f_0^2 & B/f_0^2 & D/f_0 f \\ B/f_0^2 & C/f_0^2 & E/f_0 f \\ D/f_0 f & E/f_0 f & F/f^2 \end{pmatrix} \simeq \begin{pmatrix} A & B & (f_0/f)D \\ B & C & (f_0/f)E \\ (f_0/f)D & (f_0/f)E & (f_0/f)^2 F \end{pmatrix}. \tag{5.22}$$

If we write the elements of $\bar{\boldsymbol{Q}}$ as $\bar{A}$, $\bar{B}$, ..., it is easy to see that the equation

$$\bar{A}x^2 + 2\bar{B}xy + \bar{C}y^2 + 2f(\bar{D}x + \bar{E}y) + f^2\bar{F} = 0 \tag{5.23}$$

is identical to Eq. (5.1). Namely, using the matrix $\bar{\boldsymbol{Q}}$ instead of $\boldsymbol{Q}$ means replacing the constant f_0 with the focal length f. Suppose the camera is rotated by $\boldsymbol{R}$. From Eq. (5.15), we see that

$$\boldsymbol{H}^{-1} = \begin{pmatrix} 1/f_0 & 0 & 0 \\ 0 & 1/f_0 & 0 \\ 0 & 0 & 1/f \end{pmatrix} \boldsymbol{R} \begin{pmatrix} f_0 & 0 & 0 \\ 0 & f_0 & 0 \\ 0 & 0 & f \end{pmatrix}, \tag{5.24}$$

which maps the ellipse in the form of Eq. (5.17). Hence,

$$\begin{aligned} \boldsymbol{Q}' \simeq & \begin{pmatrix} f_0 & 0 & 0 \\ 0 & f_0 & 0 \\ 0 & 0 & f \end{pmatrix} \boldsymbol{R}^\top \begin{pmatrix} 1/f_0 & 0 & 0 \\ 0 & 1/f_0 & 0 \\ 0 & 0 & 1/f \end{pmatrix} \\ & \qquad \boldsymbol{Q} \begin{pmatrix} 1/f_0 & 0 & 0 \\ 0 & 1/f_0 & 0 \\ 0 & 0 & 1/f \end{pmatrix} \boldsymbol{R} \begin{pmatrix} f_0 & 0 & 0 \\ 0 & f_0 & 0 \\ 0 & 0 & f \end{pmatrix} \\ = & \begin{pmatrix} f_0 & 0 & 0 \\ 0 & f_0 & 0 \\ 0 & 0 & f \end{pmatrix} \boldsymbol{R}^\top \bar{\boldsymbol{Q}} \boldsymbol{R} \begin{pmatrix} f_0 & 0 & 0 \\ 0 & f_0 & 0 \\ 0 & 0 & f \end{pmatrix}, \end{aligned} \tag{5.25}$$

and consequently $\bar{\boldsymbol{Q}}' \simeq \boldsymbol{R}^\top \bar{\boldsymbol{Q}} \boldsymbol{R}$. However, $\bar{\boldsymbol{Q}}$ and $\bar{\boldsymbol{Q}}'$ are both normalized to determinant -1, and the determinant is unchanged by multiplication of rotation matrices $\boldsymbol{R}$ and $\boldsymbol{R}^\top$. Hence, we have

$$\bar{\boldsymbol{Q}}' = \boldsymbol{R}^\top \bar{\boldsymbol{Q}} \boldsymbol{R}. \tag{5.26}$$

Procedure 5.5 is obtained, using this relationship. The derivation is given in Section 5.7 below, where we first consider the case where the ellipse is in canonical form (Lemma 5.8). Then, we rotate the camera so that the ellipse has the canonical form and apply the result (Proposition 5.9). The distance to the supporting plane is determined by using the radius r of the circle we observe. If r is unknown, the supporting plane is determined up to the distance from the origin O. The 3-D position of the circle can be computed by *back-projection*, i.e., as the intersection of the ray of individual points on the ellipse with the supporting plane (↪ Problem 5.8).

5.5 PROJECTED CENTER OF CIRCLE

If we know the unit surface normal $\boldsymbol{n} = (n_i)$ to the supporting plane, we can compute the image position of the center (x_C, y_C) of the circle, which does not necessarily coincide with the center (x_c, y_c) of the observed ellipse given by Eqs. (5.5). Let $(\boldsymbol{x}, \boldsymbol{Q}\boldsymbol{x}) = 0$ be the observed ellipse. The procedure is as follows.

Procedure 5.6 (Projected center of circle)

1. Compute the following vector $\boldsymbol{m} = (m_i)$:

$$\boldsymbol{m} = \begin{pmatrix} f_0 & 0 & 0 \\ 0 & f_0 & 0 \\ 0 & 0 & f \end{pmatrix} \boldsymbol{Q}^{-1} \begin{pmatrix} f_0 & 0 & 0 \\ 0 & f_0 & 0 \\ 0 & 0 & f \end{pmatrix} \begin{pmatrix} n_1 \\ n_2 \\ n_3 \end{pmatrix}. \tag{5.27}$$

2. The projected center (x_C, y_C) of the circle is given by

$$x_C = f\frac{m_1}{m_3}, \qquad y_C = f\frac{m_2}{m_3}. \tag{5.28}$$

Comments. In terms of the matrix $\bar{\boldsymbol{Q}}$ in Eq. (5.18), the right side of Eq. (5.27) can be written as $\bar{\boldsymbol{Q}}^{-1}\boldsymbol{n}$. This implies from Eq. (5.28) the following relationship:

$$\boldsymbol{n} \simeq \bar{\boldsymbol{Q}} \begin{pmatrix} x_C \\ y_C \\ f \end{pmatrix}. \tag{5.29}$$

The proof of Procedure 5.6 is given in Section 5.7 below, where we first show that Eq. (5.29) holds if the camera is rotated so that the optical axis is perpendicular to the supporting plane (Lemma 5.10). Then, we show that the relation holds if the camera is rotated arbitrarily (Proposition 5.11).

5.6 FRONT IMAGE OF THE CIRCLE

If we compute the supporting plane of the circle in the scene, we can generate its image as if seen from the front in such a way that the center of the circle is at the image origin. Note that translation of the image is also a homography. In fact, translation $x' = x + a$ and $y' = y + b$ by a and b in the x and y directions, respectively, is the following homography:

$$\begin{pmatrix} x'/f_0 \\ y'/f_0 \\ 1 \end{pmatrix} = \begin{pmatrix} (x+a)/f_0 \\ (y+b)/f_0 \\ 1 \end{pmatrix} = \begin{pmatrix} 1 & 0 & a/f_0 \\ 0 & 1 & b/f_0 \\ 0 & 0 & 1 \end{pmatrix} \begin{pmatrix} x/f_0 \\ y/f_0 \\ 1 \end{pmatrix}. \tag{5.30}$$

Its inverse is obtained by replacing a and b by $-a$ and $-b$, respectively. The hypothetical front image of the circle is computed by the following procedure.

Procedure 5.7 (Front image of the circle)

1. Compute the projected center (x_C, y_C) of the circle by Procedure 5.6.

2. Compute a camera rotation $\boldsymbol{R}$ that makes the supporting plane parallel to the image plane, and determine the corresponding homography matrix $\boldsymbol{H}$ by Eq. (5.15).

3. Compute the projected center (x'_C, y'_C) of the circle after that camera rotation as follows:

$$\begin{pmatrix} x'_C/f_0 \\ y'_C/f_0 \\ 1 \end{pmatrix} \simeq \boldsymbol{H} \begin{pmatrix} x_C/f_0 \\ y_C/f_0 \\ 1 \end{pmatrix}. \tag{5.31}$$

4. Compute the following homography matrix that translates the point (x'_C, y'_C) to the image origin:

$$\boldsymbol{H}_0 = \begin{pmatrix} 1 & 0 & -x_C/f_0 \\ 0 & 1 & -y_C/f_0 \\ 0 & 0 & 1 \end{pmatrix}. \tag{5.32}$$

5. Define a new image buffer, and compute for each pixel (x, y) of it the point $(\bar{x}, \bar{y})$ that satisfies

$$\begin{pmatrix} \bar{x}/f_0 \\ \bar{y}/f_0 \\ 1 \end{pmatrix} \simeq \boldsymbol{H}^{-1}\boldsymbol{H}_0^{-1} \begin{pmatrix} x/f_0 \\ y/f_0 \\ 1 \end{pmatrix}. \tag{5.33}$$

   Then, copy the image value of the pixel $(\bar{x}, \bar{y})$ of the input image to the pixel (x, y) of the buffer. If the resulting coordinates $(\bar{x}, \bar{y})$ are not integers, its image value is interpolated from surrounding pixels.

Comments. The camera rotation that rotates the unit vector $\boldsymbol{n}$ to the optical axis direction is not unique, since there is an indeterminacy of rotations around the optical axis (Fig. 5.5). We can choose any such rotation, but the simplest one is the rotation around an axis perpendicular to both $\boldsymbol{n}$ and the optical axis direction (= the Z-axis) by the angle Ω made by $\boldsymbol{n}$ and the Z-axis ($\hookrightarrow$ Problem 5.9). Combining it with the translation of Eq. (5.32), we can obtain the homography matrix $\boldsymbol{H}_0\boldsymbol{H}$, which maps the ellipse to a circle centered at the image origin as if we are viewing the circle from the front.

As is well known, in order to generate a new image from a given image by image processing, the transformation equation that maps an old image to a new image is not sufficient. For digital image processing, we first define a new image buffer in which the generated image is to be stored and then give a computational procedure to define the image value at each pixel of this buffer. This is done by first computing the inverse of the image generating transformation and then copying to the buffer the image value of the inversely transformed pixel position. In the above procedure, the image generating transformation is the composite homography $\boldsymbol{H}_0\boldsymbol{H}$, whose inverse is $\boldsymbol{H}^{-1}\boldsymbol{H}_0^{-1}$. The inverse $\boldsymbol{H}^{-1}$ is given by Eq. (5.24), and the inverse $\boldsymbol{H}_0^{-1}$ is obtained from Eq. (5.32) by changing the signs of x_C and y_C. When the computed image coordinates are not integers, we may simply round them to integers, but a more accurate way is to use bilinear interpolation, i.e., proportional allocation in the x and y directions, of the values of the surrounding pixels. (↪ Problem 5.10).

5.7 DERIVATIONS

We first consider the 3-D analysis of an ellipse in canonical form, i.e., centered at the image origin o having the major and minor axes in the x and y direction.

Lemma 5.8 (Reconstruction in canonical form) *If the projected circle in the image is an ellipse in the canonical form of*

$$x^2 + \alpha y^2 = \gamma, \qquad \alpha \geq 1, \qquad \gamma > 0, \tag{5.34}$$

the inclination angle θ of the supporting plane is given by

$$\sin\theta = \pm\sqrt{\frac{\alpha - 1}{\alpha + \gamma/f^2}}, \qquad \cos\theta = \sqrt{\frac{1 + \gamma/f^2}{\alpha + \gamma/f^2}}, \tag{5.35}$$

and the distance h to the supporting plane is

$$h = \frac{fr}{\sqrt{\alpha\gamma}}. \tag{5.36}$$

Proof. The matrix $\boldsymbol{Q}$ and its normalization $\bar{\boldsymbol{Q}}$ have the following form:

$$\boldsymbol{Q} = \begin{pmatrix} 1 & 0 & 0 \\ 0 & \alpha & 0 \\ 0 & 0 & -\gamma/f_0^2 \end{pmatrix}, \qquad \bar{\boldsymbol{Q}} = \kappa \begin{pmatrix} 1 & 0 & 0 \\ 0 & \alpha & 0 \\ 0 & 0 & -\gamma/f^2 \end{pmatrix}, \qquad \kappa = (f/\sqrt{\alpha\gamma})^{2/3}. \tag{5.37}$$

Since the major axis is along the x-axis, the supporting plane is inclined along the y-axis. If the inclination angle is θ, the unit surface normal to the supporting plane is $\boldsymbol{n} = (0, \sin\theta, \cos\theta)^\top$ with the sign of θ indeterminate. If the camera is rotated around the X-axis by $-\theta$, the supporting plane becomes parallel to the image plane. Such a camera rotation is given by

$$\boldsymbol{R} = \begin{pmatrix} 1 & 0 & 0 \\ 0 & \cos\theta & \sin\theta \\ 0 & -\sin\theta & \cos\theta \end{pmatrix}. \tag{5.38}$$

After the camera rotation, we observe a circle in the form

$$x^2 + (y + c)^2 = \rho^2, \qquad c \geq 0, \qquad \rho > 0. \tag{5.39}$$

The corresponding normalized matrix is

$$\bar{Q}' = \kappa' \begin{pmatrix} 1 & 0 & 0 \\ 0 & 1 & c/f \\ 0 & c/f & (c^2 - \rho^2)/f^2 \end{pmatrix}, \qquad \kappa' = (f/\rho)^{2/3}. \tag{5.40}$$

Hence, we obtain from Eq. (5.26) the equality

$$\kappa' \begin{pmatrix} 1 & 0 & 0 \\ 0 & 1 & c/f \\ 0 & c/f & (c^2 - \rho^2)/f^2 \end{pmatrix} = \kappa \begin{pmatrix} 1 & 0 & 0 \\ 0 & \cos\theta & -\sin\theta \\ 0 & \sin\theta & \cos\theta \end{pmatrix} \begin{pmatrix} 1 & 0 & 0 \\ 0 & \alpha & 0 \\ 0 & 0 & -\gamma/f^2 \end{pmatrix} \begin{pmatrix} 1 & 0 & 0 \\ 0 & \cos\theta & \sin\theta \\ 0 & -\sin\theta & \cos\theta \end{pmatrix}. \tag{5.41}$$

Comparing the $(1,1)$ elements on both sides, we see that $\kappa = \kappa'$ and hence $\rho = \sqrt{\alpha\gamma}$. Comparing the remaining elements, we obtain

$$\begin{pmatrix} 1 & c/f \\ c/f & (c^2 - \rho^2)/f^2 \end{pmatrix} = \begin{pmatrix} \cos\theta & -\sin\theta \\ \sin\theta & \cos\theta \end{pmatrix} \begin{pmatrix} \alpha & 0 \\ 0 & -\gamma/f^2 \end{pmatrix} \begin{pmatrix} \cos\theta & \sin\theta \\ -\sin\theta & \cos\theta \end{pmatrix}. \tag{5.42}$$

This implies that the matrix on the left side has eigenvalues α and $-\gamma/f^2$ with corresponding unit eigenvectors $(\cos\theta, \sin\theta)^\top$ and $(-\sin\theta, \cos\theta)^\top$. Since the trace and the determinant are invariant under the congruent transformation of Eq. (5.42), which is also the singular value decomposition, we obtain

$$1 + \frac{c^2 - \rho^2}{f^2} = \alpha - \frac{\gamma}{f^2}, \qquad \frac{c^2 - \rho^2}{f^2} - \frac{c^2}{f^2} = -\frac{\alpha\gamma}{f^2}. \tag{5.43}$$

Hence, $\rho = \sqrt{\alpha\gamma}$ and $c = \sqrt{(\alpha - 1)(\gamma + f^2)}$. Since $(\cos\theta, \sin\theta)^\top$ is the eigenvector for eigenvalue α, the following holds:

$$\begin{pmatrix} 1 & c/f \\ c/f & (c^2 - \rho^2)/f^2 \end{pmatrix} \begin{pmatrix} \cos\theta \\ \sin\theta \end{pmatrix} = \alpha \begin{pmatrix} \cos\theta \\ \sin\theta \end{pmatrix}. \tag{5.44}$$

Thus, we obtain

$$\tan\theta = \frac{\alpha - 1}{c/f} = \sqrt{\frac{\alpha - 1}{1 + \gamma/f^2}}, \tag{5.45}$$

from which we obtain Eq. (5.35). Comparing the radius ρ of the circle on the image plane, which is in distance f from the viewpoint O (Fig. 5.3), and the true radius r on the supporting plane, the distance h to the supporting plane is $h = fr/\rho$. Hence, we obtain Eq. (5.36). □

Next, we consider the general case. We rotate the camera so that the ellipse has the canonical form. This is done by first rotating the camera so that the optical axis passes through the center of the ellipse and next rotating the camera around the optical axis so that the major and minor axes are in the x and y direction. Then, we apply Lemma 5.8.

Proposition 5.9 (Reconstruction in general position) *Equations (5.20) and (5.21) hold in the general case.*

Proof. If the observed ellipse is not in the from of Eq. (5.34), we rotate the camera by some rotation $\boldsymbol{R}$ so that it has the form of Eq. (5.34). This process corresponds to the following diagonalization of the normalized matrix $\bar{\boldsymbol{Q}}$ in the form of Eq. (5.26):

$$\boldsymbol{R}^\top \bar{\boldsymbol{Q}} \boldsymbol{R} = \begin{pmatrix} \lambda_1 & 0 & 0 \\ 0 & \lambda_2 & 0 \\ 0 & 0 & \lambda_3 \end{pmatrix}. \tag{5.46}$$

Since the determinant of $\bar{\boldsymbol{Q}}$ is normalized to -1, we have $\lambda_1\lambda_2\lambda_3 = -1$. We are assuming that the three eigenvalues are arranged in the order $\lambda_2 \geq \lambda_1 > 0 > \lambda_3$, so Eq. (5.23) implies that this ellipse has the form

$$x^2 + \frac{\lambda_2}{\lambda_1} y^2 = -f^2 \frac{\lambda_3}{\lambda_1}. \tag{5.47}$$

Comparing this with Eq. (5.34), we see that $\alpha = \lambda_2/\lambda_1$ (≥ 1) and $\gamma = f^2\lambda_3/\lambda_1$ (> 0). Thus, the inclination angle θ is given by Eq. (5.35). The y- and the z-axes after the camera rotation are, respectively, in the directions $\boldsymbol{u}_2$ and $\boldsymbol{u}_3$, which are the second and the third columns of the matrix $\boldsymbol{R}$ in Eq. (5.46). Hence, the unit surface normal $\boldsymbol{n}$ to the supporting plane is given by $\boldsymbol{n} = \boldsymbol{u}_2 \sin\theta + \boldsymbol{u}_3 \cos\theta$. Rewriting the α and γ in Eqs. (5.35) and (5.36) in terms of λ_1, λ_2, and λ_3, we obtain Eq. (5.21). □

We now consider the projection of the center of the circle in the scene. We first consider the front parallel case and then the general case by applying the camera rotation homography.

Lemma 5.10 (Front parallel projection) *Equation (5.29) holds when the supporting plane of the circle is parallel to the image plane.*

Proof. If the supporting plane is parallel to the image plane, the circle is imaged in the form of $(x - x_c)^2 + (y - y_c)^2 = \rho^2$ for some (x_c, y_c) and ρ. This circle corresponds to the matrix $\bar{\boldsymbol{Q}}$ in the form

$$\bar{\boldsymbol{Q}} \simeq \begin{pmatrix} 1 & 0 & -x_c/f \\ 0 & 1 & -y_c/f \\ -x_c/f & -y_c/f & (x_c^2 + y_c^2 - \rho^2)/f^2 \end{pmatrix}. \tag{5.48}$$

Since $(x_c, y_c) = (x_C, y_C)$, i.e., the center of the circle in the scene is projected to the center of the imaged circle, the right side of Eq. (5.29) is $(0, 0, -\rho^2/f)^\top$, which is a vector orthogonal to the image plane. □

Proposition 5.11 (General projection) *Equation (5.29) holds if the camera is arbitrarily rotated around the viewpoint.*

Proof. Suppose we observe a circle on the supporting plane with unit surface normal $\boldsymbol{n}$. If the camera is rotated by $\boldsymbol{R}$ around the viewpoint, the unit surface normal is $\boldsymbol{n}' = \boldsymbol{R}^\top \boldsymbol{n}$ relative to the camera after the rotation. Suppose the projected center (x_C, y_C) moves to (x'_C, y'_C) after the camera rotation. Their ray directions $(x_C, y_C, f)^\top$ and $(x'_C, y'_C, f)^\top$ are related by

$$\begin{pmatrix} x'_C \\ y'_C \\ f \end{pmatrix} \simeq \boldsymbol{R}^\top \begin{pmatrix} x_C \\ y_C \\ f \end{pmatrix} \tag{5.49}$$

(see Fig. 5.4). Multiplying Eq. (5.29) by $\boldsymbol{R}^\top$ on both sides and noting Eq. (5.26), we obtain

$$\boldsymbol{n}' = \boldsymbol{R}^\top \boldsymbol{n} \simeq \boldsymbol{R}^\top \bar{\boldsymbol{Q}} \begin{pmatrix} x_C \\ y_C \\ f \end{pmatrix} \simeq (\boldsymbol{R}^\top \bar{\boldsymbol{Q}} \boldsymbol{R}) \boldsymbol{R}^\top \begin{pmatrix} x_C \\ y_C \\ f \end{pmatrix} \simeq \bar{\boldsymbol{Q}}' \begin{pmatrix} x'_C \\ y'_C \\ f \end{pmatrix}, \tag{5.50}$$

which means that Eq. (5.29) also holds after the camera rotation. □

5.8 SUPPLEMENTAL NOTE

As described in most geometry textbooks, the figures that Eq. (5.1) represents include:

(i) a real quadratic curve (ellipse, hyperbola, or parabola);

(ii) an imaginary ellipse;

(iii) two real lines that are intersecting or parallel;

(iv) a real line; and

(v) imaginary two lines that are intersecting at a real point or parallel.

From the standpoint of projective geometry, however, two ellipses always intersect at four points, which may be real or imaginary. Similarly, an ellipse and a line always intersect at two points; a tangent point is regarded as a degenerate double intersection, and non-existence of intersections is interpreted to be intersecting at imaginary points. A well-known textbook on classical projective geometry is Semple and Roth [1949]. The analysis of general algebraic curves in the complex number domain is called *algebraic geometry*; see the classical textbook of Semple and Kneebone [1952].

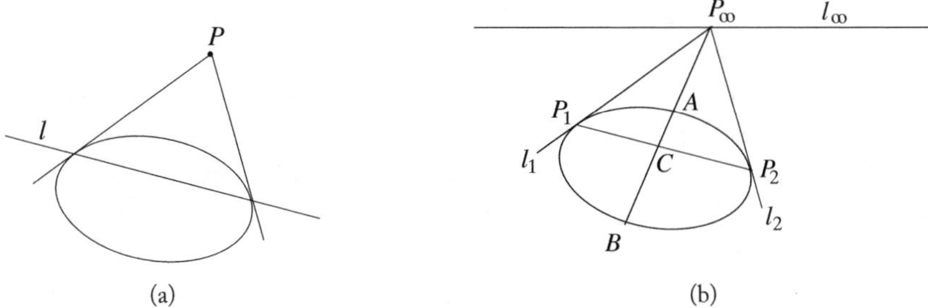

Figure 5.6: (a) The pole P and the polar l of an ellipse. (b) The ellipse center, tangent lines, vanishing point, and vanishing line.

The expression of the tangent line in Eq. (5.8) holds for a general conic. If the point (x_0, y_0) is not on the conic of Eq. (5.1), then Eq. (5.8), or $\boldsymbol{n} \simeq \boldsymbol{Q}\boldsymbol{x}_0$, defines a line, called the *polar* of the conic of Eq. (5.1) at (x_0, y_0); the point (x_0, y_0) is called the *pole* of the line $n_1x + n_2y + n_1f_0 = 0$. For a point (x_0, y_0) outside an ellipse, there exist two lines passing through it and tangent to the ellipse (Fig. 5.6a). The line passing through the two tangent points is the polar of (x_0, y_0). The pole is on the polar, if and only if the pole is on the conic and the polar is the tangent line there. The tangent line (and the polar in general) is obtained by the *polar decomposition* of the conic, the process of replacing x^2, xy, y^2, x, and y of the conic equation by x_0x, $(x_0y + xy_0)/2$, y_0y, $(x + x_0)/2$, and $(y + y_0)/2$, respectively.

The poles and polars of an ellipse are closely related to the 3-D interpretation of the ellipse. Suppose an ellipse in the image is an oblique view of an ellipse (or a circle) in scene. Let C be the true center of the ellipse, where by "true" we mean the projection of 3-D properties. Consider an arbitrary chord P_1P_2 passing through C (Fig. 5.6b). Let l_1 and l_2 be the tangent line to the ellipse at P_1 and P_2, respectively. These are parallel tangent lines to the "true" ellipse. Their intersection P_∞ in the image is the *vanishing point*, which is infinitely far away on the "true" supporting plane. The chord P_1P_2 is arbitrary, so each choice of it defines its vanishing point. All such vanishing points are on a line called the *vanishing line*, which is the "horizon" or the infinitely far away boundary of the supporting plane. In the image, the vanishing line l_∞ is the polar of the center C, which is the pole of the vanishing line l_∞. Procedure 5.6 is a consequence of this interpretation.

Let A and B be the intersection of the ellipse with the line passing through the center C and the vanishing point P_∞. Then, the set $[P_\infty, A, C, B]$ is an *harmonic range*, meaning that it has cross ratio -1; the *cross-ratio* of four distinct collinear (i.e., on a common line) points A, B, C, D in that order is defined by

$$\frac{AC}{BC} \Big/ \frac{AD}{BD}, \tag{5.51}$$

where AC, BD, etc. are signed distance along an arbitrarily fixed direction (hence $CA = -AC$, etc.). A similar relation holds for the vanishing line l_∞, the tangent lines l_1 and l_2, and the axis $P_\infty C$, and the set $[l_\infty, l_1, P_\infty C, l_2]$ is a *harmonic pencil*, meaning that it has cross-ratio -1; the *cross-ratio* of four distinct concurrent (i.e., having a common intersection) lines is defined by the cross-ratio of their intersections with an arbitrary line (the value does not depend on that line as long as it intersects at four distinct points). For more details, see Kanatani [1993a].

Procedure 5.5 for 3-D reconstruction of a circle was first presented by Forsyth et al. [1991]. The result was extended to 3-D reconstruction of an ellipse by Kanatani and Liu [1993]. These analyses are based on the image transformation induced by camera rotation, for which see Kanatani [1990, 1993a] for the details.

PROBLEMS

5.1. Show that when $|\boldsymbol{Q}| \neq 0$, the equation $(\boldsymbol{x}, \boldsymbol{Q}\boldsymbol{x}) = 0$ represents an ellipse (including an imaginary ellipse) if and only if

$$AC - B^2 > 0. \tag{5.52}$$

Also, show that $AC - B^2 = 0$ and $AC - B^2 < 0$ correspond to a parabola and a hyperbola, respectively.

5.2. (1) Show that for an arbitrary square matrix $\boldsymbol{A}$, the identity

$$|\lambda \boldsymbol{I} + \boldsymbol{A}| = \lambda^3 + \lambda^2 \mathrm{tr}[\boldsymbol{A}] + \lambda \mathrm{tr}[\boldsymbol{A}^\dagger] + |\boldsymbol{A}| \tag{5.53}$$

holds, where $\mathrm{tr}[\,\cdot\,]$ denotes the matrix trace and $\boldsymbol{A}^\dagger$ is the *cofactor matrix* of $\boldsymbol{A}$, i.e., its (i, j) equals the determinant of the matrix obtained from $\boldsymbol{A}$ by removing the row and the column containing A_{ji} and multiplying it by $(-1)^{i+j}$:

$$\boldsymbol{A}^\dagger = \begin{pmatrix} A_{22}A_{33} - A_{32}A_{23} & A_{32}A_{13} - A_{12}A_{33} & A_{12}A_{23} - A_{22}A_{13} \\ A_{31}A_{23} - A_{21}A_{33} & A_{11}A_{33} - A_{31}A_{13} & A_{12}A_{23} - A_{21}A_{13} \\ A_{21}A_{32} - A_{31}A_{22} & A_{31}A_{12} - A_{11}A_{32} & A_{11}A_{22} - A_{21}A_{12} \end{pmatrix}. \tag{5.54}$$

(2) Show that the following identity holds for arbitrary square matrices $\boldsymbol{A}$ and $\boldsymbol{B}$:

$$|\lambda \boldsymbol{A} + \boldsymbol{B}| = \lambda^3 |\boldsymbol{A}| + \lambda^2 \mathrm{tr}[\boldsymbol{A}^\dagger \boldsymbol{B}] + \lambda \mathrm{tr}[\boldsymbol{A}\boldsymbol{B}^\dagger] + |\boldsymbol{B}|. \tag{5.55}$$

5.3. Show that if $|\boldsymbol{Q}| = 0$ and $B^2 - AC > 0$, Eq. (5.1) defines the following two lines:

$$Ax + (B - \sqrt{B^2 - AC})y + \Big(D - \frac{BD - AE}{\sqrt{B^2 - AC}}\Big) f_0 = 0,$$
$$Ax + (B + \sqrt{B^2 - AC})y + \Big(D + \frac{BD - AE}{\sqrt{B^2 - AC}}\Big) f_0 = 0. \tag{5.56}$$

5.4. Describe the procedure for computing the two intersections (x_1, y_1) and (x_2, y_2) of the ellipse of Eq. (5.1) with the line $n_1 x + n_2 y + n_3 f_0 = 1$.

5.5. Show that the tangent line $n_1 x + n_2 y + n_3 f_0 = 0$ to the quadratic curve of Eq. (5.1) at (x_0, y_0) is given by Eq. (5.8).

5.6. Describe the procedure for iteratively computing the foot of the perpendicular to an ellipse drawn from a given point by modifying the ellipse fitting procedure by geometric distance minimization given in Chapter 3.

5.7. Show that $(\boldsymbol{A}^{-1})^\top = (\boldsymbol{A}^\top)^{-1}$ holds for an arbitrary nonsingular matrix $\boldsymbol{A}$.

5.8. Show that a point (x, y) in the image is back-projected onto a plane with unit surface normal $\boldsymbol{n}$ and distance h from the origin O in the following form:

$$\begin{pmatrix} X \\ Y \\ Z \end{pmatrix} = \frac{h}{n_1 x + n_2 y + n_3 f} \begin{pmatrix} x \\ y \\ f \end{pmatrix}. \tag{5.57}$$

5.9. Find a rotation matrix $\boldsymbol{R}$ that rotates a unit vector $\boldsymbol{n}$ into the direction of the Z-axis.

5.10. Show how the value of the pixel with non-integer image coordinates (x, y) is determined from surrounding pixels by bilinear interpolation.

CHAPTER 6

Experiments and Examples

We show some simulation examples of different ellipse fitting methods described in Chapters 1–3 and do statistical accuracy evaluation, repeating a large number of trials using different artificial noise. We also see some real image examples. Next, we show how the RANSAC procedure described in Chapter 4 can robustly fit an ellipse to edge segments that contain non-elliptic parts. We then see how the ellipse-specific methods described in Chapter 4 enforce the fit to be an ellipse in the presence of large noise and conclude that they do not have much practical value. Finally, we show some application examples of the ellipse-based 3-D computation described in Chapter 5.

6.1 ELLIPSE FITTING EXAMPLES

We first show some simulated ellipse fitting examples to see how in the presence of noise different methods described in Chapters 1–3 can produce different ellipses for the same point sequence. We also compare the number of iterations for different iterative methods.

We define 30 equidistant points on the ellipse shown in Fig. 6.1a. The major and minor axis are set to 100 and 50 pixels, respectively. We add independent Gaussian noise of mean 0 and standard deviation σ (pixels) to the x and y coordinates of each point and fit an ellipse by the following methods:

1. least squares (LS) (Procedure 1.1),
2. iterative reweight (Procedure 2.1),
3. Taubin method ($\hookrightarrow$ Problem 2.1),

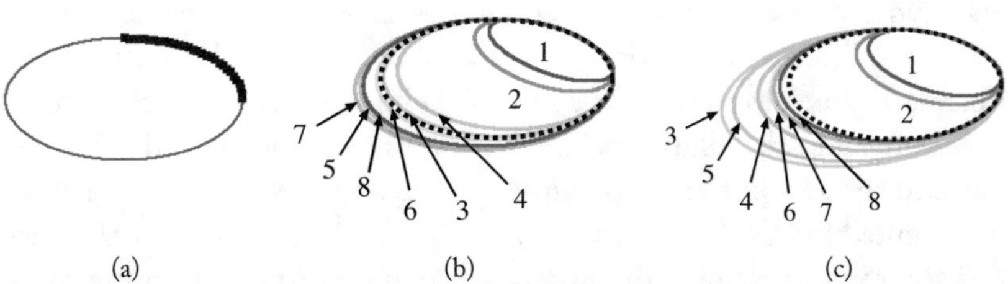

Figure 6.1: (a) 30 points on an ellipse. (b), (c) Fitted ellipses for different noise instances of $\sigma = 0.5$ (pixels): (1) LS, (2) iterative reweight, (3) Taubin, (4) renormalization, (5) HyperLS, (6) hyper-renormalization, (7) FMS, (8) hyperaccurate correction. The dotted lines indicate the true shape.

4. renormalization (Procedure 2.2),
5. HyperLS (↪ Problem 2.2),
6. hyper-renormalization (Procedure 2.3),
7. FNS (Procedure 3.1), and
8. hyperaccurate correction (Procedure 3.3).

Since the solution of geometric distance minimization (Procedure 3.2) is nearly identical to the FNS solution, it is not picked out as a different method.

Figure 6.1b,c shows fitted ellipses for different noise instances of $\sigma = 0.5$ (pixels); different ellipses result for different noise, even though the noise level is the same. The dotted lines indicate the true shape. We see that least squares and iterative reweight have large bias, producing much smaller ellipses than the true shape. The closest ellipse is given by hyper-renormalization in Fig. 6.1b and by hyperaccurate correction in Fig. 6.1c. The number of iterations of these methods is:

method		2	4	6	7/8
# of iterations	(b)	4	4	4	9
	(c)	4	4	4	8

Note that least squares, the Taubin method, and HyperLS are analytically computed without iterations. Also, hyperaccurate correction is an analytical procedure, so it does not add any iterations. We see that FNS and its hyperaccurate correction require about twice as many iterations as iterative reweight, renormalization, and hyper-renormalization.

6.2 STATISTICAL ACCURACY COMPARISON

Since every method sometimes returns a good fit and sometimes a poor fit, we need for fair comparison statistical evaluation over a large number of repeated trials, each time using different noise. From Fig. 6.1, we see that all the ellipses fit fairly well to the *data points*, meaning that not much difference exists among their geometric distances, i.e., the sums of the square distances to the data points from the fitted ellipse. Rather, the deviation is large in the part where no data points exists. This implies that the geometric distance is not a good measure of ellipse fitting. On the other hand, $\boldsymbol{\theta}$ expresses the coefficients of the ellipse equation, so the error $\Delta\boldsymbol{\theta}$ evaluates how the *ellipse equation*, i.e., the ellipse itself, differs. We are also interested in the accuracy of the center, the radii, and the area of the fitted ellipse specified by $\boldsymbol{\theta}$ as well as the accuracy of its 3-D interpretation computed from $\boldsymbol{\theta}$ (see Chapter 5). In view of this, we evaluate the error in $\boldsymbol{\theta}$. Since the computed $\boldsymbol{\theta}$ and the true $\bar{\boldsymbol{\theta}}$ are both normalized to unit norm, we measure their discrepancy $\Delta\boldsymbol{\theta}$ by the orthogonal component to $\bar{\boldsymbol{\theta}}$ (Fig. 6.2),

$$\Delta^{\perp}\boldsymbol{\theta} = \boldsymbol{P}_{\bar{\boldsymbol{\theta}}}\boldsymbol{\theta}, \qquad \boldsymbol{P}_{\bar{\boldsymbol{\theta}}} \equiv \boldsymbol{I} - \bar{\boldsymbol{\theta}}\bar{\boldsymbol{\theta}}^{\top}, \tag{6.1}$$

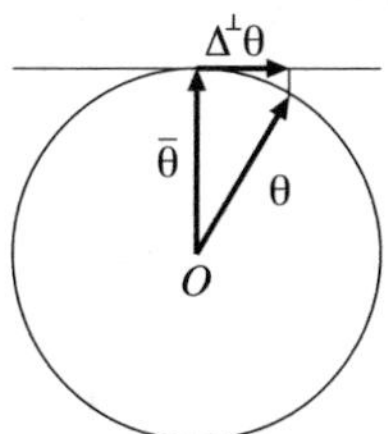

Figure 6.2: The true value $\bar{\boldsymbol{\theta}}$, the computed value $\boldsymbol{\theta}$, and its orthogonal component $\Delta^{\perp}\boldsymbol{\theta}$ of $\bar{\boldsymbol{\theta}}$.

where $\boldsymbol{P}_{\bar{\boldsymbol{\theta}}}$ is the projection matrix onto the plane perpendicular to $\bar{\boldsymbol{\theta}}$ ($\hookrightarrow$ Problem 6.1). We generate M independent noise instances and evaluate the bias B and the root-mean-square (RMS) error D defined by

$$B = \left\| \frac{1}{M} \sum_{a=1}^{M} \Delta^{\perp}\boldsymbol{\theta}^{(a)} \right\|, \qquad D = \sqrt{\frac{1}{M} \sum_{a=1}^{M} \|\Delta^{\perp}\boldsymbol{\theta}^{(a)}\|^2}, \tag{6.2}$$

where $\boldsymbol{\theta}^{(a)}$ is the solution in the ath trial. The KCR lower bound, which we will discuss in Chapter 10, implies that the RMS error D is bounded by

$$D \geq \frac{\sigma}{\sqrt{N}} \sqrt{\mathrm{tr}[\bar{\boldsymbol{M}}^{-}]}, \tag{6.3}$$

where tr$[\,\cdot\,]$ denotes the matrix trace. The matrix $\bar{\boldsymbol{M}}$ is the true value of $\boldsymbol{M}$ in the second row of Eq. (2.18), and $\bar{\boldsymbol{M}}^{-}$ is the pseudoinverse of $\bar{\boldsymbol{M}}$, which has rank 5 with the true $\bar{\boldsymbol{\theta}}$ as its

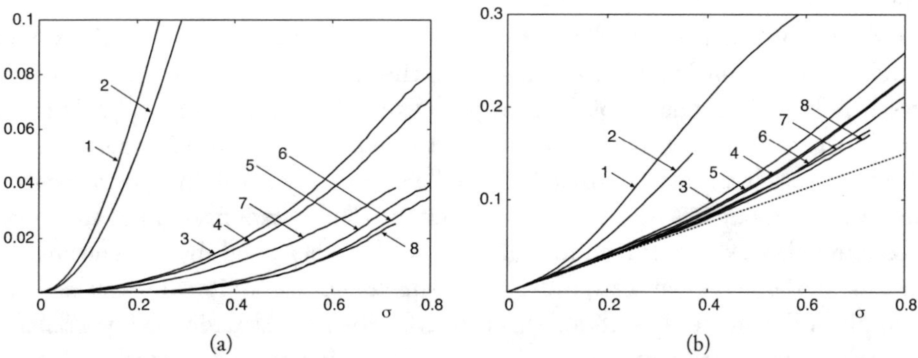

Figure 6.3: The bias (a) and the RMS error (b) of the fitted ellipse for the standard deviation σ of the noise added to the data in Fig. 6.1a over 10,000 independent trials. (1) LS, (2) iterative reweight, (3) Taubin, (4) renormalization, (5) HyperLS, (6) hyper-renormalization, (7) FNS, (8) hyperaccurate correction. The dotted line in (b) indicates the KCR lower bound.

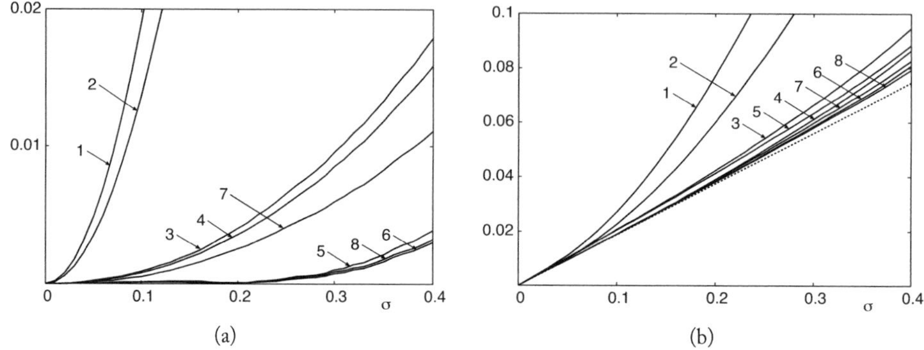

Figure 6.4: (a) Enlargement of Fig. 6.3a. (b) Enlargement of Fig. 6.3b.

null vector (we discuss these in more details in Chapters 8–10). Figure 6.3a,b plots the bias B and the RMS error D, respectively, over 10,000 independent trials for each σ. The dotted line in Fig. 6.3b is the KCR lower bound of Eq. (6.3). The interrupted plots for iterative reweight, FNS, and hyperaccurate correction indicate that the iterations did not converge beyond that noise level. Our convergence criterion is $\|\boldsymbol{\theta} - \boldsymbol{\theta}_0\| < 10^{-6}$ for the current value $\boldsymbol{\theta}$ and the value $\boldsymbol{\theta}_0$ in the preceding iteration; their signs are adjusted before subtraction. If this criterion is not satisfied after 100 iterations, we stopped. For each σ, we regarded the iterations as not convergent if any among the 10,000 trials did not converge. We see from Fig. 6.3a that least squares and iterative reweight have very large bias, while the bias of the Taubin method and renormalization is very small (pay attention to the scale of the vertical axis; the unit is pixels). The bias of HyperLS, hyper-renormalization, and hyperaccurate correction is still smaller and is even smaller than FNS. Theoretically, their bias is $O(\sigma^4)$, so their plots touch the horizontal axis near $\sigma \approx 0$ with a fourth-order contact. In contrast, the bias of the Taubin method, renormalization, and FNS is $O(\sigma^2)$, so their plots make a second-order contact.

It can be shown that the leading covariance is common to iterative reweight, renormalization, and hyper-renormalization (we will discuss this in Chapters 8 and 9). Hence, the RMS error directly reflects the influence of the bias, as shown in Fig. 6.3b. Figure 6.4 enlarges Fig. 6.3 for the small σ part. A close examination reveals that hyper-renormalization outperforms FNS. The highest accuracy is achieved, although the difference is very small, by hyperaccurate correction. However, it first requires the FNS solution, but the FNS iterations may not always converge above a certain noise level, as shown in Fig. 6.3. On the other hand, hyper-renormalization is robust to noise in the sense that it requires a much smaller number of iterations, as demonstrated in the example of the preceding section. This is because the initial solution is HyperLS, which is itself highly accurate as seen from Figs. 6.3 and 6.4. For this reason, it is concluded that hyper-renormalization is the best method for practical computations in terms of accuracy and noise robustness.

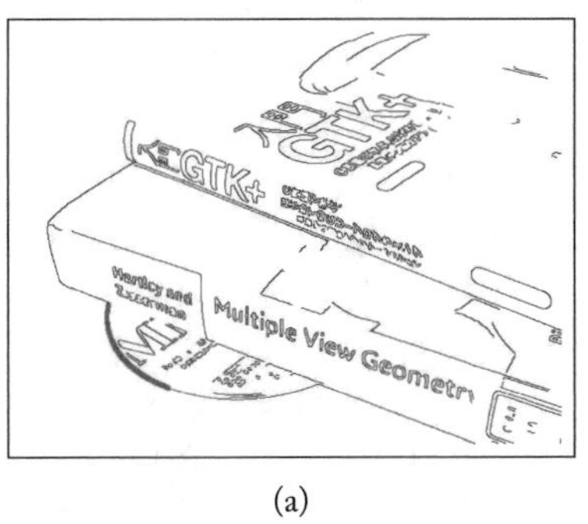

(a)

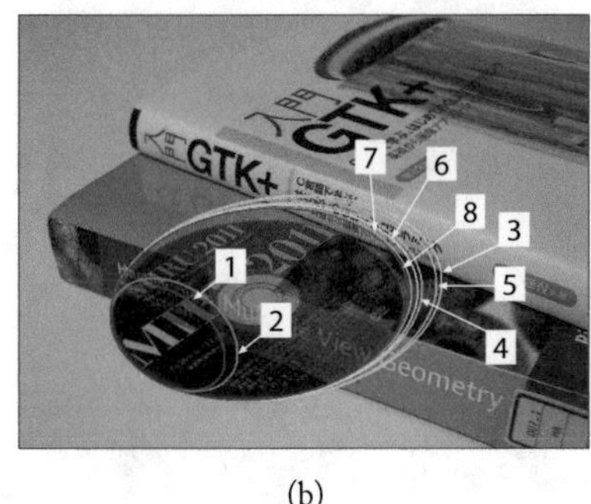

(b)

Figure 6.5: (a) An edge image of a scene with a circular object. An ellipse is fitted to the 160 edge points indicated. (b) Fitted ellipses superimposed on the original image. The occluded part is artificially composed for visual ease. (1) LS, (2) iterative reweight, (3) Taubin method, (4) renormalization, (5) HyperLS, (6) hyper-renormalization, (7) FNS, (8) hyperaccurate correction.

6.3 REAL IMAGE EXAMPLES 1

Figure 6.5a shows an edge image of a scene with a circular object. We fitted an ellipse to the 160 edge points indicated there, using different methods. Figure 6.5b shows the fitted ellipses superimposed on the original image, where the occluded part is artificially composed for visual ease. We see that least squares and iterative reweight produce much smaller ellipses than the true shape as in Fig. 6.1b,c. All other fits are very close to the true ellipse, and FNS gives the best fit in this particular instance. The number of iterations before convergence was:

method	2	4	6	7/8
# of iterations	4	3	3	6

Again, FNS and hyperaccurate correction required about twice as many iterations as other methods.

6.4 ROBUST FITTING

We now see how the RANSAC procedure described in Chapter 4 can robustly fit an ellipse to edge segments that are not necessarily elliptic arcs. The upper row of Fig. 6.6 shows examples of edge segments that do not entirely consist of elliptic arcs. Regarding those non-elliptic parts as outliers, we fit an ellipse to inlier arcs, using RANSAC. The lower row of Fig. 6.6 depicts fitted ellipses. We see that the segments that constitute an ellipse are automatically selected.

6.5 ELLIPSE-SPECIFIC METHODS

We test the ellipse-specific methods discussed in Chapter 4, i.e., the methods that enforce the fit to be an ellipse when standard methods produce a hyperbola in the presence of large noise. We compare the following four methods:

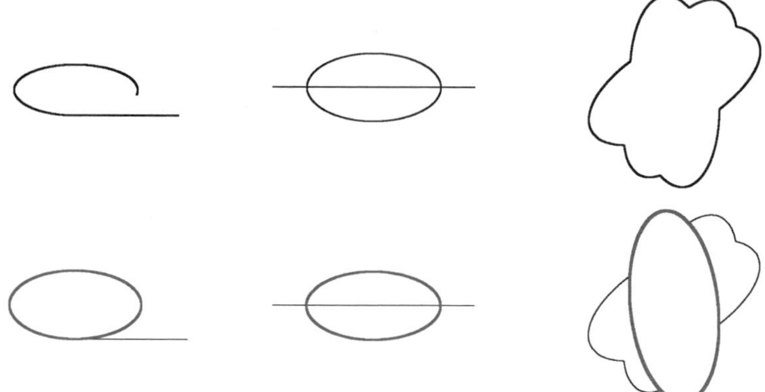

Figure 6.6: Upper row: Input edge segments. Lower row: Ellipses fitted by RANSAC.

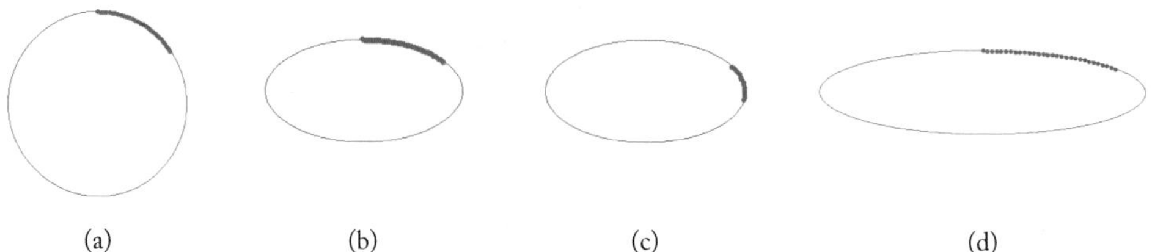

Figure 6.7: Point sequences for our experiment. The number of points is 30, 30, 15, and 30 and the average distance between neighboring points is 2.96, 3.31, 2.72, and 5.72 pixels for (a), (b), (c), and (d), respectively.

1. the method of Fitzgibbon et al. [1999] (Procedure 4.2),
2. hyper-renormalization (Procedure 2.3),
3. the method of Szpak et al. [2015], and
4. random sampling (Procedure 4.3).

As mentioned in the Supplemental Note in Chapter 4 (page 34), the method of Szpak et al. minimizes the Sampson error with a penalty term that diverges as the solution approach a hyperbola.

We generated four-point sequences shown in Fig. 6.7. The points have equal arc length separations on each ellipse. Random Gaussian noise of mean 0 and standard deviation σ is added independently to the x and y coordinates of each point, and an ellipse is fitted.

Figure 6.8 shows fitting examples for a particular noise when hyper-renormalization returns a hyperbola. The *relative noise level* at which that occurred is indicated in the caption, where we define it to be the noise level σ divided by the average distance between neighboring points. What is conspicuous is that the method of Fitzgibbon et al. always fits a very small and flat ellipse, just as

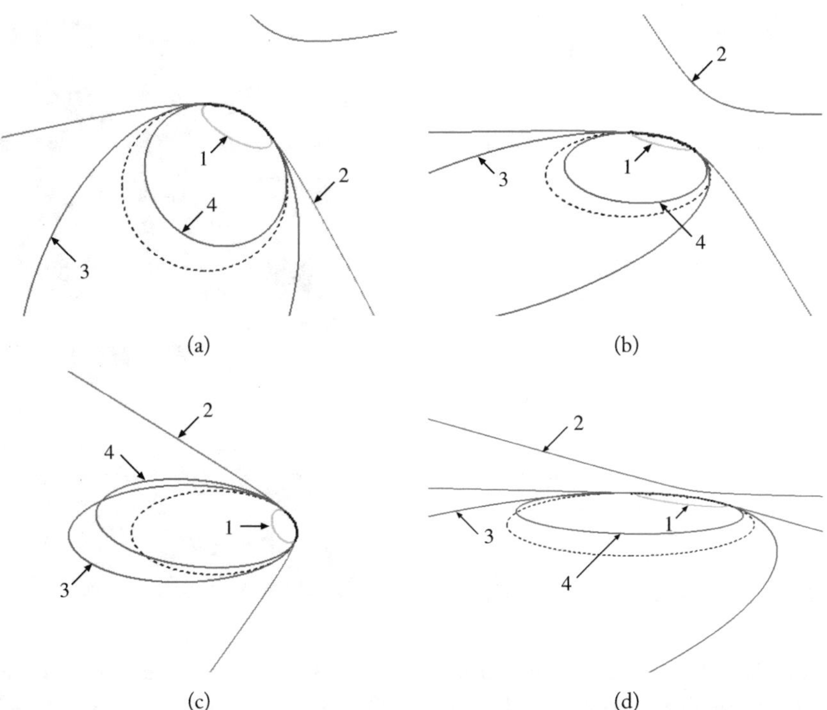

Figure 6.8: Fitting examples for a particular noise when hyper-renormalization returns a hyperbola. (1) Fitzgibbon et al., (2) hyper-renormalization, (3) Szpak et al., (4) random sampling. The dotted lines indicate the true shapes. The relative noise level ϵ is 0.169, 0.151, 0.092, and 0.087 for (a), (b), (c), and (d), respectively.

least squares and iterative reweight in Sections 6.1 and 6.3. In contrast, the method of Szpak et al. fits a large ellipse close to the fitted hyperbola. Random sampling returns an ellipse is in between. However, the fact that hyper-renormalization returns a parabola indicates that the segment does not have sufficient information for fitting an ellipse. Even though random sampling returns a relatively reasonable ellipse, we cannot expect to obtain a good fit by forcing the solution to be an ellipse using ellipse-specific methods.

6.6 REAL IMAGE EXAMPLES 2

Figure 6.9a shows edge images of real scenes. We fitted an ellipse to the edge points indicated there (200 pixels above and 140 pixels below) by different methods. In Fig. 6.9b, fitted ellipses are superimposed on the original images. In the above example, hyper-renormalization returns an ellipse, in which case random sampling returns the same ellipse. The fit is very close to the true shape as expected. The method of Szpak et al. [2015] also fits an ellipse close to it. However, the method of Fitzgibbon et al. [1999] fits a small and flat ellipse. In the lower example, hyper-renormalization returns a hyperbola, and the method of Szpak et al. fits a very large ellipse close

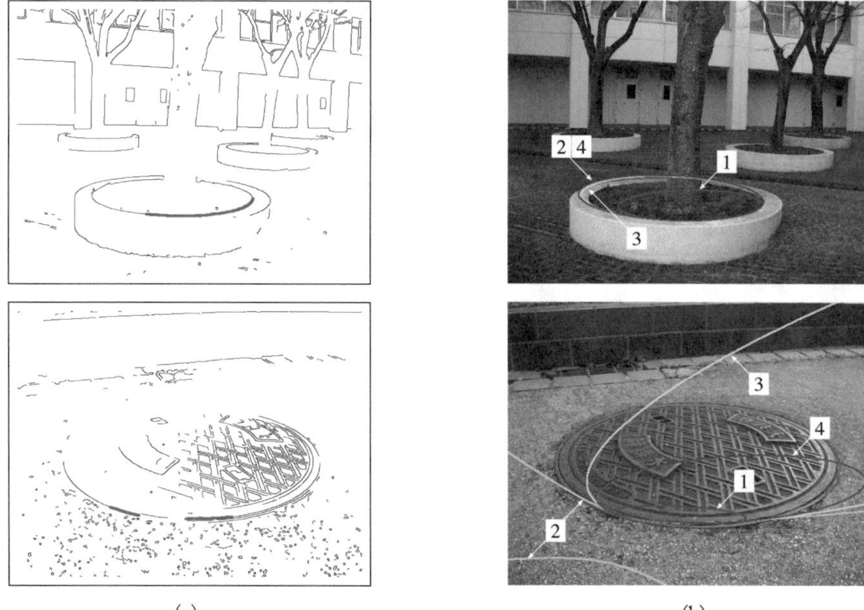

Figure 6.9: (a): Edges extracted from real images. We used 200 pixels above and 140 pixels below indicated there for fitting an ellipse. (b) Fitted ellipses superimposed on the original image. (1) Fitzgibbon et al., (2) hyper-renormalization, (3) Szpak et al., (4) random sampling.

to that hyperbola. Again, the method of Fitzgibbon et al. fits a very small and flat ellipse. The random sampling fit is somewhat in between.

Generally speaking, if hyper-renormalization fits an ellipse, we should adopt it as the best fit. If a hyperbola is returned, it indicates that the data points do not have sufficient information for fitting an ellipse. Hence, the effort to fit an ellipse to them does not make sense; forcing the solution to be an ellipse, using ellipse-specific method, does not produce any meaningful result. If, for some reason, we want an ellipse by all means, perhaps random sampling may give the least intolerable result. As mentioned in Section 4.2, pathological cases in which any five points define a hyperbola could be conceivable in theory. In practice, we can ignore such points as incapable of approximating an ellipse. In fact, it is even not easy to find an elliptic segment obtained by applying an edge filter to a real image such that a standard method fits a hyperbola, unless parts of it are artificially cut out (Fig. 6.9(b) was created in that way), much less a segment incapable of approximating an ellipse (we have never encountered one).

6.7 ELLIPSE-BASED 3-D COMPUTATION EXAMPLES

We show some applications of the ellipse-based 3-D computation techniques described in Chapter 5.

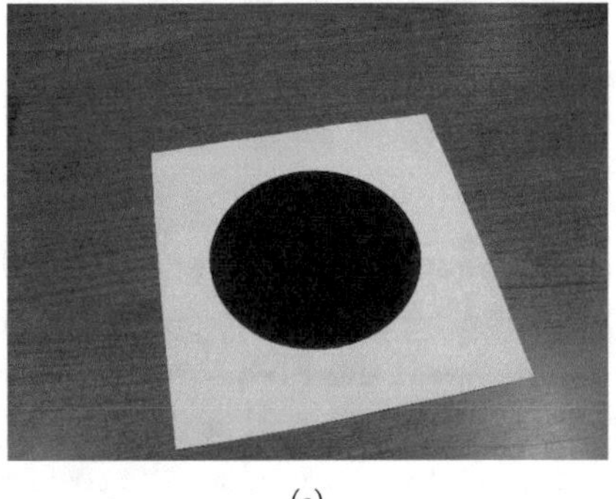

(a)

(b)

Figure 6.10: (a) An image of a circle on a planar surface. (b) A 3-D graphics object is displayed in a position compatible to the surface in (a).

(a)

(b)

Figure 6.11: (a) An image of a planar board, on which a circular mark (encircled by a white line) is painted. (b) A front image of the board generated by computing its relative orientation to the camera by Procedure 5.5, using the circular mark, and virtually rotating the camera by Procedure 5.7.

Figure 6.10a is an image of a circle drawn on a planar surface. Detecting the circle boundary by edge detection and fitting an ellipse to it, we can compute the position and orientation of the surface relative to the camera by Procedure 5.5. Using that knowledge, Fig. 6.10b displays a 3-D graphics object placed as if it were placed on the planar surface.

Figure 6.11a is an outdoor scene of a planar board, on which a circular mark (encircled by a white line in the figure) is painted. Detecting its boundary by edge detection and fitting an ellipse to it, we can compute the position and orientation of the board relative to the camera by

Procedure 5.5. Using that knowledge, we can generate its front image by virtual camera rotation, using Procedure 5.7; for visual ease, the image is appropriately translated.

6.8 SUPPLEMENTAL NOTE

Possible non-convergence is the main disadvantage of iterative methods, and efforts have been made to guarantee convergence. For minimization search, however, non-convergence is in reality an indication that *the cost function does not have a clear minimum*. If the FNS for Sampson error minimization does not converge, for example, we tend to think that we should use instead, say, the Levenberg-Marquadt method [Press et al., 2007], which is guaranteed to reduce the cost at each step. According to the authors' experiences, however, if FNS does not converge in the presence of large noise, we do not obtain a solution in most cases even by the Levenberg-Marquadt method, because convergence is too slow. For example, although the cost is constantly decreasing by a tiny amount at each step, the step size, which is also very small, does not reduce much, as if always proceeding at a snail's pace after hundreds and thousands of steps. In such a case, we have observed that the FNS iterations oscillate around some value back and forth indefinitely. Such a phenomenon is not the defect of the algorithm but rather the property of the problem itself. If the cost function has a very flat bottom without a clear minimum, any iterative search has a problem. If that is the case, we should use a non-iterative algebraic method and accept the value as an approximation to the true minimum.

One interesting issue of HyperLS, hyper-renormalization, and hyperaccurate correction is the effect of the vector $\boldsymbol{e}$ defined by Eq. (2.12). According to the authors' observation, letting $\boldsymbol{e} = \boldsymbol{0}$ did not cause differences in that the plots in Figs. 6.3 and 6.4 did not show any visible change.

We can see from Fig. 6.6 that using RANSAC elliptic arcs are automatically selected in the presence of non-elliptic segments, i.e., outliers. However, this does not always work when non-elliptic segments are dominant. The limitation of RANSAC is that it only deals with individual points without considering the fact that inliers and outliers are both contiguous segments. The RANSAC principle is the same if the data points are continuously connected or not. In view of this, various techniques have been proposed for classifying edge segments into elliptic and non-elliptic arcs, e.g., see Masuzaki et al. [2015].

PROBLEMS

6.1. Show that the projection of a vector $\boldsymbol{v}$ onto a plane with unit surface normal $\boldsymbol{u}$ is given by $\boldsymbol{P}_{\boldsymbol{u}}\boldsymbol{v}$ (Fig. 6.12), where $\boldsymbol{P}_{\boldsymbol{u}}$ is the projection matrix given by

$$\boldsymbol{P}_{\boldsymbol{u}} \equiv \boldsymbol{I} - \boldsymbol{u}\boldsymbol{u}^{\top}. \tag{6.4}$$

6.2. The projection matrix $\boldsymbol{P}_{\boldsymbol{u}}$ of Eq. (6.4) is symmetric by definition. Show that it is also *idempotent*, i.e.,

$$\boldsymbol{P}_{\boldsymbol{u}}^2 = \boldsymbol{P}_{\boldsymbol{u}}, \tag{6.5}$$

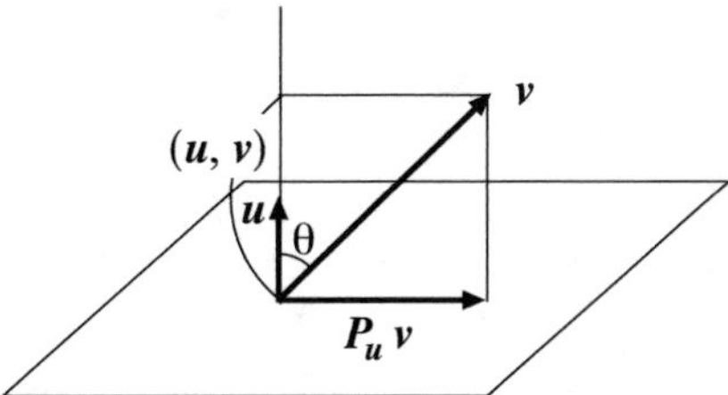

Figure 6.12: Projection $\boldsymbol{P_u v}$ of vector $\boldsymbol{v}$ onto the plane with unit surface normal $\boldsymbol{u}$.

which states that once projected, things remain there if projected again, as geometric interpretation implies.

CHAPTER 7

Extension and Generalization

Study of ellipse fitting is important not merely for extracting elliptic shapes in the image. It is also a prototype of many geometric estimation problems for computer vision applications. To illustrate this, we show two typical problems that have the same mathematical structure as ellipse fitting: computing the fundamental matrix from two images and computing the homography between two planar surface images. They are both themselves indispensable tasks for 3-D scene analysis by computer vision. We show how they are computed by extending and generalizing the ellipse fitting procedure.

7.1 FUNDAMENTAL MATRIX COMPUTATION

7.1.1 FORMULATION

Suppose we take images of the same scene using two cameras. If a particular point in the scene is imaged at (x, y) by one camera and at (x', y') by the other, it can be shown that the two points satisfy

$$\left(\begin{pmatrix} x/f_0 \\ y/f_0 \\ 1 \end{pmatrix}, \boldsymbol{F}\begin{pmatrix} x'/f_0 \\ y'/f_0 \\ 1 \end{pmatrix}\right) = 0, \tag{7.1}$$

where f_0 is a constant for adjusting the scale, just as in the ellipse fitting case. The 3×3 matrix $\boldsymbol{F}$ is called the *fundamental matrix*. It is determined solely by the relative position of the two cameras and their internal parameters, such as the focal length, independent of the scene content. Equation (7.1) is called the *epipolar constraint* or the *epipolar equation*. Since any nonzero scalar multiple of the fundamental matrix $\boldsymbol{F}$ defines the same epipolar equation, we normalize it to unit matrix norm:

$$\|\boldsymbol{F}\| \left(\equiv \sqrt{\sum_{i,j=1,3} F_{ij}^2}\right) = 1. \tag{7.2}$$

If we define 9-D vectors

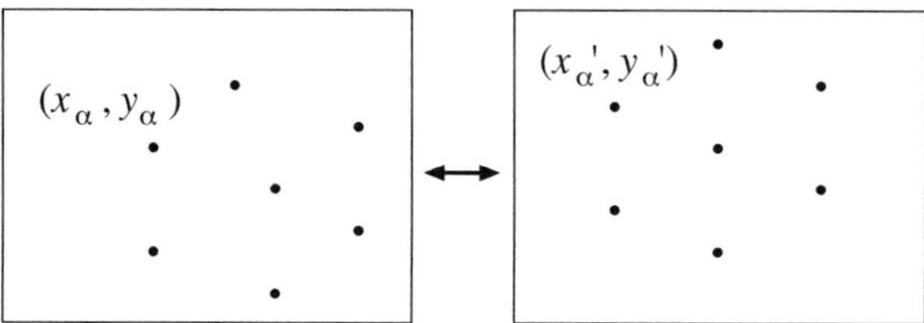

Figure 7.1: Computing the fundamental matrix from noisy point correspondences.

$$\boldsymbol{\xi} = \begin{pmatrix} xx' \\ xy' \\ f_0 x \\ yx' \\ yy' \\ f_0 y \\ f_0 x' \\ f_0 y' \\ f_0^2 \end{pmatrix}, \qquad \boldsymbol{\theta} = \begin{pmatrix} F_{11} \\ F_{12} \\ F_{13} \\ F_{21} \\ F_{22} \\ F_{23} \\ F_{31} \\ F_{32} \\ F_{33} \end{pmatrix}, \tag{7.3}$$

it is easy to see that the left side of Eq. (7.1) is $(\boldsymbol{\xi}, \boldsymbol{\theta})/f_0^2$. Hence, the epipolar equation of Eq. (7.1) is written in the form

$$(\boldsymbol{\xi}, \boldsymbol{\theta}) = 0. \tag{7.4}$$

The vector $\boldsymbol{\theta}$ has scale indeterminacy, and Eq. (7.2) is equivalent to normalizing $\boldsymbol{\theta}$ to unit norm: $\|\boldsymbol{\theta}\| = 1$. Thus, the epipolar equation has the same form as the ellipse equation of Eq. (1.9).

Computing the fundamental matrix $\boldsymbol{F}$ from point correspondences over two image is the first step of many computer vision applications. In fact, from the computed $\boldsymbol{F}$, we can determine the relative position and orientation of the two cameras and their focal lengths. Finding a matrix $\boldsymbol{F}$ that satisfies Eq. (7.1) for corresponding points (x_α, y_α) and (x'_α, y'_α), $\alpha = 1, ..., N$, in the presence of noise (Fig. 7.1) can be mathematically formulated as finding a unit vector $\boldsymbol{\theta}$ such that

$$(\boldsymbol{\xi}_\alpha, \boldsymbol{\theta}) \approx 0, \qquad \alpha = 1, ..., N, \tag{7.5}$$

where $\boldsymbol{\xi}_\alpha$ is the value of the 9-D vector $\boldsymbol{\xi}$ obtained by replacing x, y, x', and y' in Eq. (7.3) by x_α, y_α, x'_α, and y'_α, respectively. We regard the data x_α, y_α, x'_α, and y'_α as the corrupted values of their true values $\bar{x}_\alpha$, $\bar{y}_\alpha$, $\bar{x}'_\alpha$, and $\bar{y}'_\alpha$ by noise terms Δx_α, Δy_α, $\Delta x'_\alpha$, and $\Delta y'_\alpha$, respectively, and write

$$x_\alpha = \bar{x}_\alpha + \Delta x_\alpha, \quad y_\alpha = \bar{y}_\alpha + \Delta y_\alpha, \quad x'_\alpha = \bar{x}'_\alpha + \Delta x'_\alpha, \quad y'_\alpha = \bar{y}'_\alpha + \Delta y'_\alpha. \tag{7.6}$$

Substituting these into $\boldsymbol{\xi}_\alpha$ obtained from Eq. (7.3), we obtain

$$\boldsymbol{\xi}_\alpha = \bar{\boldsymbol{\xi}}_\alpha + \Delta_1 \boldsymbol{\xi}_\alpha + \Delta_2 \boldsymbol{\xi}_\alpha, \tag{7.7}$$

where $\bar{\xi}_\alpha$ is the value of ξ_α obtained by replacing x_α, y_α, x'_α, and y'_α in its components by their true values $\bar{x}_\alpha$, $\bar{y}_\alpha$, $\bar{x}'_\alpha$, and $\bar{y}'_\alpha$, respectively, while $\Delta_1\xi_\alpha$ and $\Delta_2\xi_\alpha$ are, respectively, the first- and the second-order noise terms. After expansion, we obtain

$$\Delta_1\xi_\alpha = \begin{pmatrix} \bar{x}'_\alpha \Delta x_\alpha + \bar{x}_\alpha \Delta x'_\alpha \\ \bar{y}'_\alpha \Delta x_\alpha + \bar{x}_\alpha \Delta y'_\alpha \\ f_0 \Delta x_\alpha \\ \bar{x}'_\alpha \Delta y_\alpha + \bar{y}_\alpha \Delta x'_\alpha \\ f_0 \Delta y_\alpha \\ f_0 \Delta x'_\alpha \\ f_0 \Delta y'_\alpha \\ 0 \end{pmatrix}, \qquad \Delta_2\xi_\alpha = \begin{pmatrix} \Delta x_\alpha \Delta x'_\alpha \\ \Delta x_\alpha \Delta y'_\alpha \\ 0 \\ \Delta y_\alpha \Delta x'_\alpha \\ \Delta y_\alpha \Delta y'_\alpha \\ 0 \\ 0 \\ 0 \\ 0 \end{pmatrix}. \tag{7.8}$$

We regard Δx_α and Δy_α as random variables and define the covariance matrix of ξ_α by

$$V[\xi_\alpha] = E[\Delta_1\xi_\alpha \Delta_1\xi_\alpha^\top], \tag{7.9}$$

where $E[\,\cdot\,]$ denotes expectation over their distribution. If Δx_α, Δy_α, $\Delta x'_\alpha$, and $\Delta y'_\alpha$ are subject to an independent Gaussian distribution of mean 0 and variance σ^2, we have

$$\begin{aligned} E[\Delta x_\alpha] = E[\Delta y_\alpha] = E[\Delta x'_\alpha] = E[\Delta y'_\alpha] = 0, \\ E[\Delta x_\alpha^2] = E[\Delta y_\alpha^2] = E[\Delta x'^2_\alpha] = E[\Delta y'^2_\alpha] = \sigma^2, \\ E[\Delta x_\alpha \Delta y_\alpha] = E[\Delta x'_\alpha \Delta y'_\alpha] = E[\Delta x_\alpha \Delta y'_\alpha] = E[\Delta x'_\alpha \Delta y_\alpha] = 0. \end{aligned} \tag{7.10}$$

Hence, we can write from Eq. (7.8) the covariance matrix of Eq. (7.9) in the form

$$V[\xi_\alpha] = \sigma^2 V_0[\xi_\alpha], \tag{7.11}$$

where we have taken out the common multiplier σ^2 and written the remaining part as $V_0[\xi_\alpha]$. This matrix, which we call the *normalized covariance matrix* as in ellipse fitting, has the form

$$V_0[\xi_\alpha] = \begin{pmatrix} \bar{x}_\alpha^2 + \bar{x}'^2_\alpha & \bar{x}'_\alpha \bar{y}'_\alpha & f_0 \bar{x}'_\alpha & \bar{x}_\alpha \bar{y}_\alpha & 0 & 0 & f_0 \bar{x}_\alpha & 0 & 0 \\ \bar{x}'_\alpha \bar{y}'_\alpha & \bar{x}_\alpha^2 + \bar{y}'^2_\alpha & f_0 \bar{y}'_\alpha & 0 & \bar{x}_\alpha \bar{y}_\alpha & 0 & 0 & f_0 \bar{x}_\alpha & 0 \\ f_0 \bar{x}'_\alpha & f_0 \bar{y}'_\alpha & f_0^2 & 0 & 0 & 0 & 0 & 0 & 0 \\ \bar{x}_\alpha \bar{y}_\alpha & 0 & 0 & \bar{y}_\alpha^2 + \bar{x}'^2_\alpha & \bar{x}'_\alpha \bar{y}'_\alpha & f_0 \bar{x}'_\alpha & f_0 \bar{y}_\alpha & 0 & 0 \\ 0 & \bar{x}_\alpha \bar{y}_\alpha & 0 & \bar{x}'_\alpha \bar{y}'_\alpha & \bar{y}_\alpha^2 + \bar{y}'^2_\alpha & f_0 \bar{y}'_\alpha & 0 & f_0 \bar{y}_\alpha & 0 \\ 0 & 0 & 0 & f_0 \bar{x}'_\alpha & f_0 \bar{y}'_\alpha & f_0^2 & 0 & 0 & 0 \\ f_0 \bar{x}_\alpha & 0 & 0 & f_0 \bar{y}_\alpha & 0 & 0 & f_0^2 & 0 & 0 \\ 0 & f_0 \bar{x}_\alpha & 0 & 0 & f_0 \bar{y}_\alpha & 0 & 0 & f_0^2 & 0 \\ 0 & 0 & 0 & 0 & 0 & 0 & 0 & 0 & 0 \end{pmatrix}. \tag{7.12}$$

As in the ellipse fitting case, we need not consider the second-order term $\Delta_2\boldsymbol{\xi}_\alpha$ in the covariance matrix of Eq. (7.9). Also, the true values $\bar{x}_\alpha$, $\bar{y}_\alpha$, $\bar{x}'_\alpha$, and $\bar{y}'_\alpha$ in Eq. (7.12) are, in actual computation, replaced by the observed values x_α, y_α, x'_α, and y'_α, respectively.

Thus, computing the fundamental matrix $\boldsymbol{F}$ from noisy correspondences can be formalized as computing the unit vector $\boldsymbol{\theta}$ that satisfies Eq. (7.5) by considering the noise properties described by the covariance matrices $V[\boldsymbol{\xi}_\alpha]$. Mathematically, this problem is identical to ellipse fitting. Hence, the algebraic methods (least squares, the Taubin method, HyperLS, iterative reweight, renormalization, and hyper-renormalization) and the geometric methods (FNS, geometric distance minimization, and hyperaccurate correction) can be applied directly.

7.1.2 RANK CONSTRAINT

There is, however, one aspect for fundamental matrix computation that does not exist for ellipse fitting: it can be shown from a geometric consideration that the fundamental matrix $\boldsymbol{F}$ must have rank 2 and hence

$$\det \boldsymbol{F} = 0, \tag{7.13}$$

which is called the *rank constraint*. Generally, three approaches exist for enforcing this rank constraint:

A posteriori correction: We compute $\boldsymbol{\theta}$ without considering the rank constraint, using a standard (algebraic or geometric) method. If the data are exact, Eq. (7.13) is automatically satisfied whatever method is used, and if the point correspondences are sufficiently accurate, we obtain a solution such that $\det \boldsymbol{F} \approx 0$. So, we modify the solution $\boldsymbol{F}$ afterward to enforce the rank constraint.

Internal access: Introducing *hidden variables* $\boldsymbol{u}$, we express each component of $\boldsymbol{\theta}$ in terms of $\boldsymbol{u}$ in such a way that $\boldsymbol{\theta}(\boldsymbol{u})$ identically satisfies the rank condition. Then, we search for an optimal value of $\boldsymbol{u}$, e.g., minimize the Sampson error.

External access: We do iterations without using hidden variables in such a way that $\boldsymbol{\theta}$ approaches the true value at each iteration and at the same time the rank constraint is automatically satisfied when the iterations have converged.

Geometrically, these approaches are interpreted as illustrated in Fig.7.2: we seek a solution that minimizes some cost, e.g., the least-square error, the Sampson error, or the geometric distance, subject to the rank constraint $\det \boldsymbol{F} = 0$. For *a posteriori* correction, we first go to the point in the solution space where the cost is minimum, without considering the rank constraint, and then move to the hypersurface defined by the rank constraint $\det \boldsymbol{F} = 0$ (Fig. 7.2a). It is easy to find the closest point in the hypersurface using the singular value decomposition (SVD) (↪ Problem 7.1), but this is not an optimal solution. The optimal solution is obtained by moving in the direction along which the cost increases the least. The internal access approach first parameterizes the hypersurface using the hidden variable $\boldsymbol{u}$, which can be seen as the surface coordinates of the

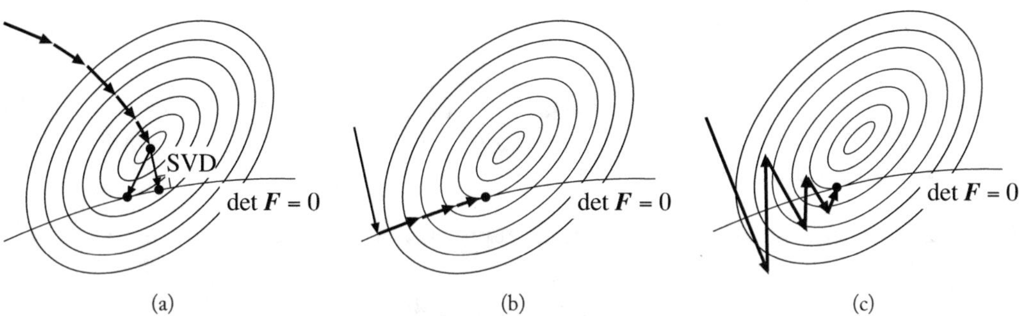

Figure 7.2: (a) A posteriori correction: We first go to the minimum of the cost without considering the rank constraint and then move to the hypersurface defined by $\det \boldsymbol{F} = 0$. (b) Internal access: We parameterize the hypersurface of $\det \boldsymbol{F} = 0$ and optimize the surface coordinates on it. (c) External access: We do iterations in the outside space, moving in the direction of decreasing the cost at each step in such a way that in the end the rank constraint is exactly satisfied.

hypersurface. Then, we search the hypersurface to minimize the cost (Fig. 7.2b). The external access, on the other hand, does iterations in the outside space, moving in the direction of decreasing the cost at each step in such a way that in the end the rank constraint is exactly satisfied (Fig. 7.2c). In each approach, various different schemes have been studied in the past; see Supplemental Note (page 77).

7.1.3 OUTLIER REMOVAL

For extracting point correspondences between two images of the same scene, we look for similarly appearing points in them and match them, using some similarity measure. For this, various methods have been studied. However, existing methods are not all perfect, sometimes matching wrong points. Such false matches are called *outliers*; correct matches are called *inliers*. Since fundamental matrix computation has mathematically the same form as ellipse fitting, the RANSAC procedure in Section 4.1 can be used for outlier removal. The underlying idea is, for a given set of point pairs, to find a fundamental matrix such that *the number of point pairs that approximately satisfy the epipolar equation is as large as possible*. Note that the fundamental matrix $\boldsymbol{F}$ has nine elements. Hence, if eight point pairs are given, we can determine $\boldsymbol{F}$ from the resulting eight epipolar equations of the form of Eq. (7.1) up to scale. The RANSAC procedure goes as follows.

Procedure 7.1 (RANSAC)

1. From among the input point pairs randomly select eight, and let $\boldsymbol{\xi}_1, \boldsymbol{\xi}_2, \ldots, \boldsymbol{\xi}_8$ be their vector representations in the form of $\boldsymbol{\xi}$ of Eq. (7.3).

2. Compute the unit eigenvector $\boldsymbol{\theta}$ of the matrix

$$M_8 = \sum_{\alpha=1}^{8} \xi_\alpha \xi_\alpha^\top, \tag{7.14}$$

for the smallest eigenvalue.

3. Store that $\boldsymbol{\theta}$ as a candidate, and count the number n of point pairs in the input that satisfy

$$\frac{(\xi, \boldsymbol{\theta})^2}{(\boldsymbol{\theta}, V_0[\xi]\boldsymbol{\theta})} < 2d^2, \tag{7.15}$$

where d is a threshold for admissible deviation of each point of a corresponding pair, e.g., $d = 2$ (pixels). Store that n.

4. Select a new set of eight point pairs from the input, and do the same. Repeat this many times, and return from among the stored candidates the one for which n is the largest.

Comments. Step 2 computes the fundamental matrix by least squares from the eight point pairs selected in Step 1. The rank constraint of Eq. (7.13) is not considered, because speed is more important than accuracy for repeated voting. Step 3 tests to what extent each point pair satisfies the epipolar equation for the candidate $\boldsymbol{\theta}$. The left side of Eq. (7.15), which has the dimension of square length (note that both ξ and $V_0[\xi]$ have the dimension of square length), is an approximation of the square sum of the minimum distances necessary to move the point pair (x, y) and (x', y') to $(\bar{x}, \bar{y})$ and $(\bar{x}', \bar{y}')$ so that the epipolar equation is satisfied (the derivation is the same as that of Eq. (3.2) for ellipse fitting). As in ellipse fitting, we can directly go on to the next sampling if the count n is smaller than the stored count, and we can stop if the current value of n is not updated over a fixed number of sampling. In the end, those point pairs that do not satisfy Eq. (7.15) for the chosen $\boldsymbol{\theta}$ are removed as outliers.

7.2 HOMOGRAPHY COMPUTATION

7.2.1 FORMULATION

Suppose we take images of a planar surface by two cameras. If point (x, y) in one images corresponds to point (x', y') in the other, it can be shown that they are related in the form

$$x' = f_0 \frac{H_{11}x + H_{12}y + H_{13}f_0}{H_{31}x + H_{32}y + H_{33}f_0}, \qquad y' = f_0 \frac{H_{21}x + H_{22}y + H_{23}f_0}{H_{31}x + H_{32}y + H_{33}f_0}, \tag{7.16}$$

for some constants H_{ij}. As in ellipse fitting and fundamental matrix computation, f_0 is a scaling constant. Equation (7.16) can be equivalently written as

$$\begin{pmatrix} x'/f_0 \\ y'/f_0 \\ 1 \end{pmatrix} \simeq \begin{pmatrix} H_{11} & H_{12} & H_{13} \\ H_{21} & H_{22} & H_{23} \\ H_{31} & H_{32} & H_{33} \end{pmatrix} \begin{pmatrix} x/f_0 \\ y/f_0 \\ 1 \end{pmatrix}, \tag{7.17}$$

where $\simeq$ denotes equality up to a nonzero constant. As mentioned in Chapter 6, this mapping from (x, y) to (x', y') is called a *homography* (or *projective transformation*), when the matrix $\boldsymbol{H} = (H_{ij})$ is nonsingular (see Eq. (5.16)). It can be shown that the matrix $\boldsymbol{H}$ is determined by the relative positions of the two cameras and their intrinsic parameters, such as the focal length, and the position and orientation of the planar scene. Since the same homography is represented if $\boldsymbol{H}$ multiplied by a nonzero constant, we normalize it to

$$\|\boldsymbol{H}\| \left(\equiv \sqrt{\sum_{i,j=1,3} H_{ij}^2} \right) = 1. \tag{7.18}$$

Equation (7.17) implies the left and right sides are parallel vectors, so we may rewrite it as

$$\begin{pmatrix} x'/f_0 \\ y'/f_0 \\ 1 \end{pmatrix} \times \begin{pmatrix} H_{11} & H_{12} & H_{13} \\ H_{21} & H_{22} & H_{23} \\ H_{31} & H_{32} & H_{33} \end{pmatrix} \begin{pmatrix} x/f_0 \\ y/f_0 \\ 1 \end{pmatrix} = \begin{pmatrix} 0 \\ 0 \\ 0 \end{pmatrix}. \tag{7.19}$$

If we define the 9-D vectors

$$\boldsymbol{\theta} = \begin{pmatrix} H_{11} \\ H_{12} \\ H_{13} \\ H_{21} \\ H_{22} \\ H_{23} \\ H_{31} \\ H_{32} \\ H_{33} \end{pmatrix}, \quad \boldsymbol{\xi}^{(1)} = \begin{pmatrix} 0 \\ 0 \\ 0 \\ -f_0 x \\ -f_0 y \\ -f_0^2 \\ xy' \\ yy' \\ f_0 y' \end{pmatrix}, \quad \boldsymbol{\xi}^{(2)} = \begin{pmatrix} f_0 x \\ f_0 y \\ f_0^2 \\ 0 \\ 0 \\ 0 \\ -xx' \\ -yx' \\ -f_0 x' \end{pmatrix}, \quad \boldsymbol{\xi}^{(3)} = \begin{pmatrix} -xy' \\ -yy' \\ -f_0 y' \\ xx' \\ yx' \\ f_0 x' \\ 0 \\ 0 \\ 0 \end{pmatrix}, \tag{7.20}$$

the vector equation of Eq. (7.19) has the following three components:

$$(\boldsymbol{\xi}^{(1)}, \boldsymbol{\theta}) = 0, \qquad (\boldsymbol{\xi}^{(2)}, \boldsymbol{\theta}) = 0, \qquad (\boldsymbol{\xi}^{(3)}, \boldsymbol{\theta}) = 0. \tag{7.21}$$

The vector $\boldsymbol{\theta}$ has scale indeterminacy, and Eq. (7.18) is equivalent to normalizing $\boldsymbol{\theta}$ to unit norm: $\|\boldsymbol{\theta}\| = 1$. However, we should note that the three equations of Eq. (7.21) are *not linearly independent* ($\hookrightarrow$ Problem 7.2). This means that if the first and the second equations in Eq. (7.21) are satisfied, for example, the third one is automatically satisfied.

Computing the homography matrix $\boldsymbol{H}$ from point correspondences of two planar scene images is the first step of many computer vision applications. In fact, from the computed $\boldsymbol{H}$, we can determine the relative position and orientation of the two cameras and the positions the planar surface relative to the two cameras. Mathematically, computing the matrix $\boldsymbol{H}$ that satisfies Eq. (7.16) for corresponding points (x_α, y_α) and (x'_α, y'_α), $\alpha = 1, ..., N$, in the presence of noise

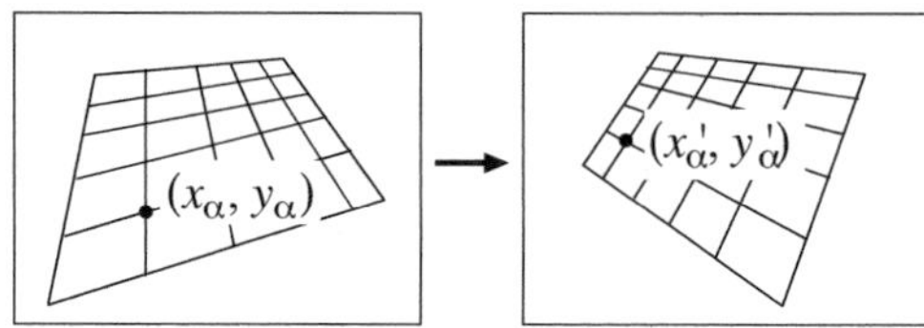

Figure 7.3: Computing a homography from noisy point correspondences.

(Fig. 7.3) is equivalent to computing a unit vector $\boldsymbol{\theta}$ such that

$$(\boldsymbol{\xi}_\alpha^{(1)}, \boldsymbol{\theta}) \approx 0, \qquad (\boldsymbol{\xi}_\alpha^{(2)}, \boldsymbol{\theta}) \approx 0, \qquad (\boldsymbol{\xi}_\alpha^{(3)}, \boldsymbol{\theta}) \approx 0, \qquad \alpha = 1, ..., N, \tag{7.22}$$

where $\boldsymbol{\xi}_\alpha^{(k)}$ is the value of the 9-D vector $\boldsymbol{\xi}^{(k)}$ in Eq. (7.20) obtained by substituting x_α, y_α, x'_α, and y'_α for x, y, x', and y', respectively. We regard the data x_α, y_α, x'_α, and y'_α as deviations of their true values $\bar{x}_\alpha$, $\bar{y}_\alpha$, and $\bar{x}'_\alpha$, by noise terms Δx_α, Δy_α, $\Delta x'_\alpha$, and $\Delta y'_\alpha$, respectively, and write

$$x_\alpha = \bar{x}_\alpha + \Delta x_\alpha, \qquad y_\alpha = \bar{y}_\alpha + \Delta y_\alpha, \qquad x'_\alpha = \bar{x}'_\alpha + \Delta x'_\alpha, \qquad y'_\alpha = \bar{y}'_\alpha + \Delta y'_\alpha. \tag{7.23}$$

If we substitute these into $\boldsymbol{\xi}_\alpha^{(k)}$ obtained from Eq. (7.20), we have

$$\boldsymbol{\xi}_\alpha^{(k)} = \bar{\boldsymbol{\xi}}_\alpha^{(k)} + \Delta_1 \boldsymbol{\xi}_\alpha^{(k)} + \Delta_2 \boldsymbol{\xi}_\alpha^{(k)}, \tag{7.24}$$

where $\bar{\boldsymbol{\xi}}_\alpha^{(k)}$ is the true value of $\boldsymbol{\xi}_\alpha^{(k)}$ obtained by replacing x_α, y_α, x'_α, and y'_α by their true values $\bar{x}_\alpha$, $\bar{y}_\alpha$, $\bar{x}'_\alpha$, and $\bar{y}'_\alpha$, respectively, while $\Delta_1 \boldsymbol{\xi}_\alpha^{(k)}$ and $\Delta_2 \boldsymbol{\xi}_\alpha^{(k)}$ are, respectively, the first- and the second-order noise terms. We regard the noise terms Δx_α and Δy_α as random variables and define the covariance matrices of $\boldsymbol{\xi}_\alpha^{(k)}$ and $\boldsymbol{\xi}_\alpha^{(l)}$ by

$$V^{(kl)}[\boldsymbol{\xi}_\alpha] = E[\Delta_1 \boldsymbol{\xi}_\alpha^{(k)} \Delta_1 \boldsymbol{\xi}_\alpha^{(l)\top}], \tag{7.25}$$

where $E[\cdot]$ denotes expectation for their probability distribution. If we regard Δx_α, Δy_α, $\Delta x'_\alpha$, and $\Delta y'_\alpha$ as independent Gaussian variables of mean 0 and standard deviation σ, Eq. (7.10) holds. Using this relationship, we can express the covariance matrix $V^{(kl)}[\boldsymbol{\xi}_\alpha]$ in the form

$$V^{(kl)}[\boldsymbol{\xi}_\alpha] = \sigma^2 V_0^{(kl)}[\boldsymbol{\xi}_\alpha], \qquad V_0^{(kl)}[\boldsymbol{\xi}_\alpha] = \boldsymbol{T}_\alpha^{(k)} \boldsymbol{T}_\alpha^{(l)\top}, \tag{7.26}$$

where $\boldsymbol{T}_\alpha^{(k)}$ is the 9×4 matrix defined by

$$\boldsymbol{T}_\alpha^{(k)} = \left(\frac{\partial \boldsymbol{\xi}^{(k)}}{\partial x} \quad \frac{\partial \boldsymbol{\xi}^{(k)}}{\partial y} \quad \frac{\partial \boldsymbol{\xi}^{(k)}}{\partial x'} \quad \frac{\partial \boldsymbol{\xi}^{(k)}}{\partial y'} \right) \Bigg|_\alpha . \tag{7.27}$$

Here, $(\cdot)|_\alpha$ means that the expression is evaluated at $x = x_\alpha$, $y = y_\alpha$, $x' = x'_\alpha$, and $y' = y'_\alpha$. As in the ellipse and fundamental matrix cases, we call $V_0^{(kl)}[\boldsymbol{\xi}_\alpha]$ the *normalized covariance matrices*.

Computing the homography matrix $\boldsymbol{H}$ from noisy point correspondences means computing the unit vector $\boldsymbol{\theta}$ that satisfies (7.22) by considering the noise properties described by the covariance matrices $V^{(kl)}[\xi_\alpha]$. This is the same as ellipse fitting and fundamental matrix computation except that the number of equations is three, rather than 1. It can be shown that after appropriate modification, we can apply the algebraic methods (least squares, the Taubin method, HyperLS, iterative reweight, renormalization, and hyper-renormalization) and the geometric methods (FNS, geometric distance minimization, and hyperaccurate correction). For instance, all algebraic methods solve Eq. (2.17), but the matrix $\boldsymbol{M}$ is modified to

$$\boldsymbol{M} = \frac{1}{N}\sum_{\alpha=1}^{N}\sum_{k,l=1}^{3} W_\alpha^{(kl)} \boldsymbol{\xi}_\alpha^{(k)} \boldsymbol{\xi}_\alpha^{(l)\top}. \tag{7.28}$$

For least squares, the Taubin method, ana HyperLS, the weight $W_\alpha^{(kl)}$ is the Kronecker delta δ_{kl}, taking 1 for $k = l$ and 0 otherwise. For iterative reweight, renormalization, and hyper-renormalization, $W_\alpha^{(kl)}$ is given by

$$W_\alpha^{(kl)} = \Big((\boldsymbol{\theta}, V_0^{(kl)}\boldsymbol{\theta})\Big)_2^-. \tag{7.29}$$

The right side is a symbolic abbreviation, meaning the (kl) element of the pseudoinverse of truncated rank 2 of the matrix whose (kl) element is $(\boldsymbol{\theta}, V_0^{(kl)}\boldsymbol{\theta})$. The use of the pseudoinverse of truncated rank 2 reflects the fact that only two equations in Eq. (7.21) are linearly independent. The form of the matrix $\boldsymbol{N}$ depends on the method. For example, $\boldsymbol{N} = \boldsymbol{I}$ (the identity) for least squares and iterative reweight. For renormalization, it has the form

$$\boldsymbol{N} = \frac{1}{N}\sum_{\alpha=1}^{N}\sum_{k,l=1}^{3} W_\alpha^{(kl)} V_0^{(kl)} V_0[\boldsymbol{\xi}_\alpha] \tag{7.30}$$

where the weight $W_\alpha^{(kl)}$ is given by Eq. (7.29); the Taubin method results if $W_\alpha^{(kl)}$ is replaced by δ_{kl}. For HyperLS and hyper-renormalization, $\boldsymbol{N}$ has a slightly complicated form (see the Supplemental Note of Chapter 8) (page 90). For geometric fitting, the Sampson error of Eq. (3.3) is modified to

$$J = \frac{1}{N}\sum_{\alpha=1}^{N}\sum_{k,l=1}^{3} W_\alpha^{(kl)} (\boldsymbol{\xi}_\alpha^{(k)}, \boldsymbol{\theta})(\boldsymbol{\xi}_\alpha^{(l)}, \boldsymbol{\theta}), \tag{7.31}$$

with the weight $W_\alpha^{(kl)}$ define by Eq. (7.29). The FNS procedure for minimizing this goes basically the same as Procedure 3.1, where the matrix $\boldsymbol{M}$ in Eq. (3.4) is given by Eq. (7.28) with the weight $W_\alpha^{(kl)}$ of Eq. (7.29). The matrix $\boldsymbol{L}$ in Eq. (3.4) is modified to

$$\boldsymbol{L} = \frac{1}{N}\sum_{\alpha=1}^{N}\sum_{k,l=1}^{3} v_\alpha^{(k)} v_\alpha^{(l)} V_0^{(kl)}[\boldsymbol{\xi}_\alpha], \tag{7.32}$$

where $v_\alpha^{(k)}$ is defined by

$$v_\alpha^{(k)} = \sum_{l=1}^{3} W_\alpha^{(kl)}(\boldsymbol{\xi}_\alpha^{(l)}, \boldsymbol{\theta}), \tag{7.33}$$

using the weight $W_\alpha^{(kl)}$ in Eq. (7.29). The geometric distance minimization also goes basically the same as Procedure 3.2 with slight modifications (we omit the details).

7.2.2 OUTLIER REMOVAL

Homography computation requires extraction of corresponding points between two images, but, as in fundamental matrix computation, existing extraction algorithms often produce wrong matches, i.e., outliers. Since the mathematical principle is the same for fundamental matrix computation and homography computation, we can apply the RANSAC of Procedure 7.1 with appropriate modifications. Note that the homography matrix $\boldsymbol{H}$ has nine elements. Hence, if four point pairs are given, we can determine $\boldsymbol{H}$ from the resulting four pairs of homography equations of the form of Eq. (7.16) up to scale. Procedure 7.1 is modified as follows.

Procedure 7.2 (RANSAC)

1. From among the input point pairs randomly select four, and let $\boldsymbol{\xi}_1^{(k)}$, $\boldsymbol{\xi}_2^{(k)}$, $\boldsymbol{\xi}_3^{(k)}$, and $\boldsymbol{\xi}_4^{(k)}$, k = 1, 2, 3, be their vector representations in the form of $\boldsymbol{\xi}^{(k)}$ in Eq. (7.20).
2. Compute the eigenvector $\boldsymbol{\theta}$ of the matrix

$$\boldsymbol{M}_4 = \sum_{\alpha=1}^{4}\sum_{k=1}^{3} \boldsymbol{\xi}_\alpha^{(k)}\boldsymbol{\xi}_\alpha^{(k)\top}, \tag{7.34}$$

   for the smallest eigenvalue.
3. Store that $\boldsymbol{\theta}$ as a candidate, and count the number n of point pairs in the input that satisfy

$$\sum_{k,l=1}^{3} W^{(kl)}(\boldsymbol{\xi}^{(k)}, \boldsymbol{\theta})(\boldsymbol{\xi}^{(l)}, \boldsymbol{\theta}) < 2d^2, \tag{7.35}$$

   where the weight $W^{(kl)}$ is defined by Eq. (7.29) for that pair, and d is a threshold for admissible deviation of each point of a corresponding pair, e.g., d = 2 (pixels). Store that n.
4. Select a new set of four point pairs from the input, and do the same. Repeat this many times, and return from among the stored candidates the one for which n is the largest.

Comments. Step 2 computes the homography matrix by least squares from the four point pairs selected in Step 1. Step 3 evaluates, for each point pair (x, y) and (x', y'), the square distances necessary to move them to the positions $(\bar{x}, \bar{y})$ and $(\bar{x}', \bar{y}')$ that satisfy the homography equation for the candidate value of $\boldsymbol{\theta}$. Since both $\boldsymbol{\xi}$ and $V_0[\boldsymbol{\xi}]$ have the dimension of square length, the left side of Eq. (7.34) has the dimension of square length. As in ellipse fitting and fundamental matrix computation, we can directly go on to the next sampling if the count n is smaller than the stored count, and we can stop if the current value of n is not updated over a fixed number of sampling. In the end, those point pairs that do not satisfy Eq. (7.35) for the chosen $\boldsymbol{\theta}$ are removed as outliers.

7.3 SUPPLEMENTAL NOTE

The epipolar equation of Eq. (7.1) is one of the most important foundations of computer vision and is explained in many textbooks, e.g., Hartley and Zisserman [2003], Kanatani [1993a, 1996]. The fundamental matrix $\boldsymbol{F}$ can be determined up to scale by solving eight epipolar equations of the form of Eq. (7.1) determined by eight corresponding point pairs, as shown in the first two steps of the RANSAC (Procedure 7.1). The rank constraint can be imposed by SVD. This is the most classical method for fundamental matrix computation and is known as the *8-point algorithm*. The same procedure can be applied to any number of point pairs, using least squares followed by SVD, so this is also-called the "8-point algorithm." The principle of optimal *a posteriori* correction is stated in Kanatani [1996], and its application to fundamental matrix computation is described in Kanatani and Ohta [2003], Kanatani and Sugaya [2007a,b]. Many variants exist for parameterize the rank constraint, but the most direct approach is the use of the SVD of $\boldsymbol{F}$; see Sugaya and Kanatani [2007a], Sugaya [2007b]. A typical method of the external access is the *extended FNS*, or *EFNS* (see Kanatani and Matsunaga [2013] for the details), which is an extension of the FNS of Chojnacki et al. [2000]. Application of EFNS to fundamental matrix computation is given in Kanatani and Sugaya [2010b].

The homography of Eq. (7.16) between two images of a planar scene is also one of the most fundamental principles of computer vision and is discussed in many textbooks, e.g., Hartley and Zisserman [2003], Kanatani [1993a, 1996]. The method of renormalization, which was initially considered for ellipse fitting and fundamental matrix computation [Kanatani, 1993b, 1996], was extended to homographies by Kanatani et al. [2000, 2014]. The Taubin method, which was originally intended for curve and surface fitting [Taubin, 1991], was extended to homographies by Rangarajan and Papamichalis [2009]. The HyperLS for homography computation was presented by Kanatani et al. [2011] and later generalized to hyper-renormalization by Kanatani et al. [2014]. The FNS of Chojnacki et al. [2000], which was initially considered for ellipse fitting and fundamental matrix computation, was extended symbolically to homographies by Scoleri et al. [2005]. It was reduced to a compact computational scheme by Kanatani and Niitsuma [2011]. The hyperaccurate correction for ellipse fitting [Kanatani, 2006, 2008] was extended to homographies by Kanatani and Sugaya [2013].

For ellipse fitting, sophisticate methods based on high order error analysis, such as HyperLS, hyper-renormalization, and hyperaccurate correction, exhibit superior performance to other methods, as demonstrated in the preceding chapter. However, these methods do not lead to accuracy improvement very much for fundamental matrices and homographies; the accuracy is nearly the same as FNS or EFNS. It is surmised that this is partly due to the consequence of the constraint on fundamental matrices and homographies being *bilinear* in the variables: the quadratic terms in Eqs. (7.3) and (7.20) are xx', xy', $x'y$, etc., but no terms of x^2, y^2, x'^2, and y'^2 are included. Since noise in *different* images is regarded as independent, the noise in xx', xy', $x'y$, etc. has expectation 0, i.e., these terms are unbiased. This is a big contrast to the ellipse equation, which contains the square terms x^2 and y^2. One of the consequences of this for fundamental matrix computation is that the vector $\boldsymbol{e}$ defined by Eq. (2.15) is $\mathbf{0}$, as easily seen from Eqs. (7.8) and (7.10).

PROBLEMS

7.1. (1) Show that if the matrix norm is defined by Eq. (7.2), we can write $\|\boldsymbol{F}\|^2$ for an 3×3 matrix $\boldsymbol{F}$ as

$$\|\boldsymbol{F}\|^2 = \sigma_1^2 + \sigma_2^2 + \sigma_3^2, \tag{7.36}$$

where σ_i, $i = 1, 2, 3$, are the singular values of $\boldsymbol{F}$.

(2) Describe the procedure to force a nonsingular matrix $\boldsymbol{F}$ to $\det \boldsymbol{F} = 0$ and $\|\boldsymbol{F}\| = 1$, using SVD.

7.2. Show that the three equations of Eq. (7.21) are linearly dependent.

CHAPTER 8

Accuracy of Algebraic Fitting

We analyze the accuracy of algebraic methods for ellipse fitting in a generalized framework. We do a detailed error analysis and derive explicite expressions for the covariance and bias of the solution. The hyper-renormalization procedure is derived in this framework. In order that the result directly applies to the fundamental matrix computation described in Section 7.1, we treat $\boldsymbol{\theta}$ and $\boldsymbol{\xi}_\alpha$ as n-D vectors (n = 6 for ellipse fitting, and n = 9 for fundamental matrix computation) and do not use particular properties of ellipse fitting.

8.1 ERROR ANALYSIS

As pointed out in Section 2.4, all algebraic methods for estimating $\boldsymbol{\theta}$ solve the equation in the form:

$$\boldsymbol{M}\boldsymbol{\theta} = \lambda \boldsymbol{N}\boldsymbol{\theta}, \tag{8.1}$$

where the $n \times n$ matrices $\boldsymbol{M}$ and $\boldsymbol{N}$ are defined in terms of the observations $\boldsymbol{\xi}_\alpha$, α = 1, ..., N, and the unknown $\boldsymbol{\theta}$. Here, we consider iterative reweight, renormalization, and hyper-renormalization, so $\boldsymbol{M}$ is given by (see Eq. (2.18))

$$\boldsymbol{M} = \frac{1}{N}\sum_{\alpha=1}^{N} W_\alpha \boldsymbol{\xi}_\alpha \boldsymbol{\xi}_\alpha^\top, \qquad W_\alpha = \frac{1}{(\boldsymbol{\theta}, V_0[\boldsymbol{\xi}_\alpha]\boldsymbol{\theta})}. \tag{8.2}$$

We assume that the observation $\boldsymbol{\xi}_\alpha$ is perturbed from its true value $\bar{\boldsymbol{\xi}}_\alpha$ in the form of Eq. (1.17). Accordingly, the solution $\boldsymbol{\theta}$ of Eq. (8.1) is also perturbed from its true value $\bar{\boldsymbol{\theta}}$ in the form

$$\boldsymbol{\theta} = \bar{\boldsymbol{\theta}} + \Delta_1\boldsymbol{\theta} + \Delta_2\boldsymbol{\theta} + \cdots, \tag{8.3}$$

where Δ_i denotes the ith order term in the standard deviation σ of the noise in the data. The scalar λ and the matrix $\boldsymbol{N}$ on the right side of Eq. (8.1) depend on particular methods, but we do error analysis, regarding them as yet to be determined. Substituting Eqs. (1.17) and (8.3) into Eq. (8.2), we can expand $\boldsymbol{M}$ and W_α in the form

$$\boldsymbol{M} = \bar{\boldsymbol{M}} + \Delta_1\boldsymbol{M} + \Delta_2\boldsymbol{M} + \cdots, \tag{8.4}$$

$$W_\alpha = \bar{W}_\alpha + \Delta_1 W_\alpha + \Delta_2 W_\alpha + \cdots, \tag{8.5}$$

where $\Delta_1\boldsymbol{M}$ and $\Delta_2\boldsymbol{M}$ are given by

$$\Delta_1\boldsymbol{M} = \frac{1}{N}\sum_{\alpha=1}^{N} \bar{W}_\alpha\left(\Delta_1\boldsymbol{\xi}_\alpha\bar{\boldsymbol{\xi}}_\alpha^\top + \bar{\boldsymbol{\xi}}_\alpha\Delta_1\boldsymbol{\xi}_\alpha^\top\right) + \frac{1}{N}\sum_{\alpha=1}^{N}\Delta_1\bar{W}_\alpha\bar{\boldsymbol{\xi}}_\alpha\bar{\boldsymbol{\xi}}_\alpha^\top, \tag{8.6}$$

$$
\begin{aligned}
\Delta_2 \boldsymbol{M} = & \frac{1}{N}\sum_{\alpha=1}^{N} \bar{W}_\alpha \left(\Delta_1\boldsymbol{\xi}_\alpha \Delta_1\boldsymbol{\xi}_\alpha^\top + \Delta_2\boldsymbol{\xi}_\alpha \bar{\boldsymbol{\xi}}_\alpha^\top + \bar{\boldsymbol{\xi}}_\alpha \Delta_2\boldsymbol{\xi}_\alpha^\top\right) \\
& + \frac{1}{N}\sum_{\alpha=1}^{N} \Delta_1 W_\alpha \left(\Delta_1\boldsymbol{\xi}_\alpha \bar{\boldsymbol{\xi}}_\alpha^\top + \bar{\boldsymbol{\xi}}_\alpha \Delta_1\boldsymbol{\xi}_\alpha^\top\right) + \frac{1}{N}\sum_{\alpha=1}^{N} \Delta_2 W_\alpha \bar{\boldsymbol{\xi}}_\alpha \bar{\boldsymbol{\xi}}_\alpha^\top,
\end{aligned} \tag{8.7}
$$

and $\Delta_1 W_\alpha$ and $\Delta_2 W_\alpha$ are given by

$$
\Delta_1 W_\alpha = -2\bar{W}_\alpha^2 \left(\Delta_1\boldsymbol{\theta}, V_0[\boldsymbol{\xi}_\alpha]\bar{\boldsymbol{\theta}}\right), \tag{8.8}
$$

$$
\Delta_2 W_\alpha = \frac{(\Delta_1 W_\alpha)^2}{\bar{W}_\alpha} - \bar{W}_\alpha^2 \Big((\Delta_1\boldsymbol{\theta}, V_0[\boldsymbol{\xi}_\alpha]\Delta_1\boldsymbol{\theta}) + 2(\Delta_2\boldsymbol{\theta}, V_0[\boldsymbol{\xi}_\alpha]\bar{\boldsymbol{\theta}})\Big). \tag{8.9}
$$

(See Proposition 8.1 below.) Similarly expanding λ and $\boldsymbol{N}$, we can write Eq. (8.1) in the following form:

$$
\begin{aligned}
& (\bar{\boldsymbol{M}} + \Delta_1\boldsymbol{M} + \Delta_2\boldsymbol{M} + \cdots)(\bar{\boldsymbol{\theta}} + \Delta_1\boldsymbol{\theta} + \Delta_2\boldsymbol{\theta} + \cdots) \\
& \quad = (\bar{\lambda} + \Delta_1\lambda + \Delta_2\lambda + \cdots)(\bar{\boldsymbol{N}} + \Delta_1\boldsymbol{N} + \Delta_2\boldsymbol{N} + \cdots)(\bar{\boldsymbol{\theta}} + \Delta_1\boldsymbol{\theta} + \Delta_2\boldsymbol{\theta} + \cdots).
\end{aligned} \tag{8.10}
$$

The true solution $\bar{\boldsymbol{\theta}}$ satisfies the constraint $(\bar{\boldsymbol{\xi}}_\alpha, \bar{\boldsymbol{\theta}}) = 0$ for the true observations $\bar{\boldsymbol{\xi}}_\alpha$. Hence, Eq. (8.2) implies that $\bar{\boldsymbol{M}}\bar{\boldsymbol{\theta}} = \boldsymbol{0}$. Equating the noiseless terms on both sides of Eq. (8.10), we obtain $\bar{\boldsymbol{M}}\bar{\boldsymbol{\theta}} = \bar{\lambda}\bar{\boldsymbol{N}}\bar{\boldsymbol{\theta}}$. We assume that $\bar{\boldsymbol{N}}\bar{\boldsymbol{\theta}} \neq \boldsymbol{0}$, so $\bar{\lambda} = 0$. Equating the first-order terms on both sides of Eq. (8.10), we obtain

$$
\bar{\boldsymbol{M}}\Delta_1\boldsymbol{\theta} + \Delta_1\boldsymbol{M}\bar{\boldsymbol{\theta}} = \Delta_1\lambda\bar{\boldsymbol{N}}\bar{\boldsymbol{\theta}}. \tag{8.11}
$$

Computing the inner product with $\bar{\boldsymbol{\theta}}$ on both sides, we obtain

$$
\left(\bar{\boldsymbol{\theta}}, \bar{\boldsymbol{M}}\Delta_1\boldsymbol{\theta}\right) + \left(\bar{\boldsymbol{\theta}}, \Delta_1\boldsymbol{M}\bar{\boldsymbol{\theta}}\right) = \Delta_1\lambda\left(\bar{\boldsymbol{\theta}}, \bar{\boldsymbol{N}}\bar{\boldsymbol{\theta}}\right). \tag{8.12}
$$

Note that $(\bar{\boldsymbol{\theta}}, \bar{\boldsymbol{M}}\Delta_1\boldsymbol{\theta}) = (\bar{\boldsymbol{M}}\bar{\boldsymbol{\theta}}, \Delta_1\boldsymbol{\theta}) = 0$. Equation (8.6) implies $(\bar{\boldsymbol{\theta}}, \Delta_1\boldsymbol{M}\bar{\boldsymbol{\theta}}) = 0$. Since we are assuming that $(\bar{\boldsymbol{\theta}}, \bar{\boldsymbol{N}}\bar{\boldsymbol{\theta}}) \neq 0$, we see that $\Delta_1\lambda = 0$. Noting this and equating the second-order terms on both sides of Eq. (8.10), we obtain

$$
\bar{\boldsymbol{M}}\Delta_2\boldsymbol{\theta} + \Delta_1\boldsymbol{M}\Delta_1\boldsymbol{\theta} + \Delta_2\boldsymbol{M}\bar{\boldsymbol{\theta}} = \Delta_2\lambda\bar{\boldsymbol{N}}\bar{\boldsymbol{\theta}}. \tag{8.13}
$$

8.2 COVARIANCE AND BIAS

We want to solve Eq. (8.11) (with $\Delta_1\lambda = 0$) for $\Delta_1\boldsymbol{\theta}$. However, $\bar{\boldsymbol{M}}\bar{\boldsymbol{\theta}} = \boldsymbol{0}$, so the matrix $\bar{\boldsymbol{M}}$ has rank $n-1$, $\bar{\boldsymbol{\theta}}$ being its null vector. Hence, its inverse does not exist. Instead, we consider its pseudoinverse $\bar{\boldsymbol{M}}^-$ (also rank $n-1$). Note that the product $\bar{\boldsymbol{M}}^-\bar{\boldsymbol{M}}$ (↪ Problem 8.4) equals the projection matrix $\boldsymbol{P}_{\bar{\boldsymbol{\theta}}}$ in the direction of $\bar{\boldsymbol{\theta}}$ (↪ Problem 6.1). It follows that, after multiplication of Eq. (8.11) by the pseudoinverse $\bar{\boldsymbol{M}}^-$ on both sides, $\Delta_1\boldsymbol{\theta}$ is expressed in the form

$$
\Delta_1\boldsymbol{\theta} = -\bar{\boldsymbol{M}}^-\Delta_1\boldsymbol{M}\bar{\boldsymbol{\theta}}, \tag{8.14}
$$

where we have noted that since $\boldsymbol{\theta}$ is normalized to unit norm, the first-order error $\Delta_1\boldsymbol{\theta}$ is orthogonal to $\bar{\boldsymbol{\theta}}$ and hence $\boldsymbol{P}_{\bar{\boldsymbol{\theta}}}\Delta_1\boldsymbol{\theta} = \Delta_1\boldsymbol{\theta}$. From Eq. (8.14), the covariance matrix $V[\boldsymbol{\theta}]$ of the solution $\boldsymbol{\theta}$ is given to a first approximation by

$$V[\boldsymbol{\theta}] = E\left[\Delta_1\boldsymbol{\theta}\Delta_1\boldsymbol{\theta}^\top\right] = \frac{\sigma^2}{N}\bar{\boldsymbol{M}}^-. \tag{8.15}$$

(See Proposition 8.2 below.) This coincides with the theoretical accuracy limit called the *KCR lower bound* to be discussed in Chapter 10. From Eq. (8.15), we conclude that *the solution $\boldsymbol{\theta}$ of iterative reweight, renormalization, and hyper-renormalization has the same covariance matrix, which agrees with the theoretical accuracy limit to a first approximation.* Hence, we cannot substantially improve the covariance any further. However, the total error is the sum of the covariance terms and the bias terms, and we may reduce the bias by a clever choice of the matrix $\boldsymbol{N}$.

Evidently, the first-order term $\Delta_1\boldsymbol{\theta}$ in Eq. (8.14) is unbiased, since the expectation of odd-order error terms is zero: $E[\Delta_1\boldsymbol{\theta}] = \boldsymbol{0}$. So, we focus on the second-order bias $E[\Delta_2\boldsymbol{\theta}]$. Substituting Eq. (8.14) into Eq. (8.13), we obtain

$$\Delta_2\lambda\bar{\boldsymbol{N}}\bar{\boldsymbol{\theta}} = \bar{\boldsymbol{M}}\Delta_2\boldsymbol{\theta} - \Delta_1\boldsymbol{M}\bar{\boldsymbol{M}}^-\Delta_1\boldsymbol{M}\bar{\boldsymbol{\theta}} + \Delta_2\boldsymbol{M}\bar{\boldsymbol{\theta}} = \bar{\boldsymbol{M}}\Delta_2\boldsymbol{\theta} + \boldsymbol{T}\bar{\boldsymbol{\theta}}, \tag{8.16}$$

where we define the matrix $\boldsymbol{T}$ to be

$$\boldsymbol{T} \equiv \Delta_2\boldsymbol{M} - \Delta_1\boldsymbol{M}\bar{\boldsymbol{M}}^-\Delta_1\boldsymbol{M}. \tag{8.17}$$

Because $\boldsymbol{\theta}$ is a unit vector, it has no error in the direction of itself; we are interested in the error orthogonal to it. So, we investigate the second-order error component orthogonal to $\bar{\boldsymbol{\theta}}$ (see Fig. 6.2):

$$\Delta_2^\perp\boldsymbol{\theta} \equiv \boldsymbol{P}_{\bar{\boldsymbol{\theta}}}\Delta_2\boldsymbol{\theta} = \bar{\boldsymbol{M}}^-\bar{\boldsymbol{M}}\Delta_2\boldsymbol{\theta}. \tag{8.18}$$

Note that the first-order error $\Delta_1\boldsymbol{\theta}$ in Eq. (8.14) is itself orthogonal to $\bar{\boldsymbol{\theta}}$. Multiplying Eq. (8.16) by $\bar{\boldsymbol{M}}^-$ on both, we obtain $\Delta_2^\perp\boldsymbol{\theta}$ in the following form:

$$\Delta_2^\perp\boldsymbol{\theta} = \bar{\boldsymbol{M}}^-\left(\Delta_2\lambda\bar{\boldsymbol{N}} - \boldsymbol{T}\right)\bar{\boldsymbol{\theta}}. \tag{8.19}$$

Computing the inner product of Eq. (8.16) and $\bar{\boldsymbol{\theta}}$ on both sides and noting that $(\bar{\boldsymbol{\theta}}, \bar{\boldsymbol{M}}\Delta_2\boldsymbol{\theta}) = 0$, we obtain $\Delta_2\lambda$ in the form

$$\Delta_2\lambda = \frac{\left(\bar{\boldsymbol{\theta}}, \boldsymbol{T}\bar{\boldsymbol{\theta}}\right)}{\left(\bar{\boldsymbol{\theta}}, \bar{\boldsymbol{N}}\bar{\boldsymbol{\theta}}\right)}. \tag{8.20}$$

Hence, Eq. (8.19) is rewritten as follows:

$$\Delta_2^\perp\boldsymbol{\theta} = \bar{\boldsymbol{M}}^-\left(\frac{(\bar{\boldsymbol{\theta}}, \boldsymbol{T}\bar{\boldsymbol{\theta}})}{(\bar{\boldsymbol{\theta}}, \bar{\boldsymbol{N}}\bar{\boldsymbol{\theta}})}\bar{\boldsymbol{N}}\bar{\boldsymbol{\theta}} - \boldsymbol{T}\bar{\boldsymbol{\theta}}\right). \tag{8.21}$$

Thus, the second-order bias is

$$E[\Delta_2^\perp\boldsymbol{\theta}] = \bar{\boldsymbol{M}}^-\left(\frac{(\bar{\boldsymbol{\theta}}, E[\boldsymbol{T}\bar{\boldsymbol{\theta}}])}{(\bar{\boldsymbol{\theta}}, \bar{\boldsymbol{N}}\bar{\boldsymbol{\theta}})}\bar{\boldsymbol{N}}\bar{\boldsymbol{\theta}} - E[\boldsymbol{T}\bar{\boldsymbol{\theta}}]\right). \tag{8.22}$$

8.3 BIAS ELIMINATION AND HYPER-RENORMALIZATION

From Eq. (8.22), we find a crucial fact: *if we can choose such an* $\boldsymbol{N}$ *that its noiseless value* $\bar{\boldsymbol{N}}$ *satisfied* $E[\boldsymbol{T}\bar{\boldsymbol{\theta}}] = c\bar{\boldsymbol{N}}\bar{\boldsymbol{\theta}}$ *for some constant* c*, we will have*

$$E\left[\Delta_2^{\perp}\boldsymbol{\theta}\right] = \bar{\boldsymbol{M}}^{-}\left(\frac{(\bar{\boldsymbol{\theta}}, c\bar{\boldsymbol{N}}\bar{\boldsymbol{\theta}})}{(\bar{\boldsymbol{\theta}}, \bar{\boldsymbol{N}}\bar{\boldsymbol{\theta}})}\bar{\boldsymbol{N}}\bar{\boldsymbol{\theta}} - c\bar{\boldsymbol{N}}\bar{\boldsymbol{\theta}}\right) = \mathbf{0}. \tag{8.23}$$

Then, the bias will be $O(\sigma^4)$, because the expectation of odd-order noise terms is zero. In order to choose such an $\boldsymbol{N}$, we need to evaluate the expectation $E[\boldsymbol{T}\bar{\boldsymbol{\theta}}]$. We evaluate the expectation of $\boldsymbol{T}\bar{\boldsymbol{\theta}} = \Delta_2\boldsymbol{M}\bar{\boldsymbol{\theta}} - \Delta_1\boldsymbol{M}\bar{\boldsymbol{M}}^{-}\Delta_1\boldsymbol{M}\bar{\boldsymbol{\theta}}$ term by term, using the identity

$$E\left[\Delta_1\xi_\alpha\Delta_1\xi_\beta^\top\right] = \sigma^2\delta_{\alpha\beta}V_0[\xi_\alpha], \tag{8.24}$$

which results from our assumption of independent noise for different points and the definition of the normalized covariance matrix $V_0[\xi_\alpha]$, where $\delta_{\alpha\beta}$ is the Kronecker delta, taking 1 for $\alpha = \beta$ and 0 otherwise. We also use the definition (see Eq. (2.15))

$$E[\Delta_2\xi_\alpha] = \sigma^2\boldsymbol{e} \tag{8.25}$$

of the vector $\boldsymbol{e}$ (we do not use Eq. (2.12), which holds only for ellipse fitting). In the end, we find that $E[\boldsymbol{T}\bar{\boldsymbol{\theta}}] = \sigma^2\bar{\boldsymbol{N}}\bar{\boldsymbol{\theta}}$ holds if we define $\bar{\boldsymbol{N}}$ in the form (see Lemmas 8.3 and 8.4 and Proposition 8.5 below)

$$\begin{aligned}\bar{\boldsymbol{N}} = &\frac{1}{N}\sum_{\alpha=1}^{N}\bar{W}_\alpha\left(V_0[\xi_\alpha] + 2\mathcal{S}\left[\bar{\xi}_\alpha\boldsymbol{e}^\top\right]\right)\\ &-\frac{1}{N^2}\sum_{\alpha=1}^{N}\bar{W}_\alpha^2\left(\left(\bar{\xi}_\alpha, \bar{\boldsymbol{M}}^{-}\bar{\xi}_\alpha\right)V_0[\xi_\alpha] + 2\mathcal{S}\left[V_0[\xi_\alpha]\bar{\boldsymbol{M}}^{-}\bar{\xi}_\alpha\bar{\xi}_\alpha\right]\right),\end{aligned} \tag{8.26}$$

where $\mathcal{S}[\cdot]$ denotes symmetrization ($\mathcal{S}[\boldsymbol{A}] = (\boldsymbol{A} + \boldsymbol{A}^\top)/2$).

Since the matrix $\bar{\boldsymbol{N}}$ in Eq. (8.26) is defined in terms of true values, we replace them by observations in actual computation. However, the matrix $\boldsymbol{M}$ defined by noisy observations ξ_α is no longer of rank $n-1$; it is generally positive definite with positive eigenvalues. So, we replace $\bar{\boldsymbol{M}}^{-}$ by the pseudoinverse $\boldsymbol{M}_{n-1}^{-}$ of truncated rank $n-1$ (see Eq. (2.16)). Using the resulting matrix $\boldsymbol{N}$, we obtain the hyper-renormalization scheme of Procedure 2.3. The bias of the resulting solution $\boldsymbol{\theta}$ is $O(\sigma^4)$, because replacing $\bar{\xi}_\alpha$ and $\bar{\boldsymbol{M}}$ by ξ_α and $\boldsymbol{M}$ introduces only errors of $O(\sigma^4)$, since the third-order noise terms have expectation 0.

8.4 DERIVATIONS

Proposition 8.1 **(Errors of weights)** *The first and the second error terms of W_α are given by Eqs. (8.8) and (8.9).*

Proof. The definition of W_α in Eq. (8.2) is written as $W_\alpha(\boldsymbol{\theta}, V_0[\boldsymbol{\xi}_\alpha]\boldsymbol{\theta}) = 1$. Expanding W_α and $\boldsymbol{\theta}$, we obtain

$$\left(\bar{W}_\alpha + \Delta_1 W_\alpha + \Delta_2 W_\alpha + \cdots\right)\Big((\bar{\boldsymbol{\theta}} + \Delta_1\boldsymbol{\theta} + \Delta_2\boldsymbol{\theta} + \cdots), V_0[\boldsymbol{\xi}_\alpha](\bar{\boldsymbol{\theta}} + \Delta_1\boldsymbol{\theta} + \Delta_2\boldsymbol{\theta} + \cdots)\Big) = 1. \tag{8.27}$$

Equating the noiseless terms on both sides, we obtain $\bar{W}_\alpha(\bar{\boldsymbol{\theta}}, V_0[\boldsymbol{\xi}_\alpha]\bar{\boldsymbol{\theta}}) = 1$. Equating the first-order terms on both sides, we obtain

$$\Delta_1 W_\alpha(\bar{\boldsymbol{\theta}}, V_0[\boldsymbol{\xi}_\alpha]\bar{\boldsymbol{\theta}}) + \bar{W}_\alpha(\Delta_1\boldsymbol{\theta}, V_0[\boldsymbol{\xi}_\alpha]\bar{\boldsymbol{\theta}}) + \bar{W}_\alpha(\bar{\boldsymbol{\theta}}, V_0[\boldsymbol{\xi}_\alpha]\Delta_1\bar{\boldsymbol{\theta}}) = 0, \tag{8.28}$$

from which we obtain

$$\Delta_1 W_\alpha = -\frac{2\bar{W}_\alpha(\Delta_1\boldsymbol{\theta}, V_0[\boldsymbol{\xi}_\alpha]\bar{\boldsymbol{\theta}})}{(\bar{\boldsymbol{\theta}}, V_0[\boldsymbol{\xi}_\alpha]\bar{\boldsymbol{\theta}})} = -2\bar{W}_\alpha^2(\Delta_1\boldsymbol{\theta}, V_0[\boldsymbol{\xi}_\alpha]\bar{\boldsymbol{\theta}}). \tag{8.29}$$

Thus, we obtain Eq. (8.8). Equating the second-order terms on both sides of Eq. (8.27), we obtain

$$\begin{aligned} &\Delta_2 W_\alpha(\bar{\boldsymbol{\theta}}, V_0[\boldsymbol{\xi}_\alpha]\bar{\boldsymbol{\theta}}) + \Delta_1 W_\alpha\Big((\Delta_1\boldsymbol{\theta}, V_0[\boldsymbol{\xi}_\alpha]\bar{\boldsymbol{\theta}}) + (\bar{\boldsymbol{\theta}} V_0[\boldsymbol{\xi}_\alpha], \Delta_1\boldsymbol{\theta})\Big) \\ &+\bar{W}_\alpha\Big((\Delta_1\boldsymbol{\theta}, V_0[\boldsymbol{\xi}_\alpha]\Delta_1\boldsymbol{\theta}) + (\Delta_2\boldsymbol{\theta}, V_0[\boldsymbol{\xi}_\alpha]\bar{\boldsymbol{\theta}}) + (\bar{\boldsymbol{\theta}}, V_0[\boldsymbol{\xi}_\alpha]\Delta_2\boldsymbol{\theta})\Big) = 0, \end{aligned} \tag{8.30}$$

from which we obtain

$$\begin{aligned} \Delta_2 W_\alpha =& -\frac{1}{(\bar{\boldsymbol{\theta}}, V_0[\boldsymbol{\xi}_\alpha]\bar{\boldsymbol{\theta}})}\Big(2\Delta_1 W_\alpha(\Delta_1\boldsymbol{\theta}, V_0[\boldsymbol{\xi}_\alpha]\bar{\boldsymbol{\theta}}) + \bar{W}_\alpha\Big((\Delta_1\boldsymbol{\theta}, V_0[\boldsymbol{\xi}_\alpha]\Delta_1\boldsymbol{\theta}) \\ &+ 2(\Delta_2\boldsymbol{\theta}, V_0[\boldsymbol{\xi}_\alpha]\bar{\boldsymbol{\theta}})\Big)\Big) \\ =& -\bar{W}_\alpha\Big(2\Delta_1 W_\alpha\Big(-\frac{\Delta_1 W_\alpha}{2\bar{W}_\alpha^2}\Big) + \bar{W}_\alpha\Big((\Delta_1\boldsymbol{\theta}, V_0[\boldsymbol{\xi}_\alpha]\Delta_1\boldsymbol{\theta}) + 2(\Delta_2\boldsymbol{\theta}, V_0[\boldsymbol{\xi}_\alpha]\bar{\boldsymbol{\theta}})\Big)\Big) \\ =& \frac{(\Delta_1 W_\alpha)^2}{\bar{W}_\alpha} - \bar{W}_\alpha^2\Big((\Delta_1\boldsymbol{\theta}, V_0[\boldsymbol{\xi}_\alpha]\Delta_1\boldsymbol{\theta}) + 2(\Delta_2\boldsymbol{\theta}, V_0[\boldsymbol{\xi}_\alpha]\bar{\boldsymbol{\theta}})\Big). \end{aligned} \tag{8.31}$$

Thus, we obtain Eq. (8.9). □

Proposition 8.2 **(Covariance of the solution)** *The covariance matrix of $\boldsymbol{\theta}$ is given by Eq. (8.15).*

Proof. Substituting Eq. (8.1) into Eq. (8.14) and noting that $\boldsymbol{\xi}_\alpha\boldsymbol{\theta} = 0$, we can write $\Delta_1\boldsymbol{\theta}$ in the form

$$\Delta_1\boldsymbol{\theta} = -\bar{\boldsymbol{M}}^-\Delta_1\boldsymbol{M}\bar{\boldsymbol{\theta}} = -\bar{\boldsymbol{M}}^-\left(\frac{1}{N}\sum_{\alpha=1}^N \bar{W}_\alpha(\Delta_1\boldsymbol{\xi}_\alpha, \bar{\boldsymbol{\theta}})\bar{\boldsymbol{\xi}}_\alpha\right). \tag{8.32}$$

The covariance matrix $V[\boldsymbol{\theta}] = E[\Delta_1\boldsymbol{\theta}\Delta_1\boldsymbol{\theta}^\top]$ is evaluated to be

$$
\begin{aligned}
V[\boldsymbol{\theta}] &= E\left[\bar{\boldsymbol{M}}^-\left(\frac{1}{N}\sum_{\alpha=1}^N \bar{W}_\alpha(\Delta_1\boldsymbol{\xi}_\alpha, \bar{\boldsymbol{\theta}})\bar{\boldsymbol{\xi}}_\alpha \frac{1}{N}\sum_{\beta=1}^N \bar{W}_\beta(\Delta_1\boldsymbol{\xi}_\beta, \bar{\boldsymbol{\theta}})\bar{\boldsymbol{\xi}}_\beta\right)\bar{\boldsymbol{M}}^-\right] \\
&= E\left[\bar{\boldsymbol{M}}^-\left(\frac{1}{N^2}\sum_{\alpha,\beta=1}^N \bar{W}_\alpha\bar{W}_\beta(\bar{\boldsymbol{\theta}}, \Delta_1\boldsymbol{\xi}_\alpha)(\Delta_1\boldsymbol{\xi}_\beta, \bar{\boldsymbol{\theta}})\bar{\boldsymbol{\xi}}_\alpha\bar{\boldsymbol{\xi}}_\beta\right)\bar{\boldsymbol{M}}^-\right] \\
&= \bar{\boldsymbol{M}}^-\left(\frac{1}{N^2}\sum_{\alpha,\beta=1}^N \bar{W}_\alpha\bar{W}_\beta(\bar{\boldsymbol{\theta}}, E[\Delta_1\boldsymbol{\xi}_\alpha\Delta_1\boldsymbol{\xi}_\beta]\bar{\boldsymbol{\theta}})\bar{\boldsymbol{\xi}}_\alpha\bar{\boldsymbol{\xi}}_\beta\right)\bar{\boldsymbol{M}}^- \\
&= \bar{\boldsymbol{M}}^-\left(\frac{1}{N^2}\sum_{\alpha,\beta=1}^N \bar{W}_\alpha\bar{W}_\beta(\bar{\boldsymbol{\theta}}, \sigma^2\delta_{\alpha\beta}V_0[\boldsymbol{\xi}_\alpha]\bar{\boldsymbol{\theta}})\bar{\boldsymbol{\xi}}_\alpha\bar{\boldsymbol{\xi}}_\beta\right)\bar{\boldsymbol{M}}^- \\
&= \bar{\boldsymbol{M}}^-\left(\frac{\sigma^2}{N^2}\sum_{\alpha=1}^N \bar{W}_\alpha^2(\bar{\boldsymbol{\theta}}, V_0[\boldsymbol{\xi}_\alpha]\bar{\boldsymbol{\theta}})\bar{\boldsymbol{\xi}}_\alpha\bar{\boldsymbol{\xi}}_\alpha\right)\bar{\boldsymbol{M}}^- \\
&= \frac{\sigma^2}{N}\bar{\boldsymbol{M}}^-\left(\frac{1}{N}\sum_{\alpha=1}^N \bar{W}_\alpha\bar{\boldsymbol{\xi}}_\alpha\bar{\boldsymbol{\xi}}_\alpha\right)\bar{\boldsymbol{M}}^- = \frac{\sigma^2}{N}\bar{\boldsymbol{M}}^-\bar{\boldsymbol{M}}\bar{\boldsymbol{M}}^- = \frac{\sigma^2}{N}\bar{\boldsymbol{M}}^-,
\end{aligned} \tag{8.33}
$$

where we have used the identity $\bar{\boldsymbol{M}}^-\bar{\boldsymbol{M}}\bar{\boldsymbol{M}}^- = \bar{\boldsymbol{M}}^-$ for the pseudoinverse $\bar{\boldsymbol{M}}^-$ (↪ Problem 8.3). □

In order to derive Eq. (8.26), we evaluate the expectation of Eq. (8.17) term by term.

Lemma 8.3 (Expectation of $\Delta_2\boldsymbol{M}\bar{\boldsymbol{\theta}}$)

$$
E[\Delta_2\boldsymbol{M}\bar{\boldsymbol{\theta}}] = \frac{\sigma^2}{N}\sum_{\alpha=1}^N \bar{W}_\alpha\Big(V_0[\boldsymbol{\xi}_\alpha]\bar{\boldsymbol{\theta}} + (\boldsymbol{e}, \bar{\boldsymbol{\theta}})\bar{\boldsymbol{\xi}}_\alpha\Big) + \frac{2\sigma^2}{N^2}\sum_{\alpha=1}^N \bar{W}_\alpha\bar{W}_\alpha\left(\bar{\boldsymbol{\xi}}_\alpha, \bar{\boldsymbol{M}}^-V_0[\boldsymbol{\xi}_\alpha]\bar{\boldsymbol{\theta}}\right)\bar{\boldsymbol{\xi}}_\alpha. \tag{8.34}
$$

Proof. From $(\bar{\xi}_\alpha, \bar{\theta}) = 0$ and Eq. (8.7), we obtain

$$\begin{aligned}
\Delta_2 M\bar{\theta} =& \frac{1}{N}\sum_{\alpha=1}^{N} \bar{W}_\alpha\left(\Delta_1\xi_\alpha\Delta_1\xi_\alpha^\top + \Delta_2\xi_\alpha\bar{\xi}_\alpha^\top + \bar{\xi}_\alpha\Delta_2\xi_\alpha^\top\right)\bar{\theta} \\
&+ \frac{1}{N}\sum_{\alpha=1}^{N} \Delta_1 W_\alpha\left(\Delta_1\xi_\alpha\bar{\xi}_\alpha^\top + \bar{\xi}_\alpha\Delta_1\xi_\alpha^\top\right)\bar{\theta} + \frac{1}{N}\sum_{\alpha=1}^{N}\Delta_2 W_\alpha\bar{\xi}_\alpha\bar{\xi}_\alpha^\top\bar{\theta} \\
=& \frac{1}{N}\sum_{\alpha=1}^{N} \bar{W}_\alpha\left((\Delta_1\xi_\alpha, \bar{\theta})\Delta_1\xi_\alpha + (\Delta_2\xi_\alpha, \bar{\theta})\bar{\xi}_\alpha\right) \\
&+ \frac{1}{N}\sum_{\alpha=1}^{N}\Delta_1 W_\alpha\left(\Delta_1\xi_\alpha, \bar{\theta}\right)\bar{\xi}_\alpha.
\end{aligned} \tag{8.35}$$

Hence,

$$\begin{aligned}
E\left[\Delta_2 M\bar{\theta}\right] =& \frac{1}{N}\sum_{\alpha=1}^{N}\bar{W}_\alpha\left(E\left[\Delta_1\xi_\alpha\Delta_1\xi_\alpha^\top\right]\bar{\theta} + \left(E[\Delta_2\xi_\alpha], \bar{\theta}\right)\bar{\xi}_\alpha\right) \\
&+ \frac{1}{N}\sum_{\alpha=1}^{N}\left(E[\Delta_1 W_\alpha\Delta_1\xi_\alpha], \bar{\theta}\right)\bar{\xi}_\alpha \\
=& \frac{\sigma^2}{N}\sum_{\alpha=1}^{N}\bar{W}_\alpha\left(V_0[\xi_\alpha]\bar{\theta} + (e, \bar{\theta})\bar{\xi}_\alpha\right) + \frac{1}{N}\sum_{\alpha=1}^{N}\left(E[\Delta_1 W_\alpha\Delta_1\xi_\alpha], \bar{\theta}\right)\bar{\xi}_\alpha.
\end{aligned} \tag{8.36}$$

Consider the expectation of $\Delta_1 W_\alpha \Delta_1 \xi_\alpha$. From Eqs. (8.1), (8.8), and (8.14), we see that

$$\begin{aligned}
\Delta_1 W_\alpha =& -2\bar{W}_\alpha^2\left(\Delta_1\theta, V_0[\xi_\alpha]\bar{\theta}\right) = 2\bar{W}_\alpha^2\left(\bar{M}^-\Delta_1 M\bar{\theta}, V_0[\xi_\alpha]\bar{\theta}\right) \\
=& 2\bar{W}_\alpha^2\left(\bar{M}^-\left(\frac{1}{N}\sum_{\beta=1}^{N}\bar{W}_\beta\left(\Delta_1\xi_\beta\bar{\xi}_\beta^\top + \bar{\xi}_\beta\Delta_1\xi_\beta^\top\right)\right.\right. \\
&\left.\left. + \frac{1}{N}\sum_{\beta=1}^{N}\Delta_1\bar{W}_\beta\bar{\xi}_\beta\bar{\xi}_\beta^\top\right)\bar{\theta}, V_0[\xi_\alpha]\bar{\theta}\right) \\
=& \frac{2}{N}\sum_{\beta=1}^{N}\bar{W}_\alpha^2\bar{W}_\beta(\Delta_1\xi_\beta, \bar{\theta})(\bar{M}^-\bar{\xi}_\beta, V_0[\xi_\alpha]\bar{\theta}) \\
=& \frac{2}{N}\sum_{\beta=1}^{N}\bar{W}_\alpha^2\bar{W}_\beta(\bar{\xi}_\beta, \bar{M}^- V_0[\xi_\alpha]\bar{\theta})(\Delta_1\xi_\beta, \bar{\theta}).
\end{aligned} \tag{8.37}$$

Hence,

$$
\begin{aligned}
E[\Delta_1 W_\alpha \Delta_1 \xi_\alpha] &= E\left[\frac{2}{N}\sum_{\beta=1}^{N} \bar{W}_\alpha^2 \bar{W}_\beta \left(\bar{\xi}_\beta, \bar{M}^- V_0[\xi_\alpha]\bar{\theta}\right)\left(\Delta_1\xi_\beta, \bar{\theta}\right)\Delta_1\xi_\alpha\right] \\
&= \frac{2}{N}\sum_{\beta=1}^{N} \bar{W}_\alpha^2 \bar{W}_\beta \left(\bar{\xi}_\beta, \bar{M}^- V_0[\xi_\alpha]\bar{\theta}\right) E\left[\Delta_1\xi_\alpha \Delta_1\xi_\beta^\top\right]\bar{\theta} \\
&= \frac{2}{N}\sum_{\beta=1}^{N} \bar{W}_\alpha^2 \bar{W}_\beta (\bar{\xi}_\beta, \bar{M}^- V_0[\xi_\alpha]\bar{\theta})\sigma^2\delta_{\alpha\beta} V_0[\xi_\alpha]\bar{\theta} \\
&= \frac{2\sigma^2}{N}\bar{W}_\alpha^3 (\bar{\xi}_\alpha, \bar{M}^- V_0[\xi_\alpha]\bar{\theta}) V_0[\xi_\alpha]\bar{\theta}.
\end{aligned}
\tag{8.38}
$$

It follows that

$$
\begin{aligned}
&\frac{1}{N}\sum_{\alpha=1}^{N}(E[\Delta_1 W_\alpha \Delta_1\xi_\alpha], \bar{\theta})\bar{\xi}_\alpha = \frac{1}{N}\sum_{\alpha=1}^{N}\left(\left(\frac{2\sigma^2}{N}\bar{W}_\alpha^3(\bar{\xi}_\alpha, \bar{M}^- V_0[\xi_\alpha]\bar{\theta})V_0[\xi_\alpha]\bar{\theta}\right), \bar{\theta}\right)\bar{\xi}_\alpha \\
&= \frac{2\sigma^2}{N^2}\sum_{\alpha=1}^{N}\bar{W}_\alpha^3(\bar{\xi}_\alpha, \bar{M}^- V_0[\xi_\alpha]\bar{\theta})(\bar{\theta}, V_0[\xi_\alpha]\bar{\theta})\bar{\xi}_\alpha = \frac{2\sigma^2}{N^2}\sum_{\alpha=1}^{N}\bar{W}_\alpha^2(\bar{\xi}_\alpha, \bar{M}^- V_0[\xi_\alpha]\bar{\theta})\bar{\xi}_\alpha.
\end{aligned}
\tag{8.39}
$$

Substituting Eq. (8.39) into Eq. (8.36), we obtain Eq. (8.34). □

Lemma 8.4 (Expectation of $\Delta_1 M \bar{M}^- \Delta_1 M \bar{\theta}$)

$$
\begin{aligned}
E[\Delta_1 M \bar{M}^- \Delta_1 M \bar{\theta}] =& \frac{\sigma^2}{N^2}\sum_{\alpha=1}^{N}\bar{W}_\alpha \bar{W}_\alpha (\bar{\xi}_\alpha, \bar{M}^- \bar{\xi}_\alpha) V_0[\xi_\alpha]\bar{\theta} \\
&+ \frac{3\sigma^2}{N^2}\sum_{\alpha=1}^{N}\bar{W}_\alpha \bar{W}_\alpha (\bar{\xi}_\alpha, \bar{M}^- V_0[\xi_\alpha]\bar{\theta})\bar{\xi}_\alpha.
\end{aligned}
\tag{8.40}
$$

Proof. From Eq. (8.1), we can write

$$
\begin{aligned}
\Delta_1 M \bar{\theta} &= \frac{1}{N}\sum_{\alpha=1}^{N}\bar{W}_\alpha\left(\Delta_1\xi_\alpha\bar{\xi}_\alpha^\top + \bar{\xi}_\alpha\Delta_1\xi_\alpha^\top\right)\bar{\theta} + \frac{1}{N}\sum_{\alpha=1}^{N}\Delta_1 W_\alpha\bar{\xi}_\alpha\bar{\xi}_\alpha^\top\bar{\theta} \\
&= \frac{1}{N}\sum_{\alpha=1}^{N}\bar{W}_\alpha(\Delta_1\xi_\alpha, \bar{\theta})\bar{\xi}_\alpha.
\end{aligned}
\tag{8.41}
$$

We can also write

$$
\begin{aligned}
\Delta_1 M \bar{M}^- \Delta_1 M \bar{\theta} &= \Delta_1 M \bar{M}^- \left(\frac{1}{N} \sum_{\alpha=1}^{N} \bar{W}_\alpha (\Delta_1 \xi_\alpha, \bar{\theta}) \bar{\xi}_\alpha \right) \\
&= \left(\frac{1}{N} \sum_{\beta=1}^{N} \bar{W}_\beta \left(\Delta_1 \xi_\beta \bar{\xi}_\beta^\top + \bar{\xi}_\beta \Delta_1 \xi_\beta^\top \right) + \frac{1}{N} \sum_{\beta=1}^{N} \Delta_1 \bar{W}_\beta \bar{\xi}_\beta \bar{\xi}_\beta^\top \right) \\
&\quad \bar{M}^- \left(\frac{1}{N} \sum_{\alpha=1}^{N} \bar{W}_\alpha (\Delta_1 \xi_\alpha, \bar{\theta}) \bar{\xi}_\alpha \right) \\
&= \frac{1}{N^2} \sum_{\alpha,\beta=1}^{N} \bar{W}_\alpha \bar{W}_\beta \left(\Delta_1 \xi_\beta \bar{\xi}_\beta^\top + \bar{\xi}_\beta \Delta_1 \xi_\beta^\top \right) \bar{M}^- (\Delta_1 \xi_\alpha, \bar{\theta}) \bar{\xi}_\alpha \\
&\quad + \frac{1}{N^2} \sum_{\alpha,\beta=1}^{N} \bar{W}_\alpha \Delta_1 \bar{W}_\beta \bar{\xi}_\beta \bar{\xi}_\beta^\top \bar{M}^- (\Delta_1 \xi_\alpha, \bar{\theta}) \bar{\xi}_\alpha \\
&= \frac{1}{N^2} \sum_{\alpha,\beta=1}^{N} \bar{W}_\alpha \bar{W}_\beta (\Delta_1 \xi_\alpha, \bar{\theta}) \left(\Delta_1 \xi_\beta \bar{\xi}_\beta^\top + \bar{\xi}_\beta \Delta_1 \xi_\beta^\top \right) \bar{M}^- \bar{\xi}_\alpha \\
&\quad + \frac{1}{N^2} \sum_{\alpha,\beta=1}^{N} \bar{W}_\alpha \Delta_1 \bar{W}_\beta (\Delta_1 \xi_\alpha, \bar{\theta}) \bar{\xi}_\beta \bar{\xi}_\beta^\top \bar{M}^- \bar{\xi}_\alpha \\
&= \frac{1}{N^2} \sum_{\alpha,\beta=1}^{N} \bar{W}_\alpha \bar{W}_\beta (\Delta_1 \xi_\alpha, \bar{\theta}) (\bar{\xi}_\beta, \bar{M}^- \bar{\xi}_\alpha) \Delta_1 \xi_\beta \quad (\equiv t_1) \\
&\quad + \frac{1}{N^2} \sum_{\alpha,\beta=1}^{N} \bar{W}_\alpha \bar{W}_\beta (\Delta_1 \xi_\alpha, \bar{\theta}) (\Delta_1 \xi_\beta, \bar{M}^- \bar{\xi}_\alpha) \bar{\xi}_\beta \quad (\equiv t_2) \\
&\quad + \frac{1}{N^2} \sum_{\alpha,\beta=1}^{N} \bar{W}_\alpha \Delta_1 \bar{W}_\beta (\Delta_1 \xi_\alpha, \bar{\theta}) (\bar{\xi}_\beta, \bar{M}^- \bar{\xi}_\alpha) \bar{\xi}_\beta \quad (\equiv t_3).
\end{aligned}
\tag{8.42}
$$

We evaluate the expectation of the three terms t_1, t_2, and t_3 separately. The expectation of t_1 is

$$
\begin{aligned}
E[t_1] &= \frac{1}{N^2} \sum_{\alpha,\beta=1}^{N} \bar{W}_\alpha \bar{W}_\beta (\bar{\xi}_\beta, \bar{M}^- \bar{\xi}_\alpha) E\left[\Delta_1 \xi_\beta \Delta_1 \xi_\alpha^\top \right] \bar{\theta} \\
&= \frac{1}{N^2} \sum_{\alpha,\beta=1}^{N} \bar{W}_\alpha \bar{W}_\beta (\bar{\xi}_\beta, \bar{M}^- \bar{\xi}_\alpha) \sigma^2 \delta_{\alpha\beta} V_0[\xi_\alpha] \bar{\theta} \\
&= \frac{\sigma^2}{N^2} \sum_{\alpha=1}^{N} \bar{W}_\alpha^2 (\bar{\xi}_\alpha, \bar{M}^- \bar{\xi}_\alpha) V_0[\xi_\alpha] \bar{\theta}.
\end{aligned}
\tag{8.43}
$$

The expectation of $\boldsymbol{t}_2$ is

$$E[\boldsymbol{t}_2] = \frac{1}{N^2}\sum_{\alpha,\beta=1}^{N} \bar{W}_\alpha \bar{W}_\beta \left(\bar{\boldsymbol{\theta}}, E[\Delta_1\boldsymbol{\xi}_\alpha \Delta_1\boldsymbol{\xi}_\beta]\bar{\boldsymbol{M}}^-\bar{\boldsymbol{\xi}}_\alpha\right)\bar{\boldsymbol{\xi}}_\beta$$
$$= \frac{1}{N^2}\sum_{\alpha,\beta=1}^{N} \bar{W}_\alpha \bar{W}_\beta \left(\bar{\boldsymbol{\theta}}, \sigma^2\delta_{\alpha\beta}V_0[\boldsymbol{\xi}_\alpha]\bar{\boldsymbol{M}}^-\bar{\boldsymbol{\xi}}_\alpha\right)\bar{\boldsymbol{\xi}}_\beta$$
$$= \frac{\sigma^2}{N^2}\sum_{\alpha=1}^{N} \bar{W}_\alpha^3 \left(\bar{\boldsymbol{\xi}}_\alpha, \bar{\boldsymbol{M}}^- V_0[\boldsymbol{\xi}_\alpha]\bar{\boldsymbol{\theta}}\right)\bar{\boldsymbol{\xi}}_\alpha. \tag{8.44}$$

Finally, we consider the expectation of $\boldsymbol{t}_3$. From Eq. (8.37), we can write

$$\Delta_1 W_\beta = \frac{2}{N}\sum_{\gamma=1}^{N} \bar{W}_\beta^2 \bar{W}_\gamma (\bar{\boldsymbol{\xi}}_\gamma, \bar{\boldsymbol{M}}^- V_0[\boldsymbol{\xi}_\beta]\bar{\boldsymbol{\theta}})(\Delta_1\boldsymbol{\xi}_\gamma, \bar{\boldsymbol{\theta}}). \tag{8.45}$$

Hence,

$$E[\Delta_1 W_\beta \Delta_1\boldsymbol{\xi}_\alpha] = E\left[\frac{2}{N}\sum_{\gamma=1}^{N} \bar{W}_\beta^2 \bar{W}_\gamma (\bar{\boldsymbol{\xi}}_\gamma, \bar{\boldsymbol{M}}^- V_0[\boldsymbol{\xi}_\beta]\bar{\boldsymbol{\theta}})(\Delta_1\boldsymbol{\xi}_\gamma, \bar{\boldsymbol{\theta}})\Delta_1\boldsymbol{\xi}_\alpha\right]$$
$$= \frac{2}{N}\sum_{\gamma=1}^{N} \bar{W}_\beta^2 \bar{W}_\gamma (\bar{\boldsymbol{\xi}}_\gamma, \bar{\boldsymbol{M}}^- V_0[\boldsymbol{\xi}_\beta]\bar{\boldsymbol{\theta}}) E[\Delta_1\boldsymbol{\xi}_\alpha \Delta_1\boldsymbol{\xi}_\gamma]\bar{\boldsymbol{\theta}}$$
$$= \frac{2}{N}\sum_{\gamma=1}^{N} \bar{W}_\beta^2 \bar{W}_\gamma (\bar{\boldsymbol{\xi}}_\gamma, \bar{\boldsymbol{M}}^- V_0[\boldsymbol{\xi}_\beta]\bar{\boldsymbol{\theta}})\sigma^2\delta_{\alpha\gamma} V_0[\boldsymbol{\xi}_\alpha]\bar{\boldsymbol{\theta}}$$
$$= \frac{2\sigma^2}{N}\bar{W}_\beta^2 \bar{W}_\alpha (\bar{\boldsymbol{\xi}}_\alpha, \bar{\boldsymbol{M}}^- V_0[\boldsymbol{\xi}_\beta]\bar{\boldsymbol{\theta}}) V_0[\boldsymbol{\xi}_\alpha]\bar{\boldsymbol{\theta}}. \tag{8.46}$$

It follows that

$$\left(E[\Delta_1 \bar{W}_\beta \Delta_1\boldsymbol{\xi}_\alpha], \bar{\boldsymbol{\theta}}\right) = \left(\frac{2\sigma^2}{N}\bar{W}_\alpha \bar{W}_\beta^2 (\bar{\boldsymbol{\xi}}_\alpha, \bar{\boldsymbol{M}}^- V_0[\boldsymbol{\xi}_\beta]\bar{\boldsymbol{\theta}}) V_0[\boldsymbol{\xi}_\alpha]\bar{\boldsymbol{\theta}}, \bar{\boldsymbol{\theta}}\right)$$
$$= \frac{2\sigma^2}{N}\bar{W}_\alpha \bar{W}_\beta^2 (\bar{\boldsymbol{\xi}}_\alpha, \bar{\boldsymbol{M}}^- V_0[\boldsymbol{\xi}_\beta]\bar{\boldsymbol{\theta}})(\bar{\boldsymbol{\theta}}, V_0[\boldsymbol{\xi}_\alpha]\bar{\boldsymbol{\theta}}) = \frac{2\sigma^2}{N}\bar{W}_\beta^2 (\bar{\boldsymbol{\xi}}_\alpha, \bar{\boldsymbol{M}}^- V_0[\boldsymbol{\xi}_\beta]\bar{\boldsymbol{\theta}}). \tag{8.47}$$

Thus, the expectation of $\boldsymbol{t}_3$ is

$$
\begin{aligned}
E[\boldsymbol{t}_3] &= \frac{1}{N^2}\sum_{\alpha,\beta=1}^{N} \bar{W}_\alpha \left(\frac{2\sigma^2}{N}\bar{W}_\beta^2(\bar{\xi}_\alpha, \bar{M}^- V_0[\xi_\beta]\bar{\theta})(\bar{\xi}_\beta, \bar{M}^-\bar{\xi}_\alpha)\right)\bar{\xi}_\beta \\
&= \frac{2\sigma^2}{N^3}\sum_{\alpha,\beta=1}^{N} \bar{W}_\alpha\bar{W}_\beta^2(\bar{\xi}_\alpha, \bar{M}^- V_0[\xi_\beta]\bar{\theta})(\bar{\xi}_\beta, \bar{M}^-\bar{\xi}_\alpha)\bar{\xi}_\beta \\
&= \frac{2\sigma^2}{N^3}\sum_{\alpha,\beta=1}^{N} \bar{W}_\alpha\bar{W}_\beta^2\bar{\xi}_\beta^\top\bar{M}^-\bar{\xi}_\alpha\bar{\xi}_\alpha^\top\bar{M}^- V_0[\xi_\beta]\bar{\theta}\bar{\xi}_\beta \\
&= \frac{2\sigma^2}{N^2}\sum_{\beta=1}^{N} \bar{W}_\beta^2\bar{\xi}_\beta^\top\bar{M}^-\left(\frac{1}{N}\sum_{\alpha=1}^{N}\bar{W}_\alpha\bar{\xi}_\alpha\bar{\xi}_\alpha\right)\bar{M}^- V_0[\xi_\beta]\bar{\theta}\bar{\xi}_\beta \\
&= \frac{2\sigma^2}{N^2}\sum_{\beta=1}^{N} \bar{W}_\beta^2(\bar{\xi}_\beta, \bar{M}^-\bar{M}\bar{M}^- V_0[\xi_\beta]\bar{\theta})\bar{\xi}_\beta = \frac{2\sigma^2}{N^2}\sum_{\beta=1}^{N} \bar{W}_\beta(\bar{\xi}_\beta, \bar{M}^- V_0[\xi_\beta]\bar{\theta})\bar{\xi}_\beta, \qquad (8.48)
\end{aligned}
$$

where we have used the identity $\bar{M}^-\bar{M}\bar{M}^- = \bar{M}^-$ for the pseudoinverse $\bar{M}^-$ (↪ Problem 8.3). Adding the expectations of $\boldsymbol{t}_1$, $\boldsymbol{t}_2$, and $\boldsymbol{t}_3$ together, we obtain the expectation of $\Delta_1 M\bar{M}^-\Delta_1 M\bar{\theta}$ in the form of Eq. (8.40). □

Proposition 8.5 **(Optimal $\bar{N}$)** *The identity $E[T\bar{\theta}] = \sigma^2\bar{N}\bar{\theta}$ holds if $\bar{N}$ is defined by Eq. (8.26).*

Proof. Combining the above expectations $E[\Delta_2 M\bar{\theta}]$ and $E[\Delta_1 M\bar{M}^-\Delta_1 M\bar{\theta}]$, we obtain the expectation of $T\bar{\theta}$ in the form

$$
\begin{aligned}
E[T\bar{\theta}] &= \frac{\sigma^2}{N}\sum_{\alpha=1}^{N}\bar{W}_\alpha\Big(V_0[\xi_\alpha]\bar{\theta} + (e,\bar{\theta})\bar{\xi}_\alpha\Big) + \frac{2\sigma^2}{N^2}\sum_{\alpha=1}^{N}\bar{W}_\alpha^2(\bar{\xi}_\alpha, \bar{M}^- V_0[\xi_\alpha]\bar{\theta})\bar{\xi}_\alpha \\
&\quad - \frac{\sigma^2}{N^2}\sum_{\alpha=1}^{N}\bar{W}_\alpha^2(\bar{\xi}_\alpha, \bar{M}^-\bar{\xi}_\alpha)V_0[\xi_\alpha]\bar{\theta} - \frac{3\sigma^2}{N^2}\sum_{\alpha=1}^{N}\bar{W}_\alpha^2(\bar{\xi}_\alpha, \bar{M}^- V_0[\xi_\alpha]\bar{\theta})\bar{\xi}_\alpha \\
&= \frac{\sigma^2}{N}\sum_{\alpha=1}^{N}\bar{W}_\alpha\Big(V_0[\xi_\alpha]\bar{\theta} + \bar{\xi}_\alpha e^\top\bar{\theta}\Big) - \frac{\sigma^2}{N^2}\sum_{\alpha=1}^{N}\bar{W}_\alpha^2(\bar{\xi}_\alpha, \bar{M}^-\bar{\xi}_\alpha)V_0[\xi_\alpha]\bar{\theta} \\
&\quad - \frac{\sigma^2}{N^2}\sum_{\alpha=1}^{N}\bar{W}_\alpha^2\bar{\xi}_\alpha\bar{\xi}_\alpha\bar{M}^- V_0[\xi_\alpha]\bar{\theta} \\
&= \frac{\sigma^2}{N}\sum_{\alpha=1}^{N}\bar{W}_\alpha\Big(V_0[\xi_\alpha]\bar{\theta} + (\bar{\xi}_\alpha e^\top + e\bar{\xi}_\alpha)\bar{\theta}\Big) - \frac{\sigma^2}{N^2}\sum_{\alpha=1}^{N}\bar{W}_\alpha^2(\bar{\xi}_\alpha, \bar{M}^-\bar{\xi}_\alpha)V_0[\xi_\alpha]\bar{\theta} \\
&\quad - \frac{\sigma^2}{N^2}\sum_{\alpha=1}^{N}\bar{W}_\alpha^2(\bar{\xi}_\alpha\bar{\xi}_\alpha\bar{M}^- V_0[\xi_\alpha] + V_0[\xi_\alpha]\bar{M}^-\bar{\xi}_\alpha\bar{\xi}_\alpha)\bar{\theta}. \qquad (8.49)
\end{aligned}
$$

Hence, if we define the matrix $\bar{N}$ by Eq. (8.26), the above equation is written as $E[T\bar{\theta}] = \sigma^2\bar{N}\bar{\theta}$. □

8.5 SUPPLEMENTAL NOTE

The covariance and bias analysis of algebraic ellipse fitting was first presented in Kanatani [2008]. Based on this analysis, the hyper-renormalization procedure was obtained by Kanatani et al. [2012]. The result is generalized by Kanatani et al. [2014] to multiple constraints in the form of $(\xi^{(k)}, \theta) = 0$, $k = 1, ..., L$ (see Eq. (7.21)). In this case, Eq. (8.15) still holds if the matrix $\bar{M}$ is replaced by

$$M = \frac{1}{N}\sum_{\alpha=1}^{N}\sum_{k,l=1}^{L} W_\alpha^{(kl)}\xi_\alpha^{(k)}\xi_\alpha^{(l)\top}, \qquad W_\alpha^{(kl)} = \left((\theta, V_0^{(kl)}\theta)\right)_r^-, \tag{8.50}$$

where r is the number of independent constraints (see Eqs. (7.28) and (7.29)). Equation (8.26) is generalized to

$$\begin{aligned}\bar{N} = &\frac{1}{N}\sum_{\alpha=1}^{N}\sum_{k,l=1}^{L} \bar{W}_\alpha^{(kl)}\left(V_0^{(kl)}[\xi_\alpha] + 2\mathcal{S}[\bar{\xi}_\alpha^{(k)} e_\alpha^{(l)\top}]\right)\\ &-\frac{1}{N^2}\sum_{\alpha=1}^{N}\sum_{k,l,m,n=1}^{L} \bar{W}_\alpha^{(kl)}\bar{W}_\alpha^{(mn)}\left(\left(\bar{\xi}_\alpha^{(k)}, \bar{M}^-\bar{\xi}_\alpha^{(m)}\right) V_0^{(ln)}[\xi_\alpha]\right.\\ &\left.+2\mathcal{S}\left[V_0^{(km)}[\xi_\alpha]\bar{M}^-\bar{\xi}_\alpha^{(l)}\bar{\xi}_\alpha^{(n)\top}\right]\right),\end{aligned} \tag{8.51}$$

where $\bar{W}_\alpha^{(kl)}$ is the true value of the $W_\alpha^{(kl)}$ in Eq. (8.50), and $e_\alpha^{(k)}$ is the vector defined by the relation

$$E\left[\Delta_2\xi_\alpha^{(k)}\right] = \sigma^2 e_\alpha^{(k)}. \tag{8.52}$$

Thus, the hyper-renormalization scheme can be applied to many other problems including homography computation ($L = 3$, $r = 2$) described in Section 7.2. For homography computation, however, we have $e_\alpha^{(k)} = \mathbf{0}$, because we see from Eqs. (7.18) that

$$\Delta_2\xi_\alpha^{(1)} = \begin{pmatrix} 0\\0\\0\\0\\0\\0\\ \Delta x_\alpha\Delta y'_\alpha\\ \Delta y_\alpha\Delta y'_\alpha\\ 0\end{pmatrix}, \quad \Delta_2\xi_\alpha^{(2)} = \begin{pmatrix} 0\\0\\0\\0\\0\\0\\ -\Delta x'_\alpha\Delta x_\alpha\\ -\Delta x'_\alpha\Delta y_\alpha\\ 0\end{pmatrix}, \quad \Delta_2\xi_\alpha^{(3)} = \begin{pmatrix} -\Delta y'_\alpha\Delta x_\alpha\\ -\Delta y'_\alpha\Delta y_\alpha\\ 0\\ \Delta x'_\alpha\Delta x_\alpha\\ \Delta x'_\alpha\Delta y_\alpha\\ 0\\0\\0\\0\end{pmatrix}. \tag{8.53}$$

All these have expectation $\mathbf{0}$, since we regard Δx_α, Δy_α, $\Delta x'_\alpha$, and $\Delta y'_\alpha$ as independent random variables of mean 0.

PROBLEMS

8.1. Let

$$\boldsymbol{A} = \boldsymbol{U} \begin{pmatrix} \sigma_1 & & \\ & \ddots & \\ & & \sigma_r \end{pmatrix} \boldsymbol{V}^\top \tag{8.54}$$

be the singular value decomposition of an $m \times n$ matrix $\boldsymbol{A}$, where the second matrix on the right side is an $r \times r$ diagonal matrix, $r \leq \min(m, n)$, with singular values $\sigma_1 \geq \cdots \geq \sigma_r$ (> 0) as diagonal elements in that order (all non-diagonal elements are 0). The matrices $\boldsymbol{U}$ and $\boldsymbol{V}$ are, respectively, $m \times r$ and $n \times r$ matrices consisting of orthonormal columns. Show that Eq. (8.54) can be written in the form

$$\boldsymbol{A} = \sigma_1 \boldsymbol{u}_1 \boldsymbol{v}_1^\top + \sigma_2 \boldsymbol{u}_2 \boldsymbol{v}_2^\top + \cdots + \sigma_r \boldsymbol{u}_r \boldsymbol{v}_r^\top, \tag{8.55}$$

where $\boldsymbol{u}_i$ and $\boldsymbol{v}_i$ are the ith columns of $\boldsymbol{U}$ and $\boldsymbol{V}$, respectively.

8.2. The pseudoinverse of the matrix $\boldsymbol{A}$ of Eq. (8.54) is defined to be

$$\boldsymbol{A}^- = \boldsymbol{V} \begin{pmatrix} 1/\sigma_1 & & \\ & \ddots & \\ & & 1/\sigma_r \end{pmatrix} \boldsymbol{U}^\top. \tag{8.56}$$

Show that this can be written in the form

$$\boldsymbol{A}^- = \frac{1}{\sigma_1} \boldsymbol{v}_1 \boldsymbol{u}_1^\top + \frac{1}{\sigma_2} \boldsymbol{v}_2 \boldsymbol{u}_2^\top + \cdots + \frac{1}{\sigma_r} \boldsymbol{v}_r \boldsymbol{u}_r^\top. \tag{8.57}$$

8.3. Show that the following identities holds for the pseudoinverse:

$$\boldsymbol{A}\boldsymbol{A}^-\boldsymbol{A} = \boldsymbol{A}, \qquad \boldsymbol{A}^-\boldsymbol{A}\boldsymbol{A}^- = \boldsymbol{A}^-. \tag{8.58}$$

8.4. For the matrix $\boldsymbol{A}$ of Eq. (8.54), show that the product $\boldsymbol{A}\boldsymbol{A}^-$ is the projection matrix onto the space spanned by $\boldsymbol{u}_1$, ..., $\boldsymbol{u}_r$ and that $\boldsymbol{A}^-\boldsymbol{A}$ is the projection matrix onto the space spanned by $\boldsymbol{v}_1$, ..., $\boldsymbol{v}_r$.

CHAPTER 9

Maximum Likelihood and Geometric Fitting

We discuss maximum likelihood estimation and Sampson error minimization and do high order error analysis to derive explicit expressions for the covariance and bias of the solution. The hyperaccurate correction procedure is derived in this framework.

9.1 MAXIMUM LIKELIHOOD AND SAMPSON ERROR

We are assuming that each point (x_α, y_α) is perturbed from its true position $(\bar{x}_\alpha, \bar{y}_\alpha)$ by independent Gaussian noise of mean 0 and variance σ^2. In statistical terms, the geometric distance between them

$$S = \frac{1}{N}\sum_{\alpha=1}^{N}\Big((x_\alpha - \bar{x}_\alpha)^2 + (y_\alpha - \bar{y}_\alpha)^2\Big) \tag{9.1}$$

is called the *Mahalanobis distance*. Strictly speaking, it should be called the "square Mahalanobis distance," because it has the dimension of square length, but the term "Mahalanobis distance" is widely used for simplicity, just as the term "geometric distance." Finding an ellipse that minimizes this is called *maximum likelihood* (*ML*) estimation. In fact, the probability density, or the *likelihood*, of the total noise is (constant) $\times\, e^{-\sigma^2 NS/2}$ according to our noise model, so minimizing S is equivalent to maximizing the likelihood.

By "minimizing S," we mean minimizing S with respect to the ellipse parameter $\boldsymbol{\theta}$. However, Eq. (9.1) itself does not contain $\boldsymbol{\theta}$; it is included in the ellipse equation $(\bar{\boldsymbol{\xi}}, \boldsymbol{\theta}) = 0$, subject to which Eq. (9.1) is minimized. This is a major difficulty for direct maximum likelihood estimation. This could be handled by introducing auxiliary variables (we will discuss this later), but the difficulty is resolved if we do maximum likelihood, using not the raw point coordinates (x_α, y_α) but their nonlinear mapping $\boldsymbol{\xi}_\alpha$, whose covariance matrix $V[\boldsymbol{\xi}_\alpha]$ is given by Eq. (1.21). If we assume that the observed $\boldsymbol{\xi}_\alpha$ is perturbed from its true value $\bar{\boldsymbol{\xi}}_\alpha$ by independent Gaussian noise of mean $\mathbf{0}$ and covariance matrix $V[\boldsymbol{\xi}_\alpha]$ $(= \sigma^2 V_0[\boldsymbol{\xi}_\alpha])$, maximum likelihood estimation is to minimize the Mahalanobis distance in the $\boldsymbol{\xi}$-space

$$J = \frac{1}{N}\sum_{\alpha=1}^{N}\Big(\boldsymbol{\xi}_\alpha - \bar{\boldsymbol{\xi}}_\alpha, V_0[\boldsymbol{\xi}_\alpha]^-(\boldsymbol{\xi}_\alpha - \bar{\boldsymbol{\xi}}_\alpha)\Big), \tag{9.2}$$

subject to the constraint

$$(\bar{\xi}_\alpha, \theta) = 0, \qquad \alpha = 1, ..., N. \tag{9.3}$$

In Eq. (9.2), we use the pseudoinverse $V_0[\xi_\alpha]^-$ rather than the inverse $V_0[\xi_\alpha]^{-1}$, because the covariance matrix $V[\xi_\alpha]$ is not positive definite, the last column and row consisting of 0 (see Eq. (1.21)). According to the Gaussian noise assumption for ξ_α, the probability density, or the likelihood, of the data $\{\xi_\alpha\}$ is (constant) $\times\, e^{-\sigma^2 NJ/2}$, so maximizing the likelihood is equivalent to minimizing Eq. (9.2) subject to Eq. (9.3). In this formulation, the constraint is *linear* in $\bar{\xi}_\alpha$, so that we can easily eliminate $\bar{\xi}_\alpha$, using Lagrange multipliers, to obtain

$$J = \frac{1}{N}\sum_{\alpha=1}^{N} W_\alpha (\xi_\alpha, \theta)^2, \qquad W_\alpha = \frac{1}{(\theta, V_0[\xi_\alpha]\theta)}, \tag{9.4}$$

which is simply the *Sampson error* of Eq. (3.3) (see Proposition 9.1 below). This is a function of θ, so we can minimize this by searching the θ-space.

However, ξ_α is a nonlinear mapping of (x_α, y_α), so the assumption that ξ_α is a Gaussian variable of mean $\mathbf{0}$ and covariance matrix $V[\xi_\alpha]$ $(= \sigma^2 V_0[\xi_\alpha])$ does not strictly hold, even if (x_α, y_α) are independent Gaussian variables of mean 0 and variance σ^2. Still, if the noise in (x_α, y_α) is small, the noise distribution of ξ_α is expected to have an approximately Gaussian-like form, concentrating around $\mathbf{0}$ with covariance matrix $V[\xi_\alpha]$ $(= \sigma^2 V_0[\xi_\alpha])$. It has been experimentally confirmed that it is indeed the case; the Sampson error minimization solution and the geometric distance minimization are almost identical. In fact, we can minimize the geometric distance by repeating the Sampson error minimization, as shown in Chapter 3, but the resulting solution is the same over several significant digits. Thus, we can in practice identify the Sampson error with the geometric distance. Moreover, the Gaussian noise assumption for ξ_α makes mathematical error analysis very easy, enabling us to evaluate higher order covariance and bias and derive a theoretical accuracy limit. In the following we adopt this Gaussian noise assumption for ξ_α.

9.2 ERROR ANALYSIS

We now analyze the error of the solution θ that minimizes the Sampson error J of Eq. (9.4). As in the preceding chapter, we treat θ and ξ_α as n-D vectors so that the result also holds for the fundamental matrix computation described in Section 7.1. The derivative of Eq. (9.4) with respect to θ has the form of Eq. (3.8), i.e.,

$$\nabla_\theta J = 2(\boldsymbol{M} - \boldsymbol{L})\theta, \tag{9.5}$$

where the $n \times n$ matrices $\boldsymbol{M}$ and $\boldsymbol{L}$ are given by

$$\boldsymbol{M} = \frac{1}{N}\sum_{\alpha=1}^{N} W_\alpha \xi_\alpha \xi_\alpha^\top, \tag{9.6}$$

$$L = \frac{1}{N}\sum_{\alpha=1}^{N} W_\alpha^2 (\xi_\alpha, \theta)^2 V_0[\xi_\alpha]. \tag{9.7}$$

As in the preceding chapter, we substitute Eq. (1.17) into Eq. (9.4) and (9.6) and expand M and W_α in the form of Eqs. (8.4) and (8.5), where $\Delta_i M$ and $\Delta_i W_\alpha$, $i = 1, 2$, are given by Eqs. (8.1), (8.7), (8.8), and (8.9). Similarly, we expand the matrix L in Eq. (9.7) in the form

$$L = \bar{L} + \Delta_1 L + \Delta_2 L + \cdots \tag{9.8}$$

Since $(\bar{\xi}_\alpha, \bar{\theta}) = 0$ in the absence of noise, we can see from Eq. (9.7) that $\bar{L} = \Delta_1 L = O$. The second-order term $\Delta_2 L$ is given by

$$\begin{aligned}\Delta_2 L = \frac{1}{N}\sum_{\alpha=1}^{N} \bar{W}_\alpha^2 \Big(&(\bar{\xi}_\alpha, \Delta_1\theta)^2 + (\bar{\xi}_\alpha, \Delta_1\theta)(\Delta_1\xi_\alpha, \bar{\theta}) \\ &+ (\Delta_1\xi_\alpha, \bar{\theta})(\bar{\xi}_\alpha, \Delta_1\theta) + (\Delta_1\xi_\alpha, \bar{\theta})^2 \Big) V_0[\xi_\alpha].\end{aligned} \tag{9.9}$$

At the value θ that minimizes the Sampson error J, the derivative $\nabla_\theta J$ in Eq. (9.5) vanishes, so

$$M\theta = L\theta. \tag{9.10}$$

Substituting Eqs. (8.4), (8.3), and (9.8), we expand this equality in the form

$$(\bar{M} + \Delta_1 M + \Delta_2 M + \cdots)(\bar{\theta} + \Delta_1\theta + \Delta_2\theta + \cdots) = (\Delta_2 L + \cdots)(\bar{\theta} + \Delta_1\theta + \Delta_2\theta + \cdots). \tag{9.11}$$

Equating terms of the same order on both sides, we obtain

$$\bar{M}\Delta_1\theta + \Delta_1 M\bar{\theta} = 0, \tag{9.12}$$

$$\bar{M}\Delta_2\theta + \Delta_1 M\Delta_1\theta + \Delta_2 M\bar{\theta} = \Delta_2 L\bar{\theta}. \tag{9.13}$$

Recall that $\bar{M}\bar{\theta} = 0$ in the absence of noise. So $\bar{M}$ has rank $n-1$, $\bar{\theta}$ being its null vector. Multiply Eq. (9.12) by the pseudoinverse $\bar{M}^-$ on both sides. Noting that $\bar{M}^-\bar{M} = P_{\bar{\theta}}$ (↪ Problems 6.1 and 8.4) and that $\Delta_1\theta$ is orthogonal to $\bar{\theta}$, we obtain

$$\Delta_1\theta = -\bar{M}^-\Delta_1 M\bar{\theta}, \tag{9.14}$$

which is the same as Eq. (8.14). This means that *the algebraic solution and the Sampson error minimization solution agree to a first approximation.* Hence, the covariance matrix $V[\theta]$ is also given by Eq. (8.15), achieving the KCR lower bound up to $O(\sigma^4)$. So, we focus on the second-order term. Multiplying Eq. (9.13) by $\bar{M}^-$ on both sides, we obtain

$$\Delta_2^\perp\theta = -\bar{M}^-\Delta_1 M\Delta_1\theta - \bar{M}^-\Delta_2 M\bar{\theta} + \bar{M}^-\Delta_2 L\bar{\theta}, \tag{9.15}$$

where we define $\Delta_2^\perp\theta$ by Eq. (8.18).

9.3 BIAS ANALYSIS AND HYPERACCURATE CORRECTION

The expectation of odd-order error terms is zero. In particular, $E[\Delta_1\boldsymbol{\theta}] = \mathbf{0}$. Hence, we focus on the second-order bias $E[\Delta_2^\top\boldsymbol{\theta}]$. From Eq. (9.15), we obtain

$$E[\Delta_2^\perp\boldsymbol{\theta}] = -E[\bar{\boldsymbol{M}}^-\Delta_1\boldsymbol{M}\Delta_1\boldsymbol{\theta}] - E[\bar{\boldsymbol{M}}^-\Delta_2\boldsymbol{M}\bar{\boldsymbol{\theta}}] + E[\bar{\boldsymbol{M}}^-\Delta_2\boldsymbol{L}\bar{\boldsymbol{\theta}}]. \tag{9.16}$$

We evaluate each term separately, using our noise assumption of Eq. (8.24) and the definition of the vector $\boldsymbol{e}$ in Eq. (8.25). In the end, we obtain the following expression (see Lemmas 9.2, 9.3, and 9.4 below):

$$E[\Delta_2^\perp\boldsymbol{\theta}] = -\frac{\sigma^2}{N}\bar{\boldsymbol{M}}^-\sum_{\alpha=1}^{N}\bar{W}_\alpha(\boldsymbol{e},\bar{\boldsymbol{\theta}})\bar{\boldsymbol{\xi}}_\alpha + \frac{\sigma^2}{N^2}\bar{\boldsymbol{M}}^-\sum_{\alpha=1}^{N}\bar{W}_\alpha^2(\bar{\boldsymbol{\xi}}_\alpha,\bar{\boldsymbol{M}}^-V_0[\boldsymbol{\xi}_\alpha]\bar{\boldsymbol{\theta}})\bar{\boldsymbol{\xi}}_\alpha. \tag{9.17}$$

Hence, we can improve the accuracy of the computed $\boldsymbol{\theta}$ by subtracting this expression, which we call *hyperaccurate correction*. Since Eq. (9.17) is defined in terms of true values, we replace them by observations for actual computation. The matrix $\boldsymbol{M}$ defined by observed $\boldsymbol{\xi}_\alpha$ is generally of full rank, so we replace $\bar{\boldsymbol{M}}^-$ by the pseudoinverse $\boldsymbol{M}_{n-1}^-$ of truncated rank $n-1$ (see Eq. (2.16)). Thus, we obtain the following expression for hyperaccurate correction (see Eq. (3.19)):

$$\Delta_c\boldsymbol{\theta} = -\frac{\sigma^2}{N}\boldsymbol{M}_{n-1}^-\sum_{\alpha=1}^{N}W_\alpha(\boldsymbol{e},\boldsymbol{\theta})\boldsymbol{\xi}_\alpha + \frac{\sigma^2}{N^2}\boldsymbol{M}_{n-1}^-\sum_{\alpha=1}^{N}W_\alpha^2(\boldsymbol{\xi}_\alpha,\boldsymbol{M}_{n-1}^-V_0[\boldsymbol{\xi}_\alpha]\boldsymbol{\theta})\boldsymbol{\xi}_\alpha. \tag{9.18}$$

Subtracting this, we correct $\boldsymbol{\theta}$ to

$$\boldsymbol{\theta} \leftarrow \mathcal{N}[\boldsymbol{\theta} - \Delta_c\boldsymbol{\theta}], \tag{9.19}$$

where $\mathcal{N}[\cdot]$ denotes normalization to unit norm. This operation is necessary, since $\boldsymbol{\theta}$ is defined to be a unit vector. For evaluating Eq. (9.18), we need to estimate σ^2. This is done, using the well-known fact in statistics: if $S_{\min}$ is the minimum of Eq. (9.1), then $NS_{\min}/\sigma^2$ is a χ^2 variable of $N-(n-1)$ degrees of freedom, and the expectation of a χ^2 variable equals its degree of freedom. Note that the parameter $\boldsymbol{\theta}$ has n components but is normalized to unit norm, so it has $n-1$ degrees of freedom. Hence, if we identify $E[S_{min}]$ with the minimum of the Sampson error J in Eq. (9.4), we can estimate σ^2 in the following form (see Eq. (3.18)):

$$\hat{\sigma}^2 = \frac{J}{1-(n-1)/N}. \tag{9.20}$$

By this hyperaccurate correction, the bias is removed up to $O(\sigma^4)$; replacing true values by observations in Eq. (9.18) and estimating σ^2 by Eq. (9.20) introduces only errors of $O(\sigma^4)$.

9.4 DERIVATIONS

We first derive Eq. (9.4). From Eqs. (1.8) and (7.3), we see that the last component of $\boldsymbol{\xi}$ is f_0^2, so no noise perturbation occurs in the direction of $\boldsymbol{k} \equiv (0, \ldots, 0, 1)^\top$. This means that $V_0[\boldsymbol{\xi}_\alpha]$ has rank $n-1$, $\boldsymbol{k}$ being its null vector. Hence, both $V_0[\xi_\alpha]V_0[\xi_\alpha]^-$ and $V_0[\xi_\alpha]^-V_0[\xi_\alpha]$ are equal to the projection matrix onto the subspace orthogonal to $\boldsymbol{k}$ (↪ Problem 8.4), having the form of $\boldsymbol{P}_{\boldsymbol{k}} = \boldsymbol{I} - \boldsymbol{k}\boldsymbol{k}^\top$ (↪ Problem 6.1). (However, all the following results also hold if $V_0[\xi_\alpha]$ is nonsingular).

Proposition 9.1 (Sampson error) *Minimizing Eq. (9.2) subject to Eq. (9.3) reduces to minimization of the Sampson error of Eq. (9.4).*

Proof. In minimizing Eq. (9.2) with respect to $\bar{\xi}_\alpha$, we must note that $\bar{\xi}_\alpha$ is constrained not only by Eq. (9.3) but also by $(\bar{\xi}_\alpha, \boldsymbol{k}) = f_0^2$. So, We introducing Lagrange multipliers λ_α and μ_α and consider

$$\frac{1}{N}\sum_{\alpha=1}^{N}(\xi_\alpha - \bar{\xi}_\alpha, V_0[\xi_\alpha]^-(\xi_\alpha - \bar{\xi}_\alpha)) - \sum_{\alpha=1}^{N}\lambda_\alpha(\bar{\xi}_\alpha, \boldsymbol{\theta}) - \sum_{\alpha=1}^{N}\mu_\alpha((\bar{\xi}_\alpha, \boldsymbol{k}) - f_0^2). \tag{9.21}$$

Differentiating this with respect to $\bar{\xi}_\alpha$ and setting the result to $\boldsymbol{0}$, we obtain

$$\frac{2}{N}V_0[\xi_\alpha]^-(\xi_\alpha - \bar{\xi}_\alpha) - \lambda_\alpha\boldsymbol{\theta} - \mu_\alpha\boldsymbol{k} = \boldsymbol{0}. \tag{9.22}$$

Multiply this by $V_0[\xi_\alpha]$. Note that $V_0[\xi_\alpha]V_0[\xi_\alpha]^- = \boldsymbol{P}_{\boldsymbol{k}}$ and $\boldsymbol{P}_{\boldsymbol{k}}(\xi_\alpha - \bar{\xi}_\alpha) = \boldsymbol{0}$. Also, note that $V_0[\xi_\alpha]\boldsymbol{k} = \boldsymbol{0}$. Hence, we obtain

$$\frac{2}{N}(\xi_\alpha - \bar{\xi}_\alpha) - \lambda_\alpha V_0[\xi_\alpha]\boldsymbol{\theta} = \boldsymbol{0}, \tag{9.23}$$

from which we obtain

$$\bar{\xi}_\alpha = \xi_\alpha - \frac{N\lambda_\alpha}{2}V_0[\xi_\alpha]\boldsymbol{\theta}. \tag{9.24}$$

Substituting this into Eq. (9.3), we have

$$(\xi_\alpha, \boldsymbol{\theta}) - \frac{N\lambda_\alpha}{2}(\boldsymbol{\theta}, V_0[\xi_\alpha]\boldsymbol{\theta}) = 0, \tag{9.25}$$

so

$$\lambda_\alpha = \frac{2(\xi_\alpha, \boldsymbol{\theta})}{N(\boldsymbol{\theta}, V_0[\xi_\alpha]\boldsymbol{\theta})}. \tag{9.26}$$

Substituting Eq. (9.24) into Eq. (9.2), we obtain

$$\begin{aligned} J &= \frac{1}{N}\sum_{\alpha=1}^{N}\left(\frac{N\lambda_\alpha}{2}V_0[\xi_\alpha]\boldsymbol{\theta}, V_0[\xi_\alpha]^-\frac{N\lambda_\alpha}{2}V_0[\xi_\alpha]\boldsymbol{\theta}\right) = \frac{N}{4}\sum_{\alpha=1}^{N}\lambda_\alpha^2(\boldsymbol{\theta}, V_0[\xi_\alpha]V_0[\xi_\alpha]^-V_0[\xi_\alpha]\boldsymbol{\theta}) \\ &= \frac{N}{4}\sum_{\alpha=1}^{N}\lambda_\alpha^2(\boldsymbol{\theta}, V_0[\xi_\alpha]\boldsymbol{\theta}) = \frac{1}{N}\sum_{\alpha=1}^{N}\frac{(\xi_\alpha, \boldsymbol{\theta})^2}{(\boldsymbol{\theta}, V_0[\xi_\alpha]\boldsymbol{\theta})}, \end{aligned} \tag{9.27}$$

where we have used the identity $V_0[\xi_\alpha]V_0[\xi_\alpha]^-V_0[\xi_\alpha] = V_0[\xi_\alpha]$ (↪ Problem 8.3). □

We now derive Eq. (9.17) by evaluating the right side of Eq. (9.16) term by term. To do this, we split the expression of $\Delta_1 \boldsymbol{M}$ and $\Delta_2 \boldsymbol{M}$ in Eqs. (8.1) and (8.7) into the following terms:

$$\Delta_1 \boldsymbol{M} = \Delta_1^0 \boldsymbol{M} + \Delta_1^* \boldsymbol{M}, \tag{9.28}$$

$$\Delta_2 \boldsymbol{M} = \Delta_2^0 \boldsymbol{M} + \Delta_2^* \boldsymbol{M} + \Delta_2^\dagger \boldsymbol{M}, \tag{9.29}$$

$$\Delta_1^0 \boldsymbol{M} \equiv \frac{1}{N}\sum_{\alpha=1}^{N} \bar{W}_\alpha (\Delta_1 \xi_\alpha \bar{\xi}_\alpha^\top + \bar{\xi}_\alpha \Delta_1 \xi_\alpha^\top), \tag{9.30}$$

$$\Delta_1^* \boldsymbol{M} \equiv \frac{1}{N}\sum_{\alpha=1}^{N} \Delta_1 W_\alpha \bar{\xi}_\alpha \bar{\xi}_\alpha^\top, \tag{9.31}$$

$$\Delta_2^0 \boldsymbol{M} \equiv \frac{1}{N}\sum_{\alpha=1}^{N} \bar{W}_\alpha (\Delta_1 \xi_\alpha \Delta_1 \xi_\alpha^\top + \Delta_2 \xi_\alpha \bar{\xi}_\alpha^\top + \bar{\xi}_\alpha \Delta_2 \xi_\alpha^\top), \tag{9.32}$$

$$\Delta_2^* \boldsymbol{M} \equiv \frac{1}{N}\sum_{\alpha=1}^{N} \Delta_1 W_\alpha (\Delta_1 \xi_\alpha \bar{\xi}_\alpha^\top + \bar{\xi}_\alpha \Delta_1 \xi_\alpha^\top), \tag{9.33}$$

$$\Delta_2^\dagger \boldsymbol{M} \equiv \frac{1}{N}\sum_{\alpha=1}^{N} \Delta_2 W_\alpha \bar{\xi}_\alpha \bar{\xi}_\alpha^\top. \tag{9.34}$$

Equation (9.17) is obtained by combining the following Lemmas 9.2, 9.3, and 9.4:

Lemma 9.2 (Expectation of $-\bar{\boldsymbol{M}}^- \Delta_1 \boldsymbol{M} \Delta_1 \boldsymbol{\theta}$)

$$E[-\bar{\boldsymbol{M}}^- \Delta_1 \boldsymbol{M} \Delta_1 \boldsymbol{\theta}] = \frac{\sigma^2}{N^2} \bar{\boldsymbol{M}}^- \sum_{\alpha=1}^{N} \bar{W}_\alpha^2 (\bar{\xi}_\alpha, \bar{\boldsymbol{M}}^- \bar{\xi}_\alpha) V_0[\xi_\alpha] \bar{\boldsymbol{\theta}} + \frac{3\sigma^2}{N^2} \bar{\boldsymbol{M}}^- \sum_{\alpha=1}^{N} \bar{W}_\alpha^2 (\bar{\xi}_\alpha, \bar{\boldsymbol{M}}^- V_0[\xi_\alpha] \bar{\boldsymbol{\theta}}) \bar{\xi}_\alpha. \tag{9.35}$$

Proof. From Eq. (9.28), we can write

$$-E[\bar{\boldsymbol{M}}^- \Delta_1 \boldsymbol{M} \Delta_1 \boldsymbol{\theta}] = E[\bar{\boldsymbol{M}}^- \Delta_1^0 \boldsymbol{M} \bar{\boldsymbol{M}}^- \Delta_1^0 \boldsymbol{M} \bar{\boldsymbol{\theta}}] + E[\bar{\boldsymbol{M}}^- \Delta_1^* \boldsymbol{M} \bar{\boldsymbol{M}}^- \Delta_1^0 \boldsymbol{M} \bar{\boldsymbol{\theta}}]. \tag{9.36}$$

The first term on the right side is written as follows:

$$E\left[\bar{\boldsymbol{M}}^- \Delta_1^0 \boldsymbol{M} \bar{\boldsymbol{M}}^- \Delta_1^0 \boldsymbol{M} \bar{\boldsymbol{\theta}}\right] = E\left[\frac{1}{N^2} \bar{\boldsymbol{M}}^- \sum_{\alpha,\beta=1}^{N} \bar{W}_\alpha \bar{W}_\beta \left(\Delta_1 \xi_\alpha \bar{\xi}_\alpha^\top + \bar{\xi}_\alpha \Delta_1 \xi_\alpha^\top\right) \bar{\boldsymbol{M}}^- (\Delta_1 \xi_\beta, \bar{\boldsymbol{\theta}}) \bar{\xi}_\beta\right]$$

$$= \frac{\sigma^2}{N^2}\bar{M}^- \sum_{\alpha=1}^{N} \bar{W}_\alpha^2(\bar{\xi}_\alpha, \bar{M}^-\bar{\xi}_\alpha)V_0[\xi_\alpha]\bar{\theta} + \frac{\sigma^2}{N^2}\bar{M}^- \sum_{\alpha=1}^{N} \bar{W}_\alpha^2(\bar{\theta}, V_0[\xi_\alpha]\bar{M}^-\bar{\xi}_\alpha)\bar{\xi}_\alpha. \tag{9.37}$$

From Eqs. (9.33) and (8.9), we obtain

$$\Delta_1^* M = \frac{2}{N}\sum_{\alpha=1}^{N} \bar{W}_\alpha^2(\bar{M}^-\Delta_1^0 M\bar{\theta}, V_0[\xi_\alpha]\bar{\theta})\bar{\xi}_\alpha\bar{\xi}_\alpha^\top. \tag{9.38}$$

Hence, the second term on the right side of Eq. (9.36) is

$$\begin{aligned}
&E[\bar{M}^-\Delta_1^* M\bar{M}^-\Delta_1^0 M\bar{\theta}] \\
&= E\left[\frac{2}{N}\bar{M}^-\sum_{\alpha=1}^{N} \bar{W}_\alpha^2(\bar{M}^-\Delta_1^0 M\bar{\theta}, V_0[\xi_\alpha]\bar{\theta})(\bar{\xi}_\alpha, \bar{M}^-\Delta_1^0 M\bar{\theta})\bar{\xi}_\alpha\right] \\
&= \frac{2}{N}\bar{M}^-\sum_{\alpha=1}^{N} \bar{W}_\alpha^2(\bar{\xi}_\alpha, E[\Delta_1\theta\Delta_1\theta^\top]V_0[\xi_\alpha]\bar{\theta})\bar{\xi}_\alpha \\
&= \frac{2\sigma^2}{N^2}\bar{M}^-\sum_{\alpha=1}^{N} \bar{W}_\alpha^2(\bar{\xi}_\alpha, \bar{M}^- V_0[\xi_\alpha]\bar{\theta})\bar{\xi}_\alpha,
\end{aligned} \tag{9.39}$$

where we have used using our noise assumption of Eq. (8.24). Adding Eqs. (9.33) and (9.39), we obtain Eq. (9.35). □

Lemma 9.3 (Expectation of $-\bar{M}^-\Delta_2 M\bar{\theta}$)

$$\begin{aligned}
E[-\bar{M}^-\Delta_2 M\bar{\theta}] = &-\frac{\sigma^2}{N}\bar{M}^-\sum_{\alpha=1}^{N}\bar{W}_\alpha\Big(V_0[\xi_\alpha]\bar{\theta} + (e,\bar{\theta})\bar{\xi}_\alpha\Big) \\
&-\frac{2\sigma^2}{N^2}\bar{M}^-\sum_{\alpha=1}^{N}\bar{W}_\alpha^2\left(\bar{\xi}_\alpha, \bar{M}^- V_0[\xi_\alpha]\bar{\theta}\right)\bar{\xi}_\alpha.
\end{aligned} \tag{9.40}$$

Proof. Using Eq. (9.29) and noting that $\Delta_2^\dagger M\bar{\theta} = \mathbf{0}$, we can write

$$-E[\bar{M}^-\Delta_2 M\bar{\theta}] = -E[\bar{M}^-\Delta_2^0 M\bar{\theta}] - E[\bar{M}^-\Delta_2^* M\bar{\theta}]. \tag{9.41}$$

The first term on the right side is written as

$$\begin{aligned}
-E[\bar{M}^-\Delta_2^0 M\bar{\theta}] &= -\bar{M}^-\frac{1}{N}\sum_{\alpha=1}^{N}\bar{W}_\alpha\Big(E[\Delta_1\xi_\alpha\Delta_1\xi_\alpha^\top] + \bar{\xi}_\alpha E[\Delta_2\xi_\alpha^\top]\Big)\bar{\theta} \\
&= -\frac{\sigma^2}{N}\bar{M}^-\sum_{\alpha=1}^{N}\bar{W}_\alpha\Big(V_0[\xi_\alpha]\bar{\theta} + (e,\bar{\theta})\bar{\xi}_\alpha\Big),
\end{aligned} \tag{9.42}$$

where we used the definition of the vector $\boldsymbol{e}$ in Eq. (8.25). The second term on the right side of Eq. (9.41) is written as

$$
\begin{aligned}
-E[\bar{\boldsymbol{M}}^{-}\Delta_2^{*}\boldsymbol{M}\bar{\boldsymbol{\theta}}] &= -E\left[\bar{\boldsymbol{M}}^{-}\frac{1}{N}\sum_{\alpha=1}^{N}\Delta_1 W_\alpha(\Delta_1\boldsymbol{\xi}_\alpha,\bar{\boldsymbol{\theta}})\bar{\boldsymbol{\xi}}_\alpha\right] \\
&= -2\bar{\boldsymbol{M}}^{-}\frac{1}{N}\sum_{\alpha=1}^{N}\bar{W}_\alpha^2\left(\bar{\boldsymbol{\theta}}, E[\Delta_1\boldsymbol{\xi}_\alpha(\Delta_1^0\boldsymbol{M}\bar{\boldsymbol{\theta}})^\top]\bar{\boldsymbol{M}}^{-}V_0[\boldsymbol{\xi}_\alpha]\bar{\boldsymbol{\theta}}\right)\bar{\boldsymbol{\xi}}_\alpha.
\end{aligned}
\tag{9.43}
$$

The expression $E[\Delta_1\boldsymbol{\xi}_\alpha(\Delta_1^0\boldsymbol{M}\bar{\boldsymbol{\theta}})^\top]$ in the above equation is evaluated as follows:

$$
\begin{aligned}
E\left[\Delta_1\boldsymbol{\xi}_\alpha(\Delta_1^0\boldsymbol{M}\bar{\boldsymbol{\theta}})^\top\right] &= E\left[\Delta_1\boldsymbol{\xi}_\alpha\left(\frac{1}{N}\sum_{\beta=1}^{N}\bar{W}_\beta\left(\Delta_1\boldsymbol{\xi}_\beta\bar{\boldsymbol{\xi}}_\beta^\top+\bar{\boldsymbol{\xi}}_\beta\Delta_1\boldsymbol{\xi}_\beta^\top\right)\bar{\boldsymbol{\theta}}\right)^\top\right] \\
&= \frac{1}{N}\sum_{\beta=1}^{N}\bar{W}_\beta E\left[\Delta_1\boldsymbol{\xi}_\alpha\Delta_1\boldsymbol{\xi}_\beta^\top\right]\bar{\boldsymbol{\theta}}\bar{\boldsymbol{\xi}}_\beta^\top = \frac{\sigma^2}{N}\bar{W}_\alpha V_0[\boldsymbol{\xi}_\alpha]\bar{\boldsymbol{\theta}}\bar{\boldsymbol{\xi}}_\alpha^\top.
\end{aligned}
\tag{9.44}
$$

Hence, Eq. (9.43) has the following form:

$$
\begin{aligned}
-E[\bar{\boldsymbol{M}}^{-}\Delta_2^{*}\boldsymbol{M}\bar{\boldsymbol{\theta}}] &= -\frac{2\sigma^2}{N^2}\bar{\boldsymbol{M}}^{-}\sum_{\alpha=1}^{N}\bar{W}_\alpha^3(\bar{\boldsymbol{\theta}},V_0[\boldsymbol{\xi}_\alpha]\bar{\boldsymbol{\theta}})(\bar{\boldsymbol{\xi}}_\alpha,\bar{\boldsymbol{M}}^{-}V_0[\boldsymbol{\xi}_\alpha]\bar{\boldsymbol{\theta}})\bar{\boldsymbol{\xi}}_\alpha \\
&= -\frac{2\sigma^2}{N^2}\bar{\boldsymbol{M}}^{-}\sum_{\alpha=1}^{N}\bar{W}_\alpha^2(\bar{\boldsymbol{\xi}}_\alpha,\bar{\boldsymbol{M}}^{-}V_0[\boldsymbol{\xi}_\alpha]\bar{\boldsymbol{\theta}})\bar{\boldsymbol{\xi}}_\alpha.
\end{aligned}
\tag{9.45}
$$

Thus, Eq. (9.41) can be written in the form of Eq. (9.40). □

Lemma 9.4 (Expectation of $\bar{\boldsymbol{M}}^{-}\Delta_2\boldsymbol{L}\bar{\boldsymbol{\theta}}$)

$$
E[\bar{\boldsymbol{M}}^{-}\Delta_2\boldsymbol{L}\bar{\boldsymbol{\theta}}] = -\frac{\sigma^2}{N^2}\bar{\boldsymbol{M}}^{-}\sum_{\alpha=1}^{N}\bar{W}_\alpha^2(\bar{\boldsymbol{\xi}}_\alpha,\bar{\boldsymbol{M}}^{-}\bar{\boldsymbol{\xi}}_\alpha)V_0[\boldsymbol{\xi}_\alpha]\bar{\boldsymbol{\theta}} + \frac{\sigma^2}{N}\bar{\boldsymbol{M}}^{-}\sum_{\alpha=1}^{N}\bar{W}V_0[\boldsymbol{\xi}_\alpha]\bar{\boldsymbol{\theta}}. \tag{9.46}
$$

Proof. Substituting Eq. (9.9), we can write

$$
\begin{aligned}
&E[\bar{M}^{-}\Delta_2 L\bar{\theta}] \\
=&E\left[\frac{1}{N}\bar{M}^{-}\sum_{\alpha=1}^{N}\bar{W}_\alpha^2(\bar{\xi}_\alpha,\Delta_1\theta)^2 V_0[\xi_\alpha]\bar{\theta}\right]+E\left[\frac{1}{N}\bar{M}^{-}\sum_{\alpha=1}^{N}\bar{W}_\alpha^2(\bar{\xi}_\alpha,\Delta_1\theta)(\Delta_1\xi_\alpha,\bar{\theta})V_0[\xi_\alpha]\bar{\theta}\right] \\
&+E\left[\frac{1}{N}\bar{M}^{-}\sum_{\alpha=1}^{N}\bar{W}_\alpha^2(\Delta_1\xi_\alpha,\bar{\theta})(\bar{\xi}_\alpha,\Delta_1\theta)V_0[\xi_\alpha]\bar{\theta}\right]+E\left[\frac{1}{N}\bar{M}^{-}\sum_{\alpha=1}^{N}\bar{W}_\alpha^2(\Delta_1\xi_\alpha,\bar{\theta})^2 V_0[\xi_\alpha]\bar{\theta}\right] \\
=&\frac{\sigma^2}{N^2}\bar{M}^{-}\sum_{\alpha=1}^{N}\bar{W}_\alpha^2(\bar{\xi}_\alpha,\bar{M}^{-}\bar{\xi}_\alpha)V_0[\xi_\alpha]\bar{\theta}+\frac{1}{N}\bar{M}^{-}\sum_{\alpha=1}^{N}\bar{W}_\alpha^2(\bar{\xi}_\alpha,E[\Delta_1\theta\Delta_1\xi_\alpha^\top]\bar{\theta})V_0[\xi_\alpha]\bar{\theta} \\
&+\frac{1}{N}\bar{M}^{-}\sum_{\alpha=1}^{N}\bar{W}_\alpha^2(\bar{\theta},E[\Delta_1\xi_\alpha\Delta_1\theta^\top]\bar{\xi}_\alpha)V_0[\xi_\alpha]\bar{\theta}+\frac{\sigma^2}{N}\bar{M}^{-}\sum_{\alpha=1}^{N}\bar{W}V_0[\xi_\alpha]\bar{\theta},
\end{aligned}
\tag{9.47}
$$

where we have used Eq. (8.15). The expression $E[\Delta_1\theta\Delta_1\xi_\alpha^\top]$ in the above equation can be evaluated as follows:

$$
E[\Delta_1\theta\Delta_1\xi_\alpha^\top]=-E[\bar{M}^{-}\Delta_1^0 M\bar{\theta}\Delta_1\xi_\alpha^\top]=-\frac{\sigma^2}{N}\bar{M}^{-}\bar{W}_\alpha\bar{\xi}_\alpha\bar{\theta}^\top V_0[\xi_\alpha]. \tag{9.48}
$$

Hence, Eq. (9.47) has the form of Eq. (9.46). □

Substituting Eqs. (9.35), (9.40), and (9.46) into Eq. (9.16), we obtain Eq. (9.17).

9.5 SUPPLEMENTAL NOTE

The hyperaccurate correction technique was first presented by Kanatani [2006], and detailed covariance and bias analysis was given by Kanatani [2008]. However, the terms that contain the vector e were omitted in these analyses. It has been confirmed by experiments that the vector e plays no significant role in the final results. Later, the hyperaccurate correction technique was generalized by Kanatani and Sugaya [2013] to the problem with multiple constraints $(\xi^{(k)},\theta)=0$, $k=1,\ldots,L$, in which case Eq. (9.18) is replaced by

$$
\begin{aligned}
\Delta_c\theta=&-\frac{\sigma^2}{N}M_{n-1}^{-}\sum_{\alpha=1}^{N}\sum_{k,l=1}^{L}W_\alpha^{(kl)}(e_\alpha^{(k)},\theta)\xi_\alpha^{(l)} \\
&+\frac{\sigma^2}{N^2}M_{n-1}^{-}\sum_{\alpha=1}^{N}\sum_{k,l=1}^{L}W_\alpha^{(km)}W_\alpha^{(ln)}(\xi_\alpha^{(l)},M_{n-1}^{-}V_0^{(mn)}[\xi_\alpha]\theta)\xi_\alpha^{(k)},
\end{aligned}
\tag{9.49}
$$

where the matrix M and the weights $W_\alpha^{(kl)}$ are given by Eq. (8.50). The vector $e_\alpha^{(k)}$ is defined by Eq. (8.52). Thus, the hyperaccurate correction can be applied to a wide range of problems including the homography computation ($L = 3$, $r = 2$) described in Section 7.2. However, $\mathbf{e}_\alpha^{(k)} = \mathbf{0}$ for homography computation, as pointed out in the Supplemental Note (page 90) of the preceding chapter.

CHAPTER 10

Theoretical Accuracy Limit

We derive a theoretical limit on ellipse fitting accuracy, assuming Gaussian noise for ξ_α. It is given in the form of a bound, called the "KCR lower bound," on the covariance matrix of the solution θ. The resulting form indicates that all iterative algebraic and geometric methods achieve this bound up to higher order terms in σ, meaning that these are all optimal with respect to covariance. As in Chapters 8 and 9, we treat θ and ξ_α as n-D vectors for generality, and the result of this chapter applies to a wide variety of problems including the fundamental matrix computation described in Chapter 7.

10.1 KCR LOWER BOUND

We want to estimate from noisy observations ξ_α of the true values $\bar{\xi}_\alpha$ the ellipse parameter θ that should satisfy $(\bar{\xi}_\alpha, \theta) = 0$, $\alpha = 1, \ldots, N$, in the absence of noise. Evidently, whatever method we use, the estimate $\hat{\theta}$ that we compute is a "function" of the observations ξ_α in the form $\hat{\theta} = \hat{\theta}(\{\xi_\alpha\}_{\alpha=1}^N)$. Such a function is called an *estimator* of θ. It is an *unbiased estimator* if

$$E[\hat{\theta}] = \theta, \tag{10.1}$$

where $E[\cdot]$ is the expectation over the noise distribution. The important fact is that Eq. (10.1) must be satisfied *identically* in $\bar{\xi}_\alpha$ and θ, because unbiasedness is a property of the "estimation method," not the data or the ellipse.

Adopting the Gaussian noise assumption for ξ_α (though this is not strictly true; see Section 9.1), we regard ξ_α as Gaussian random variables of mean $\mathbf{0}$ and covariance matrices $V[\xi_\alpha]$ ($= \sigma^2 V_0[\xi_\alpha]$), independent for different α. Let the computed estimate be $\hat{\theta} = \theta + \Delta\theta$, and define its covariance matrix by

$$V[\theta] = P_\theta E\left[\Delta\theta\Delta\theta^\top\right] P_\theta. \tag{10.2}$$

We introduce the projection operation $P_\theta = I - \theta\theta^\top$ to the space orthogonal to θ ($\hookrightarrow$ Problem 6.1), because θ is normalized to unit norm. To be specific, the n-D vector θ is constrained to be on the $(n-1)$-D unit sphere S^{n-1} centered at the origin, and we are interested in the error behavior of $\boldsymbol{\theta}$ in the tangent space $T_{\boldsymbol{\theta}}(S^{n-1})$ to the unit sphere S^{n-1} at $\boldsymbol{\theta}$ (see Fig. 6.2 in Chapter 6). We now derive the following result.

Theorem 10.1 **(KCR lower bound)** *If $\hat{\boldsymbol{\theta}}$ is an unbiased estimator of $\boldsymbol{\theta}$, the inequality*

$$V[\boldsymbol{\theta}] \succ \frac{\sigma^2}{N}\left(\frac{1}{N}\sum_{\alpha=1}^{N}\bar{W}_\alpha\bar{\boldsymbol{\xi}}_\alpha\bar{\boldsymbol{\xi}}_\alpha^\top\right)^-, \qquad \bar{W}_\alpha = \frac{1}{(\boldsymbol{\theta}, V_0[\boldsymbol{\xi}_\alpha]\boldsymbol{\theta})} \tag{10.3}$$

holds for the covariance matrix $V[\boldsymbol{\theta}]$ of $\boldsymbol{\theta}$ irrespective of the estimation method, where the inequality $\boldsymbol{A} \succ \boldsymbol{B}$ means that $\boldsymbol{A} - \boldsymbol{B}$ is positive semidefinite.

The right side of Eq. (10.3) has rank $n-1$ and is called the *KCR* (*Kanatani-Cramer-Rao*) *lower bound*. Comparing Eq. (10.3) with Eqs. (8.2) and (8.15), we see that the solution of iterative reweight, renormalization, and hyper-renormalization achieves this bound to a first approximation. Since Eq. (8.14) is the same as Eq. (9.14), the Sampson error minimization solution also achieves this bound to a first approximation. Thus, all iterative algebraic and geometric methods are optimal as far as covariance is concerned. We now give the proof of Theorem 10.1.

10.2 DERIVATION OF THE KCR LOWER BOUND

From our noise assumption, the probability density of $\boldsymbol{\xi}_\alpha$ is

$$p(\boldsymbol{\xi}_\alpha) = C_\alpha \exp\left(-\frac{1}{2}(\boldsymbol{\xi}_\alpha - \bar{\boldsymbol{\xi}}_\alpha), V[\boldsymbol{\xi}_\alpha]^-(\boldsymbol{\xi}_\alpha - \bar{\boldsymbol{\xi}}_\alpha)\right), \tag{10.4}$$

where C_α is a normalization constant. Here, we use the pseudoinverse $V[\boldsymbol{\xi}_\alpha]^-$ rather than the inverse $V[\boldsymbol{\xi}_\alpha]^{-1}$, considering a general case of the covariance matrix $V[\boldsymbol{\xi}_\alpha]$ not being positive definite (for ellipse fitting and homography computation, the last column and row consist of 0; see Eqs. (1.21) and (7.12)). If $\hat{\boldsymbol{\theta}}$ is an unbiased estimator, the equality

$$E[\hat{\boldsymbol{\theta}} - \boldsymbol{\theta}] = \boldsymbol{0} \tag{10.5}$$

is an *identity* in $\bar{\boldsymbol{\xi}}_\alpha$ and $\boldsymbol{\theta}$. Hence, Eq. (10.5) is invariant to infinitesimal variations in $\bar{\boldsymbol{\xi}}_\alpha$ and $\boldsymbol{\theta}$. In other words,

$$\begin{aligned}\delta\int(\hat{\boldsymbol{\theta}} - \boldsymbol{\theta})p_1\cdots p_N d\boldsymbol{\xi} &= -\int(\delta\boldsymbol{\theta})p_1\cdots p_N d\boldsymbol{\xi} + \sum_{\alpha=1}^{N}\int(\hat{\boldsymbol{\theta}} - \boldsymbol{\theta})p_1\cdots\delta p_\alpha\cdots p_N d\boldsymbol{\xi}\\ &= -\delta\boldsymbol{\theta} + \int(\hat{\boldsymbol{\theta}} - \boldsymbol{\theta})\sum_{\alpha=1}^{N}(p_1\cdots\delta p_\alpha\cdots p_N)d\boldsymbol{\xi} = 0,\end{aligned} \tag{10.6}$$

where p_α is an abbreviation of $p(\boldsymbol{\xi}_\alpha)$ and we use the shorthand $\int d\boldsymbol{\xi} = \int\cdots\int d\boldsymbol{\xi}_1\cdots d\boldsymbol{\xi}_N$. We are considering variations in $\bar{\boldsymbol{\xi}}_\alpha$ (not $\boldsymbol{\xi}_\alpha$) and $\boldsymbol{\theta}$. Since the estimator $\hat{\boldsymbol{\theta}}$ is a function of the observations

ξ_α, it is not affected by such variations. Note that the variation $\delta\boldsymbol{\theta}$ is independent of ξ_α, so it can be moved outside the integral $\int d\xi$. Also note that $\int p_1 \cdots p_N d\xi = 1$. Using the logarithmic differentiation formula, we can write the infinitesimal variation of Eq. (10.4) with respect to $\bar{\xi}_\alpha$ in the form

$$\delta p_\alpha = p_\alpha \delta \log p_\alpha = p_\alpha (\nabla_{\bar{\xi}_\alpha} \log p_\alpha, \delta \xi_\alpha) = (\boldsymbol{l}_\alpha, \delta \xi_\alpha) p_\alpha, \tag{10.7}$$

where we define the *score functions* $\boldsymbol{l}_\alpha$ by

$$\boldsymbol{l}_\alpha \equiv \nabla_{\bar{\xi}_\alpha} \log p_\alpha. \tag{10.8}$$

Substituting Eq. (10.7) into Eq. (10.6), we obtain

$$\delta\boldsymbol{\theta} = \int (\hat{\boldsymbol{\theta}} - \boldsymbol{\theta}) \sum_{\alpha=1}^{N} (\boldsymbol{l}_\alpha, \delta\bar{\xi}_\alpha) p_1 \cdots p_N d\xi = E\left[(\hat{\boldsymbol{\theta}} - \boldsymbol{\theta}) \sum_{\alpha=1}^{N} (\boldsymbol{l}_\alpha, \delta\bar{\xi}_\alpha) \right]. \tag{10.9}$$

Due to the constraint $(\bar{\xi}_\alpha, \boldsymbol{\theta}) = 0$, the infinitesimal variations $\delta\bar{\xi}_\alpha$ and $\delta\boldsymbol{\theta}$ are constrained to be

$$(\bar{\boldsymbol{\theta}}, \delta\bar{\xi}_\alpha) + (\bar{\xi}_\alpha, \delta\boldsymbol{\theta}) = 0. \tag{10.10}$$

Consider the following particular variations $\delta\bar{\xi}_\alpha$:

$$\delta\bar{\xi}_\alpha = -\sum_{l,m=1}^{L} \bar{W}_\alpha (\bar{\xi}_\alpha, \delta\boldsymbol{\theta}) V_0[\xi_\alpha] \bar{\boldsymbol{\theta}}. \tag{10.11}$$

For this $\delta\bar{\xi}_\alpha$, Eq. (10.10) is satisfied for any variation $\delta\boldsymbol{\theta}$ of $\boldsymbol{\theta}$. In fact,

$$(\bar{\boldsymbol{\theta}}, \delta\bar{\xi}_\alpha) = -\bar{W}_\alpha (\bar{\xi}_\alpha, \delta\boldsymbol{\theta}) (\bar{\boldsymbol{\theta}}, V_0[\xi_\alpha] \bar{\boldsymbol{\theta}}) = -(\bar{\xi}_\alpha, \delta\boldsymbol{\theta}). \tag{10.12}$$

Substituting Eq. (10.11) into Eq. (10.9), we obtain

$$\begin{aligned} \delta\boldsymbol{\theta} &= -E\left[(\hat{\boldsymbol{\theta}} - \boldsymbol{\theta}) \sum_{\alpha=1}^{N} \bar{W}_\alpha (\bar{\xi}_\alpha, \delta\boldsymbol{\theta}) (\boldsymbol{l}_\alpha, V_0[\xi_\alpha] \bar{\boldsymbol{\theta}}) \right] \\ &= -E\left[(\hat{\boldsymbol{\theta}} - \boldsymbol{\theta}) \sum_{\alpha=1}^{N} \bar{W}_\alpha (\boldsymbol{l}_\alpha, V_0[\xi_\alpha] \bar{\boldsymbol{\theta}}) \bar{\xi}_\alpha^\top \right] \delta\boldsymbol{\theta} = -E\left[(\hat{\boldsymbol{\theta}} - \boldsymbol{\theta}) \sum_{\alpha=1}^{N} \boldsymbol{m}_\alpha^\top \right] \delta\boldsymbol{\theta}, \end{aligned} \tag{10.13}$$

where we define

$$\boldsymbol{m}_\alpha = \bar{W}_\alpha (\boldsymbol{l}_\alpha, V_0[\xi_\alpha] \bar{\boldsymbol{\theta}}) \bar{\xi}_\alpha. \tag{10.14}$$

We now derive the core inequality.

Proposition 10.2 **(Bound on the covariance matrix $V[\boldsymbol{\theta}]$)**

$$V[\boldsymbol{\theta}] \succ \boldsymbol{M}^-, \tag{10.15}$$

where

$$M = E\left[\left(\sum_{\alpha=1}^{N} m_\alpha\right)\left(\sum_{\beta=1}^{N} m_\beta\right)^\top\right]. \tag{10.16}$$

Proof. Equation (10.13) must hold for arbitrary infinitesimal variation $\delta\boldsymbol{\theta}$ of $\boldsymbol{\theta}$. However, we must not forget that $\boldsymbol{\theta}$ is normalized to unit norm. Hence, its infinitesimal variation $\delta\boldsymbol{\theta}$ is constrained to be orthogonal to $\boldsymbol{\theta}$. So, we can write $\delta\boldsymbol{\theta} = \boldsymbol{P}_\theta \delta\boldsymbol{u}$, where $\delta\boldsymbol{u}$ is an arbitrary infinitesimal variation and $\boldsymbol{P}_\theta$ ($\equiv \boldsymbol{I} - \boldsymbol{\theta}\boldsymbol{\theta}^\top$) is the orthogonal projection matrix onto the tangent space $T_\theta(S^{n-1})$ to the unit sphere S^{n-1} at $\boldsymbol{\theta}$. We obtain from Eq. (10.13)

$$\boldsymbol{P}_\theta E\left[(\hat{\boldsymbol{\theta}} - \boldsymbol{\theta})\sum_{\alpha=1}^{N} \boldsymbol{m}_\alpha^\top\right]\boldsymbol{P}_\theta\delta\boldsymbol{u} = -\boldsymbol{P}_\theta\delta\boldsymbol{u}. \tag{10.17}$$

Note that the constraint $(\bar{\boldsymbol{\xi}}_\alpha, \boldsymbol{\theta}) = 0$ implies $\boldsymbol{P}_\theta\bar{\boldsymbol{\xi}}_\alpha = \bar{\boldsymbol{\xi}}_\alpha$, so from Eq. (10.14) we see that $\boldsymbol{P}_\theta \boldsymbol{m}_\alpha = \boldsymbol{m}_\alpha$. Since Eq. (10.17) must hold for arbitrary (unconstrained) $\delta\boldsymbol{u}$, we conclude that

$$\boldsymbol{P}_\theta E\left[(\hat{\boldsymbol{\theta}} - \boldsymbol{\theta})\sum_{\alpha=1}^{N} \boldsymbol{m}_\alpha^\top\right] = -\boldsymbol{P}_\theta, \tag{10.18}$$

from which we obtain the identity

$$\begin{aligned} &E\left[\begin{pmatrix} \boldsymbol{P}_\theta(\hat{\boldsymbol{\theta}} - \boldsymbol{\theta}) \\ \sum_{\alpha=1}^N \boldsymbol{m}_\alpha \end{pmatrix}\begin{pmatrix} \boldsymbol{P}_\theta(\hat{\boldsymbol{\theta}} - \boldsymbol{\theta}) \\ \sum_{\beta=1}^N \boldsymbol{m}_\beta \end{pmatrix}^\top\right] \\ &= \begin{pmatrix} \boldsymbol{P}_\theta E[(\hat{\boldsymbol{\theta}} - \boldsymbol{\theta})(\hat{\boldsymbol{\theta}} - \boldsymbol{\theta})^\top]\boldsymbol{P}_\theta & \boldsymbol{P}_\theta E[(\hat{\boldsymbol{\theta}} - \boldsymbol{\theta})\sum_{\alpha=1}^N \boldsymbol{m}_\alpha^\top] \\ (\boldsymbol{P}_\theta E[(\hat{\boldsymbol{\theta}} - \boldsymbol{\theta})\sum_{\alpha=1}^N \boldsymbol{m}_\alpha^\top])^\top & E\left[(\sum_{\alpha=1}^N \boldsymbol{m}_\alpha)(\sum_{\beta=1}^N \boldsymbol{m}_\beta)^\top\right] \end{pmatrix} \\ &= \begin{pmatrix} V[\boldsymbol{\theta}] & -\boldsymbol{P}_\theta \\ -\boldsymbol{P}_\theta & \boldsymbol{M} \end{pmatrix}. \end{aligned} \tag{10.19}$$

Since the inside of the expectation $E[\,\cdot\,]$ is positive semidefinite, so is the rightmost side. A positive semidefinite matrix sandwiched by any matrix and its transpose is also positive semidefinite, so the following is also positive semidefinite:

$$\begin{aligned} &\begin{pmatrix} \boldsymbol{P}_\theta & \boldsymbol{M}^- \\ & \boldsymbol{M}^- \end{pmatrix}\begin{pmatrix} V[\boldsymbol{\theta}] & -\boldsymbol{P}_\theta \\ -\boldsymbol{P}_\theta & \boldsymbol{M} \end{pmatrix}\begin{pmatrix} \boldsymbol{P}_\theta & \\ \boldsymbol{M}^- & \boldsymbol{M}^- \end{pmatrix} \\ &= \begin{pmatrix} \boldsymbol{P}_\theta V[\boldsymbol{\theta}]\boldsymbol{P}_\theta - \boldsymbol{P}_\theta^2\boldsymbol{M}^- + \boldsymbol{M}^-\boldsymbol{P}_\theta^2 & -\boldsymbol{P}_\theta^2\boldsymbol{M}^- + \boldsymbol{M}^-\boldsymbol{M}\boldsymbol{M}^- \\ -\boldsymbol{M}^-\boldsymbol{P}_\theta^2 + \boldsymbol{M}^-\boldsymbol{M}\boldsymbol{M}^- & \boldsymbol{M}^-\boldsymbol{M}\boldsymbol{M}^- \end{pmatrix} \\ &= \begin{pmatrix} V[\boldsymbol{\theta}] - \boldsymbol{M}^- & \\ & \boldsymbol{M}^- \end{pmatrix}. \end{aligned} \tag{10.20}$$

Here, we have noted that $P_\theta^2 = P_\theta$ (↪ Problems 6.2) and $P_\theta m_\alpha = m_\alpha$, hence $P_\theta M = M P_\theta = M$ from Eq. (10.16). We have also used the properties $MM^- = M^- M = P_\theta$ and $M^- M M^- = M^-$ of the matrix M whose domain is $T_\theta(S^{n-1})$ (↪ Problems 8.3 and 8.4). The fact that Eq. (10.20) is positive semidefinite implies the inequality of Eq. (10.15). □

10.3 EXPRESSION OF THE KCR LOWER BOUND

What remains is to show that the pseudoinverse M^- of the matrix M in Eq. (10.16) has the expression in Eq. (10.3). To show this, we use the following facts.

Lemma 10.3 (Expectation of score) *The score functions l_α have expectation* $\mathbf{0}$*:*

$$E[l_\alpha] = \mathbf{0}. \tag{10.21}$$

Proof. Since $\int p_\alpha d\xi = 1$ is an identity in $\bar{\xi}_\alpha$, the gradient of the left side with respect to $\bar{\xi}_\alpha$ (not ξ_α) is identically $\mathbf{0}$. Using the logarithmic differentiation formula (see Eq. (10.7)), we have

$$\nabla_{\bar{\theta}_\alpha} \int p_\alpha d\xi = \int \nabla_{\bar{\theta}_\alpha} p_\alpha d\xi = \int p_\alpha \nabla_{\bar{\theta}_\alpha} \log p_\alpha d\xi = \int p_\alpha l_\alpha d\xi = E[l_\alpha]. \tag{10.22}$$

Hence, l_α has expectation $\mathbf{0}$. □

The matrix $E[l_\alpha l_\alpha^\top]$ is called the *Fisher information matrix* of $\bar{\xi}_\alpha$. It is related to the covariance matrix of ξ_α as follows.

Lemma 10.4 (Fisher information matrix)

$$E[l_\alpha l_\alpha^\top] = \frac{1}{\sigma^2} V_0[\xi_\alpha]^-. \tag{10.23}$$

Proof. From Eq. (10.4), the score functions l_α in Eq. (10.8) satisfy

$$l_\alpha = -V[\xi_\alpha]^- \Delta\xi_\alpha = -\frac{1}{\sigma^2} V_0[\xi_\alpha]^- \Delta\xi_\alpha. \tag{10.24}$$

Hence,

$$\begin{aligned} E[l_\alpha l_\alpha^\top] =& \frac{1}{\sigma^4} V_0[\xi_\alpha]^- E[\Delta\xi_\alpha \Delta\xi_\alpha^\top] V_0[\xi_\alpha]^- \\ =& \frac{1}{\sigma^2} V_0[\xi_\alpha]^- V_0[\xi_\alpha] V_0[\xi_\alpha]^- = \frac{1}{\sigma^2} V_0[\xi_\alpha]^-, \end{aligned} \tag{10.25}$$

where we have noted the identity $V_0[\xi_\alpha]^- V_0[\xi_\alpha] V_0[\xi_\alpha]^- = V_0[\xi_\alpha]^-$ (↪ Problem 8.3). □

Now, we are ready to show the following result.

Proposition 10.5 (Bound expression) *The matrix $\boldsymbol{M}$ in Eq. (10.16) has the following pseudoinverse:*

$$\boldsymbol{M}^{-} = \frac{\sigma^2}{N}\left(\frac{1}{N}\sum_{\alpha=1}^{N}\bar{W}_\alpha\bar{\boldsymbol{\xi}}_\alpha\bar{\boldsymbol{\xi}}_\alpha^\top\right)^{-}. \tag{10.26}$$

Proof. Since $E[\boldsymbol{l}_\alpha] = \boldsymbol{0}$, we see from Eq. (10.14) that $E[\boldsymbol{m}_\alpha] = \boldsymbol{0}$. Noise in different observations is independent, so $E[\boldsymbol{m}_\alpha\boldsymbol{m}_\beta^\top] = E[\boldsymbol{m}_\alpha]E[\boldsymbol{m}_\beta]^\top = \boldsymbol{O}$ for $\alpha \neq \beta$. Hence,

$$\begin{aligned}
\boldsymbol{M} &= \sum_{\alpha,\beta=1}^{N} E[\boldsymbol{m}_\alpha\boldsymbol{m}_\beta^\top] = \sum_{\alpha=1}^{N} E[\boldsymbol{m}_\alpha\boldsymbol{m}_\alpha^\top] = \sum_{\alpha=1}^{N}\bar{W}_\alpha^2 E[(\boldsymbol{l}_\alpha, V_0[\boldsymbol{\xi}_\alpha]\bar{\boldsymbol{\theta}})^2]\bar{\boldsymbol{\xi}}_\alpha\bar{\boldsymbol{\xi}}_\alpha^\top \\
&= \sum_{\alpha=1}^{N}\bar{W}_\alpha^2(\bar{\boldsymbol{\theta}}, V_0[\boldsymbol{\xi}_\alpha]E[\boldsymbol{l}_\alpha\boldsymbol{l}_\alpha^\top]V_0[\boldsymbol{\xi}_\alpha]\bar{\boldsymbol{\theta}})\bar{\boldsymbol{\xi}}_\alpha\bar{\boldsymbol{\xi}}_\alpha^\top \\
&= \frac{1}{\sigma^2}\sum_{\alpha=1}^{N}\bar{W}_\alpha^2(\bar{\boldsymbol{\theta}}, V_0[\boldsymbol{\xi}_\alpha]V_0[\boldsymbol{\xi}_\alpha]^- V_0[\boldsymbol{\xi}_\alpha]\bar{\boldsymbol{\theta}})\bar{\boldsymbol{\xi}}_\alpha\bar{\boldsymbol{\xi}}_\alpha^\top \\
&= \frac{1}{\sigma^2}\sum_{\alpha=1}^{N}\bar{W}_\alpha^2(\bar{\boldsymbol{\theta}}, V_0[\boldsymbol{\xi}_\alpha]\bar{\boldsymbol{\theta}})\bar{\boldsymbol{\xi}}_\alpha\bar{\boldsymbol{\xi}}_\alpha^\top = \frac{N}{\sigma^2}\frac{1}{N}\sum_{\alpha=1}^{N}\bar{W}_\alpha\bar{\boldsymbol{\xi}}_\alpha\bar{\boldsymbol{\xi}}_\alpha^\top,
\end{aligned} \tag{10.27}$$

where we have used Eq. (10.23) and the identity $V_0[\boldsymbol{\xi}_\alpha]V_0[\boldsymbol{\xi}_\alpha]^- V_0[\boldsymbol{\xi}_\alpha] = V_0[\boldsymbol{\xi}_\alpha]$ (↪ Problem 8.3). Thus, we obtain Eq. (10.26). □

10.4 SUPPLEMENTAL NOTE

The KCR lower bound of Eq. (10.3) was first derived by Kanatani [1996] in a much more general framework of nonlinear constraint fitting. This KCR lower bound is closely related to the *Cramer-Rao lower bound* in traditional statistics, so in Kanatani [1996] the bound of Eq. (10.3) was simply called the "Cramer-Rao lower bound." Pointing out its difference from the Cramer-Rao lower bound, Chernov and Lesort [2004] named it the "KCR (Kanatani-Cramer-Rao) lower bond" and gave a rigorous proof in a linear estimation framework. The proof of this chapter was based on Kanatani [2008]. In Kanatani [1996], the KCR lower bound of Eq. (10.3) is generalized to the problem with multiple constraints, $(\boldsymbol{\xi}_\alpha^{(k)}, \boldsymbol{\theta}) = 0$, $k = 1, ..., L$, among which only r are independent, in the following form:

$$V[\boldsymbol{\theta}] \succ \frac{\sigma^2}{N}\left(\frac{1}{N}\sum_{\alpha=1}^{N}\sum_{k,l=1}^{L}\bar{W}_\alpha^{(kl)}\bar{\boldsymbol{\xi}}_\alpha^{(k)}\bar{\boldsymbol{\xi}}_\alpha^{(l)\top}\right)^{-}, \qquad \bar{W}_\alpha^{(kl)} = \Big((\boldsymbol{\theta}, V_0^{(kl)}[\boldsymbol{\xi}_\alpha]\boldsymbol{\theta})\Big)^{-}. \tag{10.28}$$

(The matrix on the right side of the second equation has rank r.) Thus, the KCR lower bound for homography computation ($L = 3$, $r = 2$) described in Section 7.2 is given in this form.

The difference of the KCR lower bound from the Cramer-Rao lower bound originates from the difference of geometric estimation, such as ellipse fitting, from traditional statistical estimation. In traditional statistics, we model a random phenomenon as a parameterized probability density $p(\boldsymbol{\xi}|\boldsymbol{\theta})$, which is called the *statistical model*, and estimate the parameter $\boldsymbol{\theta}$ from noisy instances $\boldsymbol{\xi}_1, \ldots, \boldsymbol{\xi}_N$ of $\boldsymbol{\xi}$ obtained by repeated sampling. In ellipse fitting, in contrast, the constraint $(\boldsymbol{\xi}, \boldsymbol{\theta}) = 0$ is an *implicit* equation of $\boldsymbol{\theta}$. If we are to deal with this problem in the traditional framework of statistics, the procedure goes as follows. Suppose the observation $\boldsymbol{\xi}_\alpha$ and the parameter $\boldsymbol{\theta}$ are both n-D vectors. We introduce m-D auxiliary variables $\boldsymbol{X}_1, \ldots, \boldsymbol{X}_N$ so that the true value $\bar{\boldsymbol{\xi}}_\alpha$ of $\boldsymbol{\xi}_\alpha$ can be expressed as a function of $\boldsymbol{X}_\alpha$ and $\boldsymbol{\theta}$ in the form of $\bar{\boldsymbol{\xi}}_\alpha = \bar{\boldsymbol{\xi}}_\alpha(\boldsymbol{X}_\alpha, \boldsymbol{\theta})$. For example, if $\boldsymbol{\xi}_\alpha$ are some image measurements of the αth point $\boldsymbol{X}_\alpha$ in the scene and $\boldsymbol{\theta}$ encodes the camera parameters, then $\bar{\boldsymbol{\xi}}_\alpha(\boldsymbol{X}_\alpha, \boldsymbol{\theta})$ is the measurements of that point we would obtain in the absence of noise by using the camera specified by $\boldsymbol{\theta}$. For ellipse fitting, $\boldsymbol{X}_\alpha$ can be chosen to be the angle ϕ_α (from a fixed direction) of the moving radius from the center of the ellipse specified by $\bar{\boldsymbol{\theta}}$. Our goal is to jointly estimate $\boldsymbol{X}_1, \ldots, \boldsymbol{X}_N$, and $\boldsymbol{\theta}$ from noisy observations $\boldsymbol{\xi}_\alpha = \bar{\boldsymbol{\xi}}_\alpha + \boldsymbol{\varepsilon}_\alpha$, where $\boldsymbol{\varepsilon}_\alpha$ indicates random noise. Let $p(\{\boldsymbol{\varepsilon}_\alpha\}_{\alpha=1}^N)$ be the probability density of the noise.

The Cramer-Rao lower bound is obtained as follows. First, consider $\log p(\{\boldsymbol{\xi}_\alpha - \bar{\boldsymbol{\xi}}_\alpha(\boldsymbol{X}_\alpha, \boldsymbol{\theta})\}_{\alpha=1}^N)$. Next, evaluate its second derivatives with respect to $\boldsymbol{X}_1, \ldots, \boldsymbol{X}_N$, and $\boldsymbol{\theta}$ (or multiply its first derivatives each other) to define an $(mN + n) \times (mN + n)$ matrix. Then, take expectation of that matrix with respect to the density $p(\{\boldsymbol{\xi}_\alpha - \bar{\boldsymbol{\xi}}_\alpha(\boldsymbol{X}_\alpha, \boldsymbol{\theta})\}_{\alpha=1}^N)$. The resulting matrix is called the *Fisher information matrix*, and its inverse is called the *Cramer-Rao lower bound* on the (joint) covariance matrix of $\boldsymbol{X}_1, \ldots, \boldsymbol{X}_N$, and $\boldsymbol{\theta}$. The auxiliary variables $\boldsymbol{X}_1, \ldots, \boldsymbol{X}_N$ are also known as the *nuisance parameters*, while $\boldsymbol{\theta}$ is called the *structural parameter* or *parameter of interest*. Usually, we are interested only in the covariance of $\boldsymbol{\theta}$, so we take out from the $(mN + n) \times (mN + n)$ joint covariance matrix the $n \times n$ lower right submatrix, which can be shown to coincide with the KCR lower bound of Eq. (10.3).

However, evaluating and inverting the large Fisher information matrix, whose size can grow quickly as the number N of observations increases, is a heavy burden both analytically and computationally. The KCR lower bound in Eq. (10.3) is expressed only in terms of the parameter $\boldsymbol{\theta}$ of interest without involving auxiliary nuisance parameters, resulting in significant analytical and computational efficiency, yet giving the same value as the Cramer-Rao lower bound.

Answers

Chapter 1

1.1. (1) We minimize $(1/N)\sum_{\alpha=1}^{N}(\xi_\alpha, \boldsymbol{n})^2$ subject to $\|\boldsymbol{n}\| = 1$. Corresponding to Procedure 1.1, the computation goes as follows.

1. Compute the 3×3 matrix

$$\boldsymbol{M} = \frac{1}{N}\sum_{\alpha=1}^{N} \xi_\alpha \xi_\alpha^\top.$$

2. Solve the eigenvalue problem $\boldsymbol{M}\boldsymbol{n} = \lambda \boldsymbol{n}$, and return the unit eigenvector $\boldsymbol{n}$ for the smallest eigenvalue λ.

(2) We obtain the following expression:

$$V[\xi_\alpha] = E[\Delta\xi_\alpha \Delta\xi_\alpha^\top] = E[\begin{pmatrix} \Delta x_\alpha \\ \Delta y_\alpha \\ 0 \end{pmatrix}\begin{pmatrix} \Delta x_\alpha \\ \Delta y_\alpha \\ 0 \end{pmatrix}^\top]$$
$$= \begin{pmatrix} E[\Delta x_\alpha^2] & E[\Delta x_\alpha \Delta y_\alpha] & 0 \\ E[\Delta y_\alpha \Delta y_\alpha] & E[\Delta y_\alpha^2] & 0 \\ 0 & 0 & 0 \end{pmatrix} = \sigma^2 \begin{pmatrix} 1 & 0 & 0 \\ 0 & 1 & 0 \\ 0 & 0 & 0 \end{pmatrix}.$$

Chapter 2

2.1. The procedure goes as follows.

1. Compute the 6×6 matrices

$$\boldsymbol{M} = \frac{1}{N}\sum_{\alpha=1}^{N} \xi_\alpha \xi_\alpha^\top, \qquad \boldsymbol{N} = \frac{1}{N}\sum_{\alpha=1}^{N} V_0[\xi_\alpha].$$

2. Solve the generalized eigenvalue problem $\boldsymbol{M}\boldsymbol{\theta} = \lambda \boldsymbol{N}\boldsymbol{\theta}$, and return the unit generalized eigenvector $\boldsymbol{\theta}$ for the smallest generalized eigenvalue λ.

2.2. The procedure goes as follows.

1. Compute the 6×6 matrices

$$
\begin{aligned}
\boldsymbol{M} &= \frac{1}{N}\sum_{\alpha=1}^{N} \boldsymbol{\xi}_\alpha \boldsymbol{\xi}_\alpha^\top, \\
\boldsymbol{N} &= \frac{1}{N}\sum_{\alpha=1}^{N}\Big(V_0[\boldsymbol{\xi}_\alpha] + 2\mathcal{S}[\boldsymbol{\xi}_\alpha \boldsymbol{e}^\top]\Big) - \frac{1}{N^2}\sum_{\alpha=1}^{N}\Big((\boldsymbol{\xi}_\alpha, \boldsymbol{M}_5^- \boldsymbol{\xi}_\alpha) V_0[\boldsymbol{\xi}_\alpha] \\
&\quad + 2\mathcal{S}[V_0[\boldsymbol{\xi}_\alpha]\boldsymbol{M}_5^- \boldsymbol{\xi}_\alpha \boldsymbol{\xi}_\alpha^\top]\Big).
\end{aligned}
$$

2. Solve the generalized eigenvalue problem $\boldsymbol{M}\boldsymbol{\theta} = \lambda \boldsymbol{N}\boldsymbol{\theta}$, and return the unit generalized eigenvector for the eigenvalue λ of the smallest absolute value.

Chapter 3

3.1. The gradient of Eq. (3.3) with respect to $\boldsymbol{\theta}$ is written as

$$
\nabla_{\boldsymbol{\theta}} J = \frac{1}{N}\sum_{\alpha=1}^{N} \frac{2(\boldsymbol{\xi}_\alpha, \boldsymbol{\theta})\boldsymbol{\xi}_\alpha}{(\boldsymbol{\theta}, V_0[\boldsymbol{\xi}_\alpha]\boldsymbol{\theta})} - \frac{1}{N}\sum_{\alpha=1}^{N} \frac{2(\boldsymbol{\xi}_\alpha, \boldsymbol{\theta})^2 V_0[\boldsymbol{\xi}_\alpha]\boldsymbol{\theta}}{(\boldsymbol{\theta}, V_0[\boldsymbol{\xi}_\alpha]\boldsymbol{\theta})^2} = 2(\boldsymbol{M} - \boldsymbol{L})\boldsymbol{\theta} = 2\boldsymbol{X}\boldsymbol{\theta},
$$

where $\boldsymbol{M}$, $\boldsymbol{L}$, and $\boldsymbol{X}$ are the matrices defined in Eqs. (3.4) and (3.5).

Chapter 5

5.1. If the curve of Eq. (5.1) is translated in the x and y directions by $-x_c$ and $-y_c$, respectively, where x_c and y_c are defined by Eq. (5.5), the ellipse is centered at the origin O in the form

$$
Ax^2 + 2Bxy + Cy^2 = c, \qquad c = Ax_c^2 + 2Bx_c y_c + Cy_c^2 - f_0 F.
$$

If the xy coordinate system is rotated around the origin by angle θ, there exists a θ such that the curve equation has the form

$$
\lambda_1 x'^2 + \lambda_2 y'^2 = c,
$$

in the rotated $x'y'$ coordinate system. As is well known in linear algebra, the values λ_1 and λ_2 are the eigenvalues of the matrix $\begin{pmatrix} A & B \\ B & C \end{pmatrix}$, and $\begin{pmatrix} \cos\theta \\ \sin\theta \end{pmatrix}$ and $\begin{pmatrix} -\sin\theta \\ \cos\theta \end{pmatrix}$ are the corresponding eigenvectors. This curve is an ellipse when λ_1 and λ_2 have the same sign, i.e., when $\lambda_1\lambda_2 > 0$. Since the eigenvalues λ_1 and λ_2 are the solutions of the secular equation

$$
\begin{vmatrix} \lambda - A & -B \\ -B & \lambda - C \end{vmatrix} = \lambda^2 - (A + C)\lambda + (AC - B^2) = 0,
$$

we have $\lambda_1\lambda_2 = AC - B^2$. Hence, the curve is an ellipse when $AC - B^2 > 0$. It is a real ellipse if λ_1 and λ_2 have the same sign as c, and an imaginary ellipse otherwise. The curve is a parabola if one of λ_1 and λ_2 is 0, i.e., $\lambda_1\lambda_2 = 0$, and is a hyperbola if λ_1 and λ_2 have different signs, i.e., $\lambda_1\lambda_2 < 0$. These correspond to $AC - B^2 = 0$ and $AC - B^2 < 0$, respectively.

5.2. (1) Expanding the left side, we can see that the cubic term in λ is λ^3. We also see that the quadratic term is $(A_{11} + A_{22} + A_{33})\lambda^2$, i.e., $\lambda^2\mathrm{tr}[\boldsymbol{A}]$, and that the coefficient of the linear term is the sum of the minors of $\boldsymbol{A}$ obtained by removing the row and column containing each diagonal element in turn, i.e., $A^\dagger_{11} + A^\dagger_{22} + A^\dagger_{33} = \mathrm{tr}[\boldsymbol{A}^\dagger]$. The constant term is obtained by letting $\lambda = 0$, i.e., $|\boldsymbol{A}|$.

(2) Since $\boldsymbol{A}^{-1} = \boldsymbol{A}^\dagger/|\boldsymbol{A}|$, we obtain

$$|\lambda\boldsymbol{A} + \boldsymbol{B}| = |\boldsymbol{A}| \cdot |\lambda\boldsymbol{I} + \boldsymbol{A}^{-1}\boldsymbol{B}| = |\boldsymbol{A}| \cdot \left|\lambda\boldsymbol{I} + \frac{\boldsymbol{A}^\dagger}{|\boldsymbol{A}|}\boldsymbol{B}\right|.$$

Evidently, the cubic term in λ is $|\boldsymbol{A}|\lambda^3$, and the coefficient of the quadratic term is, from the above result of (1), $|\boldsymbol{A}|\mathrm{tr}[(\boldsymbol{A}^\dagger/|\boldsymbol{A}|)\boldsymbol{B}] = \mathrm{tr}[\boldsymbol{A}^\dagger\boldsymbol{B}]$. Letting $\lambda = 0$, we see that the constant term is $|\boldsymbol{B}|$. On the other hand, note the equality

$$|\lambda\boldsymbol{A} + \boldsymbol{B}| = \lambda^3\left|\frac{\boldsymbol{B}}{\lambda} + \boldsymbol{A}\right|.$$

The coefficient of λ equals the coefficient of $1/\lambda^2$ in $|\boldsymbol{B}/\lambda + \boldsymbol{A}|$, which equals $\mathrm{tr}[\boldsymbol{B}^\dagger\boldsymbol{A}]$ $(= \mathrm{tr}[\boldsymbol{A}\boldsymbol{B}^\dagger])$ from the above result. Thus, we obtain Eq. (5.55). The above argument assumes that $\boldsymbol{A}$ has its inverse $\boldsymbol{A}^{-1}$ and that $\lambda \neq 0$. However, Eq. (5.55) is a polynomial in $\boldsymbol{A}$ and λ. Hence, this is a "polynomial identity," holding for all $\boldsymbol{A}$ and λ including the case of $|\boldsymbol{A}| = 0$ and $\lambda = 0$.

5.3. Equation (1.1) is rearranged in terms of x in the form

$$Ax^2 + 2(By + Df_0)x + (Cy^2 + 2f_0Ey + f_0^2F) = 0,$$

which is factorized as follows:

$$A(x - \alpha)(y - \beta) = 0,$$

$$\alpha, \beta = \frac{-(By + Df_0) \pm \sqrt{(By + Df_0)^2 - A(Cy^2 + 2f_0Ey + f_0^2F)}}{A}.$$

Since $|\boldsymbol{Q}| = 0$, the quadratic equation degenerates into the product of two linear terms. Hence, the inside of the square root

$$(B^2 - AC)y^2 + 2f_0(BD - AE)y + f_0^2(D^2 - AF)$$

is a square of a linear expression in y. If $B^2 - AC > 0$, it has the form

$$\left(\sqrt{B^2 - AC}\,y + f_0 \frac{BD - AE}{\sqrt{B^2 - AC}}\right)^2.$$

Thus, we obtain the following factorization:

$$A\left(x - \frac{-(By + Df_0) + \sqrt{B^2 - AC}\,y + f_0(BD - AE)/\sqrt{B^2 - AC}}{A}\right)$$
$$\times\left(x - \frac{-(By + Df_0) - \sqrt{B^2 - AC}\,y - f_0(BD - AE)/\sqrt{B^2 - AC}}{A}\right) = 0.$$

Equation (5.56) results from this.

5.4. If $n_2 \neq 0$, we substitute $y = -(n_1 x + n_3 f_0)/n_2$ into Eq. (5.1) to obtain

$$Ax^2 - 2Bx(n_1 x + n_3 f_0)/n_2 + C(n_1 x + n_3 f_0)^2/n_2^2$$
$$+2f_0(Dx - E(n_1 x + n_3 f_0)/n_2) + f_0^2 F = 0.$$

Expanding this, we obtain the following quadratic equation in x:

$$(An_2^2 - 2Bn_1 n_2 + Cn_1^2)x^2 + 2f_0(Dn_2^2 + Cn_1 n_3 - Bn_2 n_3 - En_1 n_2)x$$
$$+(Cn_3^2 - 2En_2 n_3 + Fn_2^2)f_0^2 = 0.$$

If we let x_i, $i = 1, 2$, be the two roots, y_i is given by $y_i = -(n_1 x_i + n_3 f_0)/n_2$. If $n_2 \approx 0$, we substitute $x = -(n_2 y + n_3 f_0)/n_1$ into Eq. (5.1) to obtain

$$A(n_2 x + n_3 f_0)^2/n_1^2 - 2Bx(n_2 y + n_3 f_0)/n_1 + Cy^2$$
$$+2f_0(-D(n_2 y + n_3 f_0)/n_1 + Ey) + f_0^2 F = 0.$$

Expanding this, we obtain the following quadratic equation in y:

$$(An_2^2 - 2Bn_1 n_2 + Cn_1^2)y^2 + 2f_0(En_1^2 + An_2 n_3 - Bn_1 n_3 - Dn_1 n_2)y$$
$$+(An_3^2 - 2Dn_1 n_3 + Fn_1^2)f_0^2 = 0.$$

If we let y_i, $i = 1, 2$, be the two roots, x_i is given by $x_i = -(n_2 x_i + n_3 f_0)/n_1$. In actual computation, in stead of considering if $n_2 \neq 0$ or $n_2 \approx 0$, we compute the former solution when$|n_2| \geq |n_1|$ and the latter solution when $|n_2| < |n_1|$. If the quadratic equation has imaginary roots, the line does not intersect the ellipse. If it has a double root, we obtain the tangent point.

5.5. The normal to the line $n_1 x + n_2 y + n_3 f_0 = 0$ is given by $(n_1, n_2)^\top$. The normal to a curve $F(x, y) = 0$ at $(x_0, y_0)^\top$ is given up to scale by $\nabla F = (\partial F/\partial x, \partial F/\partial y)$. Hence, the normal $(n_1, n_2)^\top$ to the curve of Eq. (5.1) at (x_0, y_0) is given up to scale by

$$n_1 = Ax_0 + By_0 + f_0 D, \qquad n_2 = Bx_0 + Cy_0 + f_0 E.$$

The line passing through (x_0, y_0) having normal $(n_1, n_2)^\top$ is given by

$$n_1(x - x_0) + n_2(x - x_0) + n_3 f_0 = 0.$$

After expansion using $Ax_0^2 + 2Bx_0y_0 + Cy_0^2 + 2f_0(Dx_0 + Ey_0) + f_0^2 F = 0$, we obtain the line $n_1 x + n_2 y + n_3 f_0 = 0$ given by Eq. (5.8).

5.6. We only need to read (x_α, y_α) in Procedure 3.2 as (a, b) and remove the step of updating the ellipse. Hence, we obtain the following procedure.

1. Represent the ellipse by the 6-D vector $\boldsymbol{\theta}$ as in Eq. (1.8), and let $J_0^* = \infty$ (a sufficiently large number), $\hat{a} = a$, $\hat{b} = b$, and $\tilde{a} = \tilde{b} = 0$.
2. Compute the normalized covariance matrix $V_0[\hat{\boldsymbol{\xi}}]$ obtained by replacing $\bar{x}_\alpha$ and $\bar{y}_\alpha$ of $V_0[\boldsymbol{\xi}_\alpha]$ in Eq. (1.21) by $\hat{a}$ and $\hat{b}$, respectively.
3. Compute

$$\boldsymbol{\xi}^* = \begin{pmatrix} \hat{a}^2 + 2\hat{a}\tilde{a} \\ 2(\hat{a}\hat{b} + \hat{b}\tilde{a} + \hat{a}\tilde{b}) \\ \hat{b}^2 + 2\hat{b}\tilde{b} \\ 2f_0(\hat{a} + \tilde{a}) \\ 2f_0(\hat{b} + \tilde{b}) \\ f_0 \end{pmatrix}.$$

4. Update $\tilde{a}$, $\tilde{b}$, $\hat{a}$, and $\hat{b}$ as follows:

$$\begin{pmatrix} \tilde{a} \\ \tilde{b} \end{pmatrix} \leftarrow \frac{2(\boldsymbol{\xi}^*, \boldsymbol{\theta})^2}{(\boldsymbol{\theta}, V_0[\hat{\boldsymbol{\xi}}]\boldsymbol{\theta})} \begin{pmatrix} \theta_1 & \theta_2 & \theta_4 \\ \theta_2 & \theta_3 & \theta_5 \end{pmatrix} \begin{pmatrix} \hat{a} \\ \hat{b} \\ f_0 \end{pmatrix}, \qquad \hat{a} \leftarrow a - \tilde{a}, \qquad \hat{b} \leftarrow b - \tilde{b}.$$

5. Compute

$$J^* = \tilde{a}^2 + \tilde{b}^2.$$

If $J^* \approx J_0$, return $(\hat{a}, \hat{b})$ and stop. Else, let $J_0 \leftarrow J^*$, and go back to Step 2.

5.7. Transposition of $\boldsymbol{A}\boldsymbol{A}^{-1} = \boldsymbol{I}$ on both side gives $(\boldsymbol{A}^{-1})^\top \boldsymbol{A}^\top = \boldsymbol{I}$. This means that $(\boldsymbol{A}^{-1})^\top$ is the inverse of $\boldsymbol{A}^\top$, i.e., $(\boldsymbol{A}^{-1})^\top = (\boldsymbol{A}^\top)^{-1}$.

5.8. Since $(x, y, f)^\top$ is the direction of the line of sight, we can write $X = cx$, $Y = cy$, $Z = cf$ for some c. This point is on the supporting plane $n_1 X + n_2 Y + n_3 Z = h$, so $c(n_1 x + n_2 y + n_3 f) = h$ holds. Hence, $c = h/(n_1 x + n_2 y + n_3 f)$, and X, Y, and Z are given by Eq. (5.57).

5.9. The unit vector along the Z-axis is $\boldsymbol{k} = (0, 0, 1)^\top$. Let Ω be the angle made by $\boldsymbol{n}$ and $\boldsymbol{k}$ (positive for rotating $\boldsymbol{n}$ toward $\boldsymbol{k}$ screw-wise). It is computed by

$$\Omega = \sin^{-1} \|\boldsymbol{n} \times \boldsymbol{k}\|.$$

The unit vector orthogonal to both $\boldsymbol{n}$ and $\boldsymbol{k}$ is given by

$$\boldsymbol{l} = \mathcal{N}[\boldsymbol{n} \times \boldsymbol{k}].$$

The rotion around $\boldsymbol{l}$ by angle Ω screw-wise is given by the matrix

$$\boldsymbol{R} = \begin{pmatrix} \cos\Omega + l_1^2(1-\cos\Omega) & l_1 l_2(1-\cos\Omega) - l_3\sin\Omega & l_1 l_3(1-\cos\Omega) + l_2\sin\Omega \\ l_2 l_1(1-\cos\Omega) + l_3\sin\Omega & \cos\Omega + l_2^2(1-\cos\Omega) & l_2 l_3(1-\cos\Omega) - l_1\sin\Omega \\ l_3 l_1(1-\cos\Omega) - l_2\sin\Omega & l_3 l_2(1-\cos\Omega) + l_1\sin\Omega & \cos\Omega + l_3^2(1-\cos\Omega) \end{pmatrix}.$$

5.10. Let $I(i, j)$ be the value of the pixel with integer coordinates (i, j). For non-integer coordinates (x, y), let (i, j) be their integer parts, and (ξ, η) $(= (x - i, y - j))$ their fraction parts. We compute $I(x, y)$ by the following bilinear interpolation:

$$\begin{aligned} I(x, y) = (1-\xi)(1-\eta)I(i, j) + \xi(1-\eta)I(i+1, j) \\ +(1-\xi)\eta I(i, j+1) + \xi\eta I(i+1, j+1). \end{aligned}$$

This means that we first do linear interpolation in the j-direction, combining $I(i, j)$ and $I(i, j+1)$ in the ratio $\eta : 1-\eta$, combining $I(i+1, j)$ and $I(i, j+1)$ in the ratio $\eta : 1-\eta$, and then combining these in the i-direction in the ratio $\xi : 1-\xi$. We obtain the same result if we change the order, linearly interpolating first in the i-direction and then in the j-direction.

Chapter 6

6.1 Let θ be the angle made by $\boldsymbol{u}$ and $\boldsymbol{v}$ (Fig. 6.12). The length of the projection of $\boldsymbol{v}$ onto the line in the direction of the unit vector $\boldsymbol{u}$ is given by

$$\|\boldsymbol{v}\| \cos\theta = \|\boldsymbol{u}\| \|\boldsymbol{v}\| \cos\theta = (\boldsymbol{u}, \boldsymbol{v}).$$

Hence, $\boldsymbol{v}$ has the component $(\boldsymbol{u}, \boldsymbol{v})\boldsymbol{u}$ in the $\boldsymbol{u}$ direction. It follows that the projection of $\boldsymbol{v}$ onto the plane is given by

$$\boldsymbol{u} - (\boldsymbol{u}, \boldsymbol{v})\boldsymbol{u} = \boldsymbol{u} - \boldsymbol{u}\boldsymbol{u}^\top\boldsymbol{v} = (\boldsymbol{I} - \boldsymbol{u}\boldsymbol{u}^\top)\boldsymbol{v} = \boldsymbol{P}_{\boldsymbol{u}}\boldsymbol{v}.$$

6.2 We see that

$$\begin{aligned} \boldsymbol{P}_{\boldsymbol{u}}^2 &= (\boldsymbol{I} - \boldsymbol{u}\boldsymbol{u}^\top)(\boldsymbol{I} - \boldsymbol{u}\boldsymbol{u}^\top) = \boldsymbol{I} - \boldsymbol{u}\boldsymbol{u}^\top - \boldsymbol{u}\boldsymbol{u}^\top + \boldsymbol{u}\boldsymbol{u}^\top\boldsymbol{u}\boldsymbol{u}^\top = \boldsymbol{I} - 2\boldsymbol{u}\boldsymbol{u}^\top + \boldsymbol{u}(\boldsymbol{u}, \boldsymbol{u})\boldsymbol{u}^\top \\ &= \boldsymbol{I} - 2\boldsymbol{u}\boldsymbol{u}^\top + \boldsymbol{u}\boldsymbol{u}^\top = \boldsymbol{I} - \boldsymbol{u}\boldsymbol{u}^\top = \boldsymbol{P}_{\boldsymbol{u}}. \end{aligned}$$

Chapter 7

7.1 (1) Let

$$F = U \begin{pmatrix} \sigma_1 & 0 & 0 \\ 0 & \sigma_2 & 0 \\ 0 & 0 & \sigma_3 \end{pmatrix} V^\top, \qquad \sigma_1 \geq \sigma_2 \geq \sigma_3 > 0, \qquad (*)$$

be the singular value decomposition of the matrix F. Using the identities $\mathrm{tr}[A^\top A] = \|A\|^2$ and $\mathrm{tr}[AB] = \mathrm{tr}[BA]$ about the matrix trace and noting that U and V are orthogonal matrices, we obtain the following expression:

$$\begin{aligned}
\|F\|^2 &= \mathrm{tr}[F^\top F] = \mathrm{tr}[V \begin{pmatrix} \sigma_1 & 0 & 0 \\ 0 & \sigma_2 & 0 \\ 0 & 0 & \sigma_3 \end{pmatrix} U^\top U \begin{pmatrix} \sigma_1 & 0 & 0 \\ 0 & \sigma_2 & 0 \\ 0 & 0 & \sigma_3 \end{pmatrix} V^\top] \\
&= \mathrm{tr}[V \begin{pmatrix} \sigma_1^2 & 0 & 0 \\ 0 & \sigma_2^2 & 0 \\ 0 & 0 & \sigma_3^2 \end{pmatrix} V^\top] = \mathrm{tr}[\begin{pmatrix} \sigma_1^2 & 0 & 0 \\ 0 & \sigma_2^2 & 0 \\ 0 & 0 & \sigma_3^2 \end{pmatrix} V^\top V] \\
&= \mathrm{tr} \begin{pmatrix} \sigma_1^2 & 0 & 0 \\ 0 & \sigma_2^2 & 0 \\ 0 & 0 & \sigma_3^2 \end{pmatrix} \\
&= \sigma_1^2 + \sigma_2^2 + \sigma_3^2.
\end{aligned}$$

(2) We first compute the singular value decomposition of F in the form of the above $(*)$ and replace the smallest eigenvalue σ_3 by 0 to make $\det F = 0$. Then, we change the scale so that $\|F\| = 1$. In other words, we correct F to

$$F \leftarrow U \begin{pmatrix} \sigma_1/\sqrt{\sigma_1^2 + \sigma_2^2} & 0 & 0 \\ 0 & \sigma_2/\sqrt{\sigma_1^2 + \sigma_2^2} & 0 \\ 0 & 0 & 0 \end{pmatrix} V^\top.$$

7.2 From Eq. (7.20), we see that $x'\boldsymbol{\xi}^{(1)} - y'\boldsymbol{\xi}^{(2)} = \boldsymbol{\xi}^{(3)}$. Hence, the three equations of Eq. (7.21) are related by $x'(\boldsymbol{\xi}^{(1)}, \boldsymbol{\theta}) - y'(\boldsymbol{\xi}^{(2)}, \boldsymbol{\theta}) = (\boldsymbol{\xi}^{(3)}, \boldsymbol{\theta})$, meaning that if the first and the second equations are satisfied, the third is automatically satisfied.

Chapter 8

8.1 From the rule of matrix multiplication, we observe that

$$A = \begin{pmatrix} u_1 & \cdots & u_r \end{pmatrix} \begin{pmatrix} \sigma_1 & & \\ & \ddots & \\ & & \sigma_r \end{pmatrix} \begin{pmatrix} v_1^\top \\ \vdots \\ v_r \end{pmatrix} = \sum_{i=1}^{r} \sigma_i u_i v_i^\top.$$

8.2 This is immediately obtained from the above result.

8.3 Since $\{u_i\}$ and $\{v_i\}$ are orthonormal sets, $(u_i, u_j) = \delta_{ij}$ and $(v_i, v_j) = \delta_{ij}$ hold, where δ_{ij} is the Kronecker delta (1 for $i = j$ and 0 otherwise). Hence, we observe that

$$\begin{aligned} AA^{-}A &= \sum_{i=1}^{r} \sigma_i u_i v_i^\top \sum_{j=1}^{r} \frac{1}{\sigma_j} v_j u_j^\top \sum_{k=1}^{r} \sigma_k u_k v_k^\top = \sum_{i,j,k=1}^{r} \frac{\sigma_i \sigma_k}{\sigma_j} u_i (v_i, v_j)(u_j, u_k) v_k^\top \\ &= \sum_{i,j,k=1}^{r} \frac{\sigma_i \sigma_k}{\sigma_j} \delta_{ij} \delta_{jk} u_i v_k^\top = \sum_{i=1}^{r} \sigma_i u_i v_i^\top = A, \\ A^{-}AA^{-} &= \sum_{i=1}^{r} \frac{1}{\sigma_i} v_i u_i^\top \sum_{j=1}^{r} \sigma_j u_j v_j^\top \sum_{k=1}^{r} \frac{1}{\sigma_k} v_k u_k^\top = \sum_{i,j,k=1}^{r} \frac{\sigma_j}{\sigma_i \sigma_k} v_i (u_i, u_j)(v_j, v_k) u_k^\top \\ &= \sum_{i,j,k=1}^{r} \frac{\sigma_j}{\sigma_i \sigma_k} \delta_{ij} \delta_{jk} v_i u_k^\top = \sum_{i=1}^{r} \frac{1}{\sigma_i} v_i u_i^\top = A^{-}. \end{aligned}$$

8.4 We see that

$$\begin{aligned} AA^{-} &= \sum_{i=1}^{r} \sigma_i u_i v_i^\top \sum_{j=1}^{r} \frac{1}{\sigma_j} v_j u_j^\top = \sum_{i,j=1}^{r} \frac{\sigma_i}{\sigma_j} u_i (v_i, v_j) u_j^\top = \sum_{i,j=1}^{r} \frac{\sigma_i}{\sigma_j} \delta_{ij} u_i u_j^\top = \sum_{i=1}^{r} u_i u_i^\top, \\ A^{-}A &= \sum_{i=1}^{r} \frac{1}{\sigma_i} v_i u_i^\top \sum_{j=1}^{r} \sigma_j u_j v_j^\top = \sum_{i,j=1}^{r} \frac{\sigma_j}{\sigma_i} v_i (u_i, u_j) v_j^\top = \sum_{i,j=1}^{r} \frac{\sigma_j}{\sigma_i} \delta_{ij} v_i v_j^\top = \sum_{i=1}^{r} v_i v_i^\top. \end{aligned}$$

Hence,

$$\begin{aligned} AA^{-}u_k &= \sum_{i=1}^{r} u_i (u_i, u_k) = \sum_{i=1}^{r} \delta_{i,j} u_i = \begin{cases} u_k & 1 \le k \le r \\ \mathbf{0} & r < k \end{cases}, \\ A^{-}Av_k &= \sum_{i=1}^{r} v_i (v_i, v_k) = \sum_{i=1}^{r} \delta_{i,j} v_i = \begin{cases} v_k & 1 \le k \le r \\ \mathbf{0} & r < k \end{cases}. \end{aligned}$$

This means that AA^{-} is the projection matrix onto the space spanned by u_1, ..., u_r and that $A^{-}A$ is the projection matrix onto the space spanned by v_1, ..., v_r.

Bibliography

A. Albano, Representation of digitized contours in terms of conic arcs and straight-line segments, *Computer Graphics and Image Processing*, Vol. 3, No. 1, pp. 23–33 (1973). DOI: 10.1016/0146-664x(74)90008-2. 6, 7

F. L. Bookstein, Fitting conic sections to scattered data, *Computer Graphics and Image Processing*, Vol. 9, No. 1, pp. 56–71 (1979). DOI: 10.1016/0146-664x(79)90082-0. 6, 7

N. Chernov and C. Lesort, Statistical efficiency of curve fitting algorithms, *Computational Statistics and Data Analysis*, Vol. 47, No. 4, pp. 713–728 (2004). DOI: 10.1016/j.csda.2003.11.008. 108

W. Chojnacki, M. J. Brooks, A. van den Hengel, and D. Gawley, On the fitting of surfaces to data with covariances, *IEEE Transactions on Pattern Analysis and Machine Intelligence*, Vol. 22, No. 11, pp. 1294–1303 (2000). DOI: 10.1109/34.888714. 28, 29, 77

D. R. Cooper and N. Yalabik, On the computational cost of approximating and recognizing noise-perturbed straight lines and quadratic arcs in the plane, *IEEE Transactions on Computers*, Vol. 25, No. 10, pp. 1020–1032 (1976). DOI: 10.1109/tc.1976.1674543. 6, 7

D. R. Davis, Finding ellipses using the generalized Hough transform, *Pattern Recognition Letters*, Vol. 9, No. 1, pp. 87–96 (1989). DOI: 10.1016/0167-8655(89)90041-x. 6

M. A. Fischler and R. C. Bolles, Random sample consensus: A paradigm for model fitting with applications to image analysis and automated cartography, *Commun. ACM*, Vol. 24, No. 6, pp. 381–395 (1981). DOI: 10.1145/358669.358692. 34

A. Fitzgibbon, M. Pilu, and R. B. Fisher, Direct least squares fitting of ellipses, *IEEE Transactions on Pattern Analysis and Machine Intelligence*, Vol. 21, No. 5, pp. 476–480 (1999). DOI: 10.1109/34.765658. 7, 32, 34, 60, 61

D. Forsyth, J. L. Mundy, A. Zisserman, C. Coelho, A. Heller, and C. Rothwell, Invariant descriptors for3-D object recognition and pose, *IEEE Transactions on Pattern Analysis and Machine Intelligence*, Vol. 13, No. 10, pp. 971–991 (1991). DOI: 10.1109/34.99233. 52

R. Gnanadesikan, *Methods for Statistical Data Analysis of Multivariate Observations*, Wiley, NY, U.S. (1977). DOI: 10.1002/9781118032671. 6, 7

R. Hartley, In defense of the eight-point algorithm, *IEEE Transactions on Pattern Analysis and Machine Intelligence*, Vol. 19, No. 6, pp. 580–593 (1997). DOI: 10.1109/34.601246. 7

R. Hartley and A. Zisserman, *Multiple View Geometry in Computer Vision*, 2nd ed., Cambridge University Press, Cambridge, U.K. (2003). DOI: 10.1017/cbo9780511811685. 77

P. J. Huber, *Robust Statistics*, 2nd ed., Wiley, Hoboken, NJ, U.S. (2009). DOI: 10.1002/0471725250. 34

K. Kanatani, *Group-Theoretical Methods in Image Understanding*, Springer, Berlin, Germany (1990). DOI: 10.1007/978-3-642-61275-6. 52

K. Kanatani, *Geometric Computation for Machine Vision*, Oxford University Press, Oxford, U.K. (1993). 52, 77

K. Kanatani, Renormalization for unbiased estimation, *Proc. 4th International Conference on Computer Vision*, Berlin, Germany, pp. 599–606 (1993). DOI: 10.1109/iccv.1993.378156. 16, 77

K. Kanatani, *Statistical Optimization for Geometric Computation: Theory and Practice*, Elsevier, Amsterdam, The Netherlands (1996). Reprinted by Dover, NY, U.S. (2005). DOI: 10.1109/icpr.2014.11. 16, 77, 108

K. Kanatani, Ellipse fitting with hyperaccuracy, *IEICE Transactions on Information and Systems*, Vol. E89-D, No. 10, pp. 2653–2660 (2006). DOI: 10.1093/ietisy/e89-d.10.2653. 29, 77, 101

K. Kanatani, Statistical optimization for geometric fitting: Theoretical accuracy bound and high order error analysis, *International Journal of Computer Vision*, Vol. 80, No. 2, pp. 167–188 (2008). DOI: 10.1007/s11263-007-0098-0. 29, 77, 90, 101, 108

K. Kanatani, A. Al-Sharadqah, N. Chernov, and Y. Sugaya, Renormalization returns: Hyper-renormalization and its applications, *Proc. 12th European Conference on Computer Vision*, Firenze, Italy, October (2012). DOI: 10.1007/978-3-642-33712-3_28. 16, 90

K. Kanatani and W. Liu, 3D interpretation of conics and orthogonality, *CVIGP: Image Understanding*, Vol. 58, No. 3, pp. 286–301 (1993). DOI: 10.1006/ciun.1993.1043. 52

K. Kanatani and C. Matsunaga, Computing internally constrained motion of 3-D sensor data for motion interpretation, *Pattern Recognition*, Vol. 46, No. 6, pp. 1700–1709 (2013). DOI: 10.1016/j.patcog.2012.11.023. 77

K. Kanatani and H. Niitsuma, Optimal two-view planar triangulation, *IPSJ Transactions on Computer Vision and Applications*, Vol. 3, pp. 67–79 (2011). DOI: 10.2197/ipsjtcva.3.67. 77

K. Kanatani and N. Ohta, Comparing optimal three-dimensional reconstruction for finite motion and optical flow, *Journal of Electronic Imaging*, Vol. 12, No. 3, pp. 478–488 (2003). DOI: 10.1117/1.1579018. 77

K. Kanatani, N. Ohta, and Y. Kanazawa, Optimal homography computation with a reliability measure, *IEICE Transactions on Information and Systems*, Vol. E83-D, No. 7, pp. 1369–1374 (2000). 77

K. Kanatani and P. Rangarajan, Hyper least squares fitting of circles and ellipses, *Computational Statistics and Data Analysis*, Vol. 55, No. 6, pp. 2197–2208 (2011). DOI: 10.1016/j.csda.2010.12.012. 8, 16

K. Kanatani, P. Rangarajan, Y. Sugaya, and H. Niitsuma, HyperLS and its applications, *IPSJ Transactions on Computer Vision and Applications*, Vol. 3, pp. 80–94 (2011). 8, 16, 77

K. Kanatani, A. Al-Sharadqah, N. Chernov, and Y. Sugaya, Hyper-renormalization: Non-minimization approach for geometric estimation, *IPSJ Transactions on Computer Vision and Applications*, Vol. 6, pp. 143–159 (2014). DOI: 10.2197/ipsjtcva.6.143. 16, 77, 90

K. Kanatani and Y. Sugaya, High accuracy fundamental matrix computation and its performance evaluation, *IEICE Transactions on Information and Systems*, Vol. E90-D, No. 2, pp. 579–585 (2007). DOI: 10.1093/ietisy/e90-d.2.579. 77

K. Kanatani and Y. Sugaya, Performance evaluation of iterative geometric fitting algorithms, *Computational Statistics and Data Analysis*, Vol. 52, No. 2, pp. 1208–1222 (2007). DOI: 10.1016/j.csda.2007.05.013. 29, 77

K. Kanatani and Y. Sugaya, Compact algorithm for strictly ML ellipse fitting, *Proc. 19th International Conference on Pattern Recognition*, Tampa, FL, U.S. (2008). DOI: 10.1109/icpr.2008.4761605. 29

K. Kanatani and Y. Sugaya, Unified computation of strict maximum likelihood for geometric fitting, *Journal of Mathematical Imaging and Vision*, Vol. 38, No. 1, pp. 1–13 (2010). DOI: 10.1007/s10851-010-0206-6. 29

K. Kanatani and Y. Sugaya, Compact fundamental matrix computation, *IPSJ Transactions on Computer Vision and Applications*, Vol. 2, pp. 59–70 (2010). DOI: 10.2197/ipsjtcva.2.59. 77

K. Kanatani and Y. Sugaya, Hyperaccurate correction of maximum likelihood for geometric estimation, *IPSJ Transactions on Computer Vision and Applications*, Vol. 5, pp. 19–29 (2013). DOI: 10.2197/ipsjtcva.5.19. 29, 77, 101

Y. Leedan and P. Meer, Heteroscedastic regression in computer vision: Problems with bilinear constraint, *International Journal of Computer Vision*, Vol. 37, No. 2, pp. 127–150 (2000). DOI: 10.1023/A:1008185619375. 29

J. Matei and P. Meer, Estimation of nonlinear errors-in-variables models for computer vision applications, *IEEE Transactions on Pattern Analysis and Machine Intelligence*, Vol. 28, No. 10, pp. 1537–1552 (2006). DOI: 10.1109/tpami.2006.205. 29

T. Masuzaki, Y. Sugaya and K. Kanatani, High accuracy ellipse-specific fitting, *Proc. 6th Pacific-Rim Symposium on Image and Video Technology*, Guanajuato, Mexico, pp. 314–324 (2013). DOI: 10.1007/978-3-642-53842-1_27. 34

T. Masuzaki, Y. Sugaya and K. Kanatani, Floor-wall boundary estimation by ellipse fitting, *Proc. IEEE 7th International Conference on Robotics, Automation and Mechatronics*, Angkor Wat, Cambodia, pp. 30–35 (2015). DOI: 10.1109/iccis.2015.7274592. 64

Y. Nakagawa and A. Rosenfeld, A note on polygonal and elliptical approximation of mechanical parts, *Pattern Recognition*, Vol. 11, No. 2, pp. 133–142 (1979). DOI: 10.1016/0031-3203(79)90059-1. 6

T. Okatani and K. Deguchi, On bias correction for geometric parameter estimation in computer vision, *Proc. IEEE Conference on Computer Vision and Pattern Recognition*, Miami Beach, FL, U.S., pp. 959–966 (2009). DOI: 10.1109/cvpr.2009.5206722. 29

T. Okatani and K. Deguchi, Improving accuracy of geometric parameter estimation using projected score method, *Proc. 12th International Conference on Computer Vision*, Kyoto, Japan, pp. 1733–1740 (2009). DOI: 10.1109/iccv.2009.5459388. 29

K. A. Paton, Conic sections in chromosome analysis, *Pattern Recognition*, Vol. 2, No. 1, pp. 39–51 (1970). DOI: 10.1016/0031-3203(70)90040-3. 6

W. H. Press, S. A. Teukolsky, W. T. Vetterling, and B. P. Flannery, *Numerical Recipes: The Art of Scientific Computing*, 3rd ed., Cambridge University Press, Cambridge, U.K. (2007). DOI: 10.1119/1.14981. 64

P. Rangarajan and K. Kanatani, Improved algebraic methods for circle fitting, *Electronic Journal of Statistics*, Vol. 3, pp. 1075–1082 (2009). DOI: 10.1214/09-ejs488. 8, 16

P. Rangarajan and P. Papamichalis, Estimating homographies without normalization, *Proc. International Conference on Image Processing*, Cairo, Egypt, pp. 3517–3520 (2009). DOI: 10.1109/icip.2009.5414071. 77

P. L. Rosin, A note on the least squares fitting of ellipses, *Pattern Recognition Letters*, Vol. 13, No. 10, pp. 799–808 (1993). DOI: 10.1016/0167-8655(93)90062-i. 7

P. J. Rousseeuw and A. M. Leroy, *Robust Regression and Outlier Detection*, Wiley, NY, U.S. (1987). DOI: 10.1002/0471725382. 34

P. D. Sampson, Fitting conic sections to "very scattered" data: An iterative refinement of the Bookstein Algorithm, *Computer Vision and Image Processing*, Vol. 18, No. 1, pp. 97–108 (1982). DOI: 10.1016/0146-664x(82)90101-0. 16, 28

T. Scoleri, W. Chojnacki, and M. J. Brooks, A multi-objective parameter estimation for image mosaicing, *Proc. 8th International Symposium on Signal Processing and its Applications*, Sydney, Australia, Vol. 2, pp. 551–554 (2005). DOI: 10.1109/isspa.2005.1580997. 77

J. G. Semple and G. T. Kneebone, *Algebraic Projective Geometry*, Oxford University Press, Oxford, U.K. (1952). 50

J. G. Semple and L. Roth, *Introduction to Algebraic Geometry*, Oxford University Press, Oxford, U.K. (1949). 50

Y. Sugaya and K. Kanatani, High accuracy computation of rank-constrained fundamental matrix, *Proc. 18th British Machine Vision Conference*, Coventry, U.K., Vol. 1, pp. 282–291 (2007). DOI: 10.5244/c.21.19. 77

Y. Sugaya and K. Kanatani, Highest accuracy fundamental matrix computation, *Proc. 8th Asian Conference on Computer Vision*, Tokyo, Japan, Vol. 2, pp. 311–321 (2007). DOI: 10.1007/978-3-540-76390-1_31. 77

Z. L. Szpak, W. Chojnacki, and A. van den Hengel, Guaranteed ellipse fitting with a confidence region and an uncertainty measure for centre, axes, and orientation, *Journal of Mathematical Imaging and Vision*, Vol. 52, N. 2, pp. 173–199 (2015). 35, 60, 61

G. Taubin, Estimation of planar curves, surfaces, and non-planar space curves defined by implicit equations with applications to edge and range image segmentation, *IEEE Transactions on Pattern Analysis and Machine Intelligence*, Vol. 13, No. 11, pp. 1115–1138 (1991). DOI: 10.1109/34.103273. 16, 77

Authors' Biographies

KENICHI KANATANI

Kenichi Kanatani received his B.E., M.S., and Ph.D. in applied mathematics from the University of Tokyo in 1972, 1974, and 1979, respectively. After serving as Professor of computer science at Gunma University, Gunma, Japan, and Okayama University, Okayama, Japan, he retired in 2013 and is now Professor Emeritus of Okayama University. He was a visiting researcher at the University of Maryland, U.S., (1985–1986, 1988–1989, 1992), the University of Copenhagen, Denmark (1988), the University of Oxford, U.K. (1991), INRIA at Rhone Alpes, France (1988), ETH, Switzerland (2013), University of Paris-Est, France (2014), and Linköping University, Sweden (2015). He is the author of K. Kanatani, *Group-Theoretical Methods in Image Understanding* (Springer, 1990), K. Kanatani, *Geometric Computation for Machine Vision* (Oxford University Press, 1993), K. Kanatani, *Statistical Optimization for Geometric Computation: Theory and Practice* (Elsevier, 1996; reprinted Dover, 2005), and K. Kanatani, *Understanding Geometric Algebra: Hamilton, Grassmann, and Clifford for Computer Vision and Graphics* (AK Peters/CRC Press 2015). He received many awards including the best paper awards from IPSJ (1987) , IEICE (2005), and PSIVT (2009). He is a Fellow of IEICE and IEEE.

YASUYUKI SUGAYA

Yasuuki Sugaya received his B.E., M.S., and Ph.D. in computer science from the University of Tsukuba, Ibaraki, Japan, in 1996, 1998, and 2001, respectively. After serving as Assistant Professor of computer science at Okayama University, Okayama, Japan, he is currently Associate Professor of computer science and engineering at Toyohashi University of Technology, Toyohashi, Aichi, Japan. His research interests include image processing and computer vision. He received the IEICE best paper award in 2005.

YASUSHI KANAZAWA

Yasushi Kanazawa received his B.E. and M.S. degree in information engineering from Toyohashi University of Technology in 1985 and 1987, respectively, and his Ph.D in information and computer science from Osaka University in 1997. After engaging in research and development of image processing systems at Fuji Electric Co., Tokyo, Japan, and serving as Lecturer of Information and Computer Engineering at Gunma College of Technology, Gunma, Japan, he is currently

Associate Professor of computer science and engineering at Toyohashi University of Technology, Aichi, Japan. His research interests include image processing and computer vision.

Index

Printed in the United States
by Baker & Taylor Publisher Services